CONSUMER FINANCE:
A Case History in American Business

CONSUMER FINANCE:

A Case History
in American Business

by

IRVING S. MICHELMAN

with Preface by

LEON HENDERSON

FREDERICK FELL, INC.
New York

Copyright © 1966 by Irving S. Michelman

All rights reserved

For information address:
Frederick Fell, Inc.
386 Park Avenue South
New York 16, N.Y.

Library of Congress Catalog Card No. 66-17339

Published simultaneously in Canada by
George J. McLeod, Limited, Toronto 2B, Ontario

Manufactured in the United States of America

To My Wife

FOREWORD

How unique can a business be? Take the consumer finance business back to the days of its origins. A new charitable foundation, one of America's first, decides to reform an outlaw business known as the "loan shark" business. The people behind the foundation are patrician reformers, bringing "reform from above" to turn-of-the-century America's social problems. Just a hairbreadth decision decrees a life instead of a death sentence on the fortunes of this unique business, which at first strongly resists the cloak of legitimacy. The better elements then thoroughly convert to legislation and help create a great new American business.

Brought into focus by the passage of time are the lives and personalities of some remarkable people who worked for the foundation. Men like Arthur H. Ham, Walter S. Hilborn, Leon Henderson and Rolf Nugent mixed study with practicality, theory with common sense, in order to convince state legislatures throughout the country about the need to provide agencies for small loans. The consumer finance industry is as much in debt to these brilliant, gifted men as other industries are to their captains on the production lines.

Foreword

Almost overnight the instalment way of life becomes as American as apple pie. A revolutionary change in attitudes and purchasing power takes place. The mighty economic force known as "consumer credit" is on its way to the $100 billion mark, beyond the wildest dreams of its founders. Important colorful people, Russell Sage, Huey Long, Fiorello H. La Guardia, Calvin Coolidge, Franklin D. Roosevelt, John Maynard Keynes, Senator Paul Douglas touch on its orbit. Vital public considerations, such as its effect on the business cycle, follow in its wake. Meanwhile, the outlaw loan business gets "legal" and gets "respectable," becomes a commonplace service on practically every Main Street of America. Its social work origins fade into memories. At the height of its growth it is now only a minor segment of consumer credit as it anticipates the inevitability of major changes.

I have chosen to write this history largely in terms of the ideas and the social and economic forces which accompanied the development of the consumer finance business in the twentieth century. It has been a labor of love and a repayment of debt to an intriguing creditor. It would not have been possible without the encouragement and help of my wife.

I am deeply grateful for the advice and recollections of Leon Henderson and Walter S. Hilborn, two of the principals of this history. I also acknowledge with gratitude the comments of Neil H. Jacoby, educator and former Economic Adviser to President Eisenhower, and of Sherman J. Maisel, member of the Board of Governors of the Federal Reserve System. All opinions expressed herein are, of course, my own, unless otherwise noted.

IRVING S. MICHELMAN

Los Angeles, California
March 1, 1966

8

PREFACE

I find Mr. Michelman's book to be one of the finest of its special kind about consumer credit, not only because of its unique approach, but also because he has recorded *in extenso* significant historical material which other writers in the field have overlooked, ignored or actually side-tracked. With a zeal for research unexpected from such a business executive, he has brought to light significant data worthy of recognised consumer credit experts, such as Dr. Louis N. Robinson and Rolf Nugent, some of whose works are discussed in this volume.

One of my last important services to the Russell Sage Foundation during its long period of remedial loan and consumer credit activities was in relation to its files, completed in the late Forties, after the tragic death of Director Rolf Nugent. The Library of Congress was glad to accept into its permanent collections the files from the Foundation. I am naturally pleased to note that the author has made use of this material.

Friends and admirers of Arthur H. Ham, the first Director of the Department of Remedial Loans, while their personal recollections of him may vary, as do mine, will be grateful for the

9

Preface

author's graphic portrait of this great pioneer, as well as recognition of Walter S. Hilborn for his many contributions, including his talented legal draftsmanship which is living testimony of his capacities. Mr. Michelman performed a needed service in recording the values of another pioneer, Dr. Clarence W. Wassam. Great courage was required of a social work foundation to sponsor the Uniform Small Loan Law, with its original 42% per year interest rates, and this courage came, as noted in this book, from John M. Glenn, General Director of the Sage Foundation. Not only did he authorize the required research and legal nexus, but he sturdily supported the anti-loan shark drives, the exciting legislative campaigns, but not less noteworthy, the by-products of these, which could scarcely be termed either "research" or "social work."

Mr. Michelman emphasizes many of the social and economic ideas which have accompanied the development of consumer finance as a business. He notes Nugent's *Consumer Credit and Economic Stability*, published in 1939, which was the first major work in establishing the high importance of this credit in the swings of business cycles. I am proud of having initiated this research in 1928, and especially for securing such a brilliant scholar as Rolf Nugent to handle the inquiries. It was gratifying, too, when John Maynard Keynes commented favorably on the Nugent thesis when he and I met to discuss World War II financing. I was never an out-and-out Keynesian, having never completely abandoned Adam Smith. For the United States crises, I preferred the formulae of Beardsley Ruml and his creativeness.

As I have stated many times, the inequality of bargaining power of the borrower in most consumer credit transactions distinguishes these transactions from the purchase of commodities and services. The Uniform Law was written with borrower protections as its standards, which carried much weight in court testings. A parallel factor was the task force of legal talent that emerged to be alert for violations and defense. Recognition goes

10

to the Hubacheks, *(père et fils)*, Charles Napier, Walter S. Hilborn, David J. Gallert, Albert Raphael, and Charles S. Kelly, to mention a few and slight many.

The vast figures of consumer credit volume should astound me, but I am protected by my politico-economic experience with depression and war. What does constantly astound me is the confidence demonstrated by the volume of public money invested in the business, when I recall the difficulties in passing and sustaining the enabling legislation, the repeals and rate cuts, which influenced the strains of public financing, as the author marks out. He does not need to bluntly state an evident conclusion, which is yet there for any reader who just strolls thru the accounts of disparate oppositions, ranging from the saintly Senator George Norris, along thru zealots with their biblical quotes, the holier-than-thou competitive lenders, down to threats against the persons of Foundation directors. So, to paraphrase: "he who would ignore history should read the Michelman early chapters for today's lesson."

I was given a leave of absence in 1934 for work with General Hugh S. Johnson at the National Recovery Administration. (I resigned from the Foundation in September of that year.) Since that date there has never been a two-year period that I did not have association, mostly rewarding, with the expanding consumer credit boom. We studied the entire structure of credit at TNEC (the Monopoly Committee). Both Nugent and I wrote articles for financial publications and the annals of learned societies. In 1937, I again urged Congress to pass the Uniform Law in the District of Columbia, and again, without Fiorello La Guardia (see Chapter 17) I was rebuffed. At the Securities & Exchange Commission, my knowledge of ingenious illegal lending schemes was helpful in thwarting undesirable securities registrations. I appeared as an expert witness in two important cases involving licensees; in one the New Deal was our opponent. I was treated royally before a Canadian Royal Commission, which recommended the principles of the Uniform Law. (I recall it as the only similar appearance at which some disguised loan shark opponent did not heckle me.) Once, in the late Fifties, I was consulted by some independents in the instalment finance game who wanted me to find a foundation to help their wobbly practices!

With the hearty partnership of Marriner Eccles, Chairman of the Federal Reserve Board, I presented the bold proposal to President Roosevelt to issue an Executive Order (Regulation W) for war-time control of all consumer credit. I know that his pride in the success of the New York Uniform Small Loan Law, which he helped mightily to pass, was partially responsible for his authorization for this first federal regulation of the vast business treated in this book.

My last article was written for the Duke University School of Law publication, *Law and Contemporary Problems*, in 1954. On re-reading, I have no apologies worth mentioning.

Thus I am a veteran of about forty years in consumer credit and even now am toying with two assignments in the field. Naturally, I am delighted with every bit of this engaging venture in history, even for points of view contrary to mine. The volume can be stamped as something special and unique towards understanding the great economic revolution of our times.

LEON HENDERSON

CONTENTS

Foreword 7
Preface 9
Illustrations 14

I THE MEANEST SKINFLINT 17
II MRS. SAGE'S FOUNDATION 28
III THE MAN FROM LIVERMORE FALLS 45
IV THE IMPULSE TO REFORM 53
V NEW YORK, NEW YORK 68
VI AN OLD PROFESSION 86
VII EARLY LENDING IN AMERICA 97
VIII GROWTH OF UNREGULATED LENDING 106
IX FIGHTING THE LOAN SHARKS 112
X MR. TOLMAN GOES TO JAIL 130
XI THE BEGINNINGS OF EFFECTIVE
LEGISLATION 136
XII WERE THERE ANY GOOD LOAN
SHARKS? 151
XIII THE MASSACHUSETTS STORY—A CASE
HISTORY IN REGULATION 157
XIV COLONEL HODSON'S BUREAU AND
BONDS 180
XV DEVELOPMENT OF OTHER CREDIT
AGENCIES 191
XVI THE MAN FROM MILLVILLE, NEW
JERSEY 213
XVII "THE TOUGHEST SOCIAL WORKER
I EVER MET" 231
XVIII GOVERNMENT CONTROL OF CONSUMER
CREDIT 256
XIX THE MASS CONSUMPTION SOCIETY 278
XX CONSUMER FINANCE TODAY 300
XXI THE FUTURE 313
Footnotes 320
Index 332

ILLUSTRATIONS

FOLLOWING PAGE 160:

RUSSELL SAGE AT THE TICKER TAPE. *Circa* 1900.

ARTHUR H. HAM. From Russell Sage Foundation reprint of *The Trend and Progress of the Movement to Improve Small Loan Conditions,* 1921.

ABRAHAM LINCOLN'S PROPOSED USURY LIMITATIONS. From the *Sangamo Journal* of March 9, 1832, courtesy of the Illinois State Historical Society.

PASS THE LOAN SHARK BILL! Harry Murphy's anti-loan shark cartoon in the *Chicago Examiner* of March 26, 1917.

THE USURER'S GRIP. Brochure of Arthur H. Ham's film produced in 1912.

UNREGULATED LENDERS' ADVERTISING AT THE TURN OF THE CENTURY.

THE FIRST NATIONAL AUTO FINANCING ADVERTISEMENT. From the *Saturday Evening Post* of April 8, 1916.

LEON HENDERSON IN WAR-TIME ROLE.

LOAN SHARK WAR GETS NATIONAL AID. From the *Detroit News* of June 23, 1927.

WALTER S. HILBORN AND THE AUTHOR.

CONSUMER FINANCE:

A Case History in American Business

I

THE MEANEST SKINFLINT

Russell Sage was one of the "meanest skinflints who ever lived," on the authority of no less a person than Fiorello H. La Guardia.[1] The Little Flower may have been right on this score. Sage was certainly one of the most unattractive of the tycoons of the Gilded Age, as that freebooting, expansive era following the Civil War for a period of approximately twenty years is so often called.

He made a fortune, at least $65,000,000 in nineteenth century dollars, worth about four times that amount in current dollars. After having nurtured his money through four panics and depressions, the aged millionaire had the rare sense to leave it all to his wife, Margaret Olivia, who used a good portion of it to establish the Russell Sage Foundation, which was to become the godfather of the present day consumer finance industry. In a two-volume history of the Foundation, his name is mentioned twice, once to note that he died on July 22, 1906. In the halls of the Foundation, they still speak of it as "Mrs. Sage's Foundation."

In the decades following the Civil War, the gap between the

rich and the poor was already immense. The least the very rich could do was live in a style that matched the king-size, tax-free incomes they were amassing from America's explosive industrialism, which had been catapulted decades ahead by the war itself. Most of these nabobs accommodated the rather reverent attitude of the masses below and lived it up on a princely scale duly reported in the newspapers and magazines, much as movie stars were reported in later years.

To begin with, they built palatial homes, like the seven Vanderbilt mansions within a few blocks of each other on New York's Fifth Avenue. Some of the mansions were designed to represent limestone castles of fifteenth century France, in order to house the treasures of Europe the monied nobility were collecting with the same zest otherwise reserved for railroads, traction lines and steel mills. In addition to town houses, there were yachts, summer homes, winter homes, hunting lodges and, finally, sons-in-law with European titles to be acquired by families for whom a rocking chair or a Franklin stove might have been a luxury not too long ago. With men like Ulysses S. Grant and his cronies in the White House, there was hardly a surge of moral fervor in the air. Public opinion, except for some outburts in the farmlands, was strangely passive in accepting the piracy, fraud and deceit that infected the nation, at least until the end of the century. Meanwhile, the new moguls were hardly self-conscious about their exalted position or questionable tactics. "What do I care about the law?" questioned the richest of them all, Commodore Vanderbilt, "Hain't I got the power?" Big Jim Fisk was even more cynical about the charges he misused other people's money. Settling his vast frame into his gilded carriage, he had the candor to comment: "Nothing is lost save honor." In such a gallery, even the worst rogue could be expected to have his fans, but Russell Sage played to an empty house.

The fact is Sage was pretty close to being a miser. In the Gilded Age and even beyond, you made a fortune and consumed it conspicuously. Every rich man had his magnificent indulgences, his expensive hobbies, his princely way of life. In a sense, Sage simply failed to live up to the canons of his class and so he had a bad press and bad public relations. He turned his Midas touch into something odious as far as the have-nots were concerned because he refused to invest it with the grandeur that made the gold glitter. His manner was crabby—crustaceous was the word often used—and the few photos of Sage in his prime show a hatchet-faced, beanpole of a man, studying a ticker tape, stony eyes peering from a taut skull. He spent just enough to allow himself a comfortable Fifth Avenue residence, but his frayed clothes were the laugh of the town. He cared little for public opinion, delivered no homilies, no tips, no guides for successful living. On occasion, he would grant an interview on his advanced birthdays, offering such morsels as "Any man can earn a dollar, but it takes a wise man to keep it" or "Vacations are the outgrowth of business abnormality. They will ruin the country!" [2] In the end, he died at ninety, making his long-suffering wife Margaret Olivia one of the richest women in the world. We can at least give him credit for bequeathing her a free hand to use the money as charitably as she did.

II

His career needs telling, however, since it reflects the times and outlook of his age, and since his shortcomings are probably balanced by the superb accomplishments of the Foundation bearing his name. He was born into a farmer's family in upstate New York in 1816 and neither went to high school nor to college. Instead he went to work in his brother's grocery store in Troy, New York, where he showed a keen nose for business and at the age of twenty-three was already a partner in a wholesale grocery enterprise. By 1851, he had performed his first major swindle, earning posterity for himself in the celebrated

"Warehouse Case," *Wheeler* v. *Sage,* recorded in the annals of the United States Supreme Court.[3]

Sage and two other men had a partnership named Wheeler, Sage and Slocum based in Troy, but with a western headquarters in Milwaukee under the name of Wheeler and Company. One of its debtors in Milwaukee, named Sweet, went bankrupt, but his debt was secured by a mortgage on a valuable warehouse. The Sage group foreclosed on the property but Sweet claimed Wheeler and Company owed him $12,000 for three years' rent on the warehouse. This threw a cloud on the foreclosure, as there were other creditors, and so the partners schemed to bribe Alexander Mitchell, who represented Sweet, to settle with the other creditors. Sage was appointed negotiator by his partners, but, according to the Supreme Court records, "without the knowledge of Wheeler, Sage abandoned their agreement and made one with Mitchell for his own benefit." Mitchell actually became the purchaser, agreeing to give Sage a secret interest. Sage gave his partners $12,000 each, advising them that the proceeds were $36,000. As Wheeler charged later, the property had been sold to net $105,000 and so Wheeler carried his suit against his former partner all the way to the United States Supreme Court. Justice Davis threw out the case on the grounds that Wheeler himself had acted illegally and could not seek redress from his swindling partner. The case, wrote the Justice, "is anything but creditable to the partners concerned, and it is surprising they should have been willing to give it publicity through legal proceedings."

This was small change in Sage's career, however, as he had already become Treasurer of Rensselaer County and a member of the Troy Common Council, from which vantage point he was watching the operations of the struggling twenty-three mile Schenectady and Troy railroad owned by the city of Troy. Fortunes were to be made in railroad construction and financing, and by 1860 railroading would become America's largest industry and outlet for private investment. The affairs of the Schenectady and Troy in 1848 were to give Sage experience for the furious battles in railroading which later engaged so much of his career.

Municipally owned railroads were doomed to short lives. They were an affront to the railroad capitalists who could run them better and who usually saw to it that they were so mismanaged or discriminated against they fell one after another like ripe plums into private hands. It was time for New York's separate little railroads to be consolidated anyway, as only a single system could really be efficient, regardless of who was being enriched. Meanwhile, the Schenectady and Troy was losing money at the rate of $100,000 a year.

The industrious Sage became the chairman of the committee to sell the railroad and also head of the group that bought it. As a result the road was purchased for $50,000 down, with fourteen years to pay the balance of $150,000, and then sold soon afterwards to the newly formed New York Central combination for $650,000 plus a bonus of 25% in Central bonds, according to the records of the inevitable and ineffectual legislative investigating committee. Actually, Sage and his partners had set up the deal with the Central beforehand and Sage emerged as a director of the Central for the first six years of its existence. The move was acceptable to everyone, however, and the citizens of Troy rejoiced at the prospect of the Central using their city as a major stop, since the Schenectady and Troy possessed the only railroad bridge across the Hudson river. Something of a local hero, perhaps for the only time in his life, Sage, already a lender of large sums of money to the New York State Whig political bosses, was sent to Congress in 1852.

III

Sage's Congressional career seems in retrospect the finest part of his life. Wealthy, happy with the companionship of his attractive first wife, Marie-Henrie, daughter of a prominent Troy family, Sage cut a commanding figure. The young, raw-boned Yankee dressed impeccably, sported the famous winged Troy collar made by his constituents, and held his own among the orators. Keeping a close business eye on the awarding of land-grants to railroads, he still found time to propose that Congress purchase Mount Vernon as a national shrine, thus acquiring a brief halo of patriotism.

His heart was really in the passage of the Pacific Railroad Bill, which was to make land grants available to the railroad builders who would dare extend railway transportation from the Mississippi to the Pacific coast. The bill was not signed until 1862 by President Lincoln, but Sage was already pressing for it during his two terms in the House, even managing to refer to its urgency during one of his few major speeches in Congress on the completely unrelated Kansas-Nebraska Bill.[4]

When Congress adjourned in 1857, Sage returned to Troy to find that his fellow Central directors had treacherously decided to build another railway bridge across the Hudson from Albany, thus shelving Troy's anticipated prosperity and making Sage the town villain and worse. His political career was ended, as far as public office was concerned, and he stonily turned his energies towards money-making alone, bitterly adopting an attitude of cynicism and distrust, along with a studied indifference towards his clothes and appearance.

The financier was not only busy with railroads in this period but soon made another fortune in the "bankers' panic" of 1857, which saw 5,000 banks and railroads collapse. The young speculator made millions by exchanging his gold for paper money at a discount and by selling his New York Central shares "short," anticipating the declining market. The list of Sage's similar canny tactics for the rest of the century leaves no question that this durable capitalist was one of the greatest of all stock traders and corporate jugglers in the first era of frenzied finance. In fact, panics were his specialty and he claimed to have made $10,000,000 in ten days in the Panic of 1873. Basically a lone wolf, Sage had one principal partner to whom he lent millions of dollars at high rates while operating in the background. This was the ruthless, unprincipled and generally despised Jay Gould, whose idea of a day's work was to attempt to corner the nation's gold supply in 1869, bribing the brother-in-law of Ulysses S. Grant in this pre-Goldfinger exploit. With Gould's connivance, Sage added three more giant corporations to his string of controlled companies, Western Union, the Manhattan Elevated Railroad Company and the Missouri Pacific Railroad.

Among Sage's typical railroad maneuvers was the passing of $1,000,000 in gifts to Wisconsin state officials and legislators in order to obtain the state's 1856 Congressional land grants for his own struggling Wisconsin line.[5] When the bribery was exposed, he managed to put the railroad into receivership and sell it to his new Milwaukee and Minnesota Railroad Company, which inherited the assets but not the liabilities of the bankrupt line and became the cornerstone of his railroad empire in Wisconsin, Iowa and Minnesota. Meanwhile, he had his hand in the typical railroad construction companies which were always created to enrich the railroad promoters through ignoring the conflict of interests between owners and suppliers. As a result, thousands of initial bondholders of the new railroads were relieved of the value of their investments. Years later, when Leon Henderson, representing the Russell Sage Foundation's Department of Remedial Loans, was trying to explain why the Uniform Small Loan Law should be passed to drive the loan sharks out of Minnesota, an aged legislator declared: "There are two things of which I have very bad memories in Minnesota—locusts and Russell Sage and his railroad bonds, and I will never vote to get either of them back!"[6]

To add to the irony of this tale, Russell Sage was himself actually convicted of usury. Known as "Uncle Russell" on Wall

Street, a term of opprobrium rather than affection, Sage not only was the man to go to for a loan on securities but for any loan at interest the traffic would bear. To his great surprise, Sage was arrested in August 1869, having been indicted by a Grand Jury for violating the 7% usury limits. He was alleged to have charged a stockbroker, Edward P. Scott, an additional 1% for a short period on a $230,000 loan. Appearing before Judge Albert Cardozo, the disbelieving Wizard of Wall Street heard himself being sentenced to a fine of $250 and five days in prison.[7]

Sage immediately poured his wrath upon his attorney, Samuel J. Tilden, future governor of New York and the man who would lose the Presidency by one electoral vote in 1876 after winning the popular vote. Tilden at that time was highly involved in Sage's railroad ventures and was also a private money-lender himself. Cardozo, a Tammany judge, quickly remitted the sentence[8] and a few years later resigned his position over other scandals, much to the embarrassment of his son, the future distinguished Supreme Court Justice.

IV

Sage's first wife Marie-Henrie died in 1867, six years after they had moved from Troy to New York City. In 1869, he married Margaret Olivia Slocum, the plain but aristocratic daughter of the partner he had swindled years ago in the "Warehouse Case." Slocum had lost the rest of his money in the stock market and the Panic of 1857, and was not "ruined" by Sage as often charged. Margaret Olivia, a forty-one year old schoolteacher in reduced circumstances, married the fifty-three year old legendary millionaire and put up with his vagaries for thirty-six apparently difficult years. Of a charitable disposition, she seemed to have little influence on the man whose obsession continued to be the making of another million for each year of his life and who confidently expected to reach one hundred. A sensitive person, she was embarrassed and humiliated by the old warrior's constant involvement in legal actions, including suits against Sage by his former accountant for non-payment of services and by a cook in her predecessor's employ for seduction and child support. Always in the news, Sage gained even more disfavor in 1891 when a deranged broker, claiming he bore a message from John D. Rockefeller, burst into his office and demanded $1,200,-000 in cash if Sage did not want him to explode the satchel of dynamite he was carrying. Sage grabbed a young clerk named Laidlaw and apparently using him as a shield lunged for the exit. The resulting explosion killed Sage's secretary as well as the bomber and maimed Laidlaw's leg. Sage escaped with minor injuries. Laidlaw, represented by the eminent attorney Joseph H. Choate, sued for damages, claiming he was destitute as a result. Sage refused to pay a cent and finally won a hollow victory after a long series of trials culminating in 1899 that secured his reputation for being one of America's least favorite people.

V

What should history's verdict be for Russell Sage? There have been cases of scalawags who eventually received a reverse debunking and emerged only slightly tarnished. His contemporaries, of course, buried him without honors, partly because of his meanness, but more likely because he was even then considered a speculator rather than a builder. On the credit side, one could say the man's word was as good as his bond and in the business world of his times, such minimum conduct often denoted integrity. There is even a certain redeeming quality about his having lost $7,000,000 in one of his worst moments when he reportedly had to pay out this amount in three days on Lake Shore option contracts in May 1884, and calmly taking the beating with stoic detachment. His great competitive instincts also took some of the edge off his greed for more money. He

25

once naïvely advised the press that his pursuit of millions was like the case of the small boy who wanted to win more marbles for the sake of winning. People may not have liked Mr. Sage, but they needn't have felt sorry for him. He had a good time in a lengthy life in a city that fascinated him and there is no record of his ever having been assailed by self-doubts.

Even in his heartless reaction to the Laidlaw claim, he managed to find his supporters. The verdict of the New York State Court of Appeals reversed a lower court judgment against him on the grounds that both rich and poor were entitled to equal consideration before the law and if Sage were not a rich man, there would have been no case. This was before the days of workmen's compensation acts and there were many who thought the old eccentric's fight was the good fight on behalf of all innocent employers whose employees might be blown up through no fault of their own. Why, after winning his case, he didn't take care of Laidlaw, is another question.

Preferring to work behind the scenes, Sage is generally referred to as the junior partner of Jay Gould in the cataloging of the depredations of the so-called Robber Barons. In his *History of the Great American Fortunes*, Gustavus Myers, who published his book in 1912, gives Sage a thorough going-over but largely as a representative of the capitalist class whose actions were consistent with the inherent evils of capitalism. Writing from the socialist's point of view, Myers then endorses the ruthless consolidation of railroads into the hands of the few winners on the grounds that nothing could be more wasteful than free, competitive, private enterprise in the first place. Since the people weren't smart enough to take over the basic means of production and transportation, Myers indicates they might as well let men like Sage do their central planning for them.

This leads to a similar verdict rendered by later historians without a socialist bias. It is usually agreed that the corruption and monopolies generated in the post Civil War period are morally indefensible and that the period is properly labelled "the era of good stealings" rather than "the era of good feelings." On the other hand, how else were railroads to be pushed across the continent and giant enterprises to be created in time to serve a population that would increase from 39 million in 1870 to 76 million in 1900, as America opened its doors to Europe's desperate immigrants? We now see that this richly endowed, uninhibited country had enough resources to squander them recklessly in land grants, homesteads and prizes for the fittest, and to that extent the exploits of the Carnegies, Rockefellers, Harrimans and other captains of industry are justified. Can we deny that they were any less necessary for their times than our own new class of corporate managers are necessary for today's managed capitalism? One of America's most distinguished liberal theorists, Thurman Arnold, jolted his contemporaries in his *The Symbols of Government*, published in 1935, by assigning to folklore the notion that these early capitalists were all bad. He pointed out that great constructive accomplishments have quite often been achieved by unscrupulous men and that these tycoons raised the level of productive capacity beyond the dreams of their fathers.[9]

There was something else, however, besides the great displays of managerial enterprise that distinguished Sage's century, and that was the willingness of so many people to take tremendous risks on behalf of progress. Government may not have interfered but neither did it regulate or protect, and fortunes were lost as well as made in that hectic period. To the extent that Sage was almost entirely a speculator, something of a scavenger who profited by a sixth sense of what to do about other people's disasters, he does not rank well among his fellow entrepreneurs. At the time of his death, there was little evidence that he was interested in taking any particular risks in building up the companies he and Gould had literally captured. His claim for absolution now rested in the frail hands of his second wife.

27

II

MRS. SAGE'S FOUNDATION

"I am nearly eighty years old and I feel as if I were just beginning to live," is what Mrs. Russell Sage said to a friend at the close of the first meeting of the Russell Sage Foundation, a year after her husband's death.[1] Whether or not part of her rejuvenation reflected her husband's absence, there is no question that Mrs. Sage was already showing a strong mind of her own. In the twelve remaining years of her life, she became a celebrated philanthropist. Since the will, a startlingly brief three page document, contained no restrictions, Mrs. Sage started giving away millions immediately. In the next twelve years she disposed of $35,000,000 and by the terms of her own will, bequeathed another $36,000,000 to charitable, religious and educational institutions.

Mrs. Sage showed definite tendencies towards charity while her husband was still alive. She had made many trips to the Bowery Mission, where she had prayed with the derelicts and contributed from her own funds to their feeding. She had even persuaded her husband to provide annual railroad rides and picnics for over 1,000 poor children on some of his few remaining birthdays, but as far as major giving was concerned, she bided her time. In his perversely humorous way, of course, Sage must have realized that his aged, childless wife would give his fortune to charity. He was also quite aware that the ultimate disposition of his millions was something of a national guessing game, similar to the *New York Times*' headline: "Will Russell Sage Really Pay?" at one stage of the Laidlaw case.[2] Yet the dead hand did not reach out to control his widow's actions, or to specify her advisers.

Who would her advisers be? Not her fellow executors of the will, which included Dr. John Munn, her husband's physician, or Charles Osborne, her husband's Cashier. It might have been Samuel Jones Tilden, the almost President, the patrician millionaire of Gramercy Park whose rapacious business talents were shielded behind a genteel façade. He had labored long and profitably for his clients, Russell Sage and Jay Gould, but had died in 1886, leaving the bulk of his fortune to the New York Public Library. Jay Gould himself passed on in 1892 at age fifty-six, having seen his empire reduced to seventy-seven millions.

It was time to turn to a new group and Mrs. Sage had the discrimination to select as attorney and mentor Robert W. de Forest. De Forest had been associated with philanthropic and civic enterprises in New York for years and appears to have been a man of impeccable standards and public responsibility. He had been President of the Charity Organization Society of New York, in those days before public welfare departments, since 1888. He was a board member of a number of important social agencies and had been president of the National Conference of Charities and Correction in 1903. By a most fortunate circumstance for the yet unborn regulated loan business, de Forest had been one of those benevolent aristocrats who in 1894 organized the Provident Loan Society, New York's great "philanthropic pawnshop."

II

Almost immediately after her husband's death, Mrs. Sage gave $1,000,000 to Rensselaer Polytechnic Institute in Troy, New York. The former schoolteacher naturally was interested in education and had a warm spot in her heart for the old city on the Hudson where she was living in resigned spirits at the time of her unexpected marriage. To Emma Willard School in Troy, where she had been a student, she also gave a quick million. In time, Syracuse University, New York University, Harvard, Yale, Princeton and a college to be called Russell Sage College, in Troy, received her benefactions.

One could expect the imperious, doughty old lady to indulge in some whimsical ideas of her own and she did. Her chief hobby while Sage watched the ticker tape had been bird-watching and she donated a substantial sum to save the robins on their northward migrations. She also established a natural bird refuge on about 70,000 acres in Louisiana known as Marsh Island and she often called the Central Park authorities to inquire about the circumstances of her favorite cardinal birds who usually wintered there. Not to be outdone by Russell on Mount Vernon, she impulsively acquired Constitution Island at West Point and donated it to the nation.[3]

Next, she paid for the restoration and decoration of the run-down New York City Hall, whose tax assessors had been reasonable about her husband's estate and she also gave a carefully selected library to each of the 258 firehouses in Greater New York. Certainly the spectacle of the charging black firehorses carrying the red and gold fire-wagons through the streets of New York at that time was a splendid big-city sight, but why the firehouses needed libraries and what books entered them is a matter of conjecture.

In 1903, Mrs. Sage had finally pried her husband loose from

the old residence at 506 Fifth Avenue and established the eighty-seven year old financier in a more pretentious mansion at 632 Fifth Avenue, opposite St. Patrick's Cathedral and the site of today's Rockefeller Center. Here she would spend the rest of her days, except for summers at Sag Harbor, New York. Comfortably alone in her New York town house, Mrs. Sage received visits from Mr. de Forest and her other new friends in the charitable and educational worlds, and here no doubt the idea of the Foundation was born.

Being one of the richest women in the world was not without its problems. She was soon overwhelmed with applications from both individuals and institutions all over the world, especially when it became apparent she intended to give away her money. In a day when the art of letter writing, even among the poor, was still a matter of grace and elegance as well as essential communication, Mrs. Sage received no less than 60,000 eloquently pleading letters within two years after her husband's death. In addition, there was a daily line of hopefuls at her door. Robert de Forest, in an article written in her memory, soberly recalls the appearance at her house one day of a clergyman from a far-off place with an empty carpet-bag. He refused to leave the premises for a long time, and when asked why he had brought along the empty carpet-bag, replied it was so he could "take the stuff" back with him.[4]

Mrs. Sage had hired W. Frank Persons of the Charity Organization Society to investigate these letters for her and here again a fortuitous event in the life of the loan business took place. Persons found so many letters asking for help from the victims of loan sharks that he decided to discuss the matter with de Forest, who was familiar with the problem through his continuing association with the Provident Loan Society. In a memo to de Forest, Persons stated that there was an "apparent great demand for an organized business, which would take care of this obvious need in the community, under regulated and decent auspices." [5] Here indeed was the seed of the future giant lending industry and it is interesting to note that a quarter-century later, Persons, after a distinguished social worker's career, became executive vice-president of the lenders' trade association.

III

Mr. de Forest recalls that Mrs. Sage liked to make up her own mind and, although she sought advice, was just as likely as not to call off any proposition if she felt pressured. An instance of his tact in handling Mrs. Sage is revealed in a letter written in confidence to some friends in the charitable and foundation world in October, 1906:

It has fallen to me to advise Mrs. Russell Sage, and though she may not take my advice, and I am certainly not going to press it upon her, I wish to be prepared to advise her as to the best direction, either national or local, in which some amount, say from ten to fifteen millions, can be applied, which would do the most good and at the same time be some memorial of her husband . . . . . . what would you do with it to accomplish the most good? [6]

The consensus of opinion among de Forest and his early confidantes, men like Daniel C. Gilman, president of Johns Hopkins University and John M. Glenn, a leading figure in charitable work in Baltimore, was to establish an institution to do investigative and preventive work in the field of social ills, rather than add new agencies or supply temporary relief. This of course was in keeping with the temper of the times. Johns Hopkins University, for example, was emphasizing the process of discovery and the dissemination of new knowledge over mere instructions. Mr. de Forest shared the new enthusiasm of those early years of the twentieth century in the belief that the causes of poverty, crime and disease could be tracked down and then eliminated or at least controlled. For example, he had been chairman of a

Tenement House Committee created by the Charity Organization Society in 1898 and also of the State Commission it brought about. This in turn led to the drafting and passage of the New York State Tenement House Law in 1901. Not content with that, this practical idealist accepted the position of first Tenement House Commissioner in New York City under the new law. In brief, here was a man who could set the style for any group or person who believed in analyzing a problem, using law to solve it, and then finding an honest administrator to police it. Mr. de Forest was also a founder of the National Child Labor Committee and the National Association for the Study and Prevention of Tuberculosis.

Committed firmly to the idea of finding the causes of social problems and then removing them, Mr. de Forest submitted a memorandum to Mrs. Sage in which he delicately suggested that her money ought not to go only to institutions but towards "social betterment—improvement of the hard conditions of our working classes, making homes and surroundings more healthful and comfortable and their lives happier; giving more opportunity to them and their children." [7] He then suggested the establishment of a foundation, but one devoted to the general field of social betterment instead of to a particular cause.

Foundations were still something new in America. There were only eight in existence in 1907, and none were organized for the specific purpose the Russell Sage Foundation would undertake. The first had been brought about by John D. Rockefeller's efforts to reduce his fortune which was actually increasing beyond control. Impressed by a forty year old Baptist preacher named Frederick T. Gates, Rockefeller hired him away from the pulpit and found his talents equally impressive in business. Under his spell, Rockefeller set up the first of his foundations, the General Education Board, in 1902, a broad purpose foundation which set the pattern for scientific, public giving. Gates later conceived the Rockefeller Institute for Medical Research

33

and finally the Rockefeller Foundation which was chartered in 1913 to "advance the well-being of mankind throughout the world."

Following the basic plan of the General Education Board, de Forest envisioned a large principal sum, which should always remain intact, placed in the hands of a corporation managed by a small body of self-perpetuating trustees who would spend the income to the best of their ability for a specified general purpose. The general purpose, illustrating the social scientist's approach of Robert de Forest and his associates, was to be "the improvement of social and living conditions in the United States of America."

Mrs. Sage accepted these suggestions and since the Trustees would have to be selected before the organization could be incorporated, she and Mr. de Forest produced a list of seven in addition to themselves. Inasmuch as they were persons who among other things would literally decide the fate of the licensed small loan business, they may well be recounted here.

Three were personal friends of Mrs. Sage. They were Cleveland H. Dodge, industrialist and officer of the Red Cross, Y.M.C.A., and New York's Museum of Natural History; Robert C. Ogden, an early fighter in the cause for improved educational conditions in the South, both for whites and Negroes; and Miss Helen Gould, the youngest of the group, who for years had been "like a daughter" to Mrs. Sage. Mr. de Forest provided Gertrude S. Rice, a founder of the New York Charity Organization Society; Miss Louise Schuyler, a leader in the training of nurses in America; Daniel C. Gilman and John M. Glenn. Mr. Glenn needs particular recognition as he was soon persuaded to become the general director of the new Foundation. Mr. Glenn had started his career in Baltimore as an attorney but for some years had devoted practically all of his time to public service, having preceded de Forest as a president of the National Conference of Charities and Correction. When asked to leave

Baltimore, he was president of the Board of Supervisors of City Charities of Baltimore, chairman of the Executive Committee of the Baltimore Charity Organization Society, president of St. Paul's Guild House, and lecturer at the Johns Hopkins University. Mr. Glenn served as general director until 1931 and was a pillar of strength in support of the Foundation's activities in the lending field. In 1932, when Leon Henderson was breathlessly guiding the Uniform Small Loan Law into existence in New York, after sixteen years of embarrassingly futile efforts in the Foundation's home state, Governor Franklin D. Roosevelt cheerfully told him: "Don't worry. If Mr. Glenn wants it done, I'll do it!" [8]

IV

The announcement of the Foundation, along with Mrs. Sage's initial gift of $10,000,000, was received with acclaim in newspapers throughout the country, many of them commenting on the discretion given to the Trustees to pursue such a wide range of inquiry. Social workers felt particularly honored that their calling should have received such recognition. Teachers of the social sciences felt that their day had finally arrived. The leading publication in the social work field, bearing the archaic name *Charities and the Commons*, published two issues devoted to effusions on behalf of the new Foundation, one by the social workers and another by educators.

To get an idea of the formidable aura of eminence and authority the Foundation received almost congenitally, one might review some of the personages who offered their tributes to Mrs. Sage's Foundation in the issues of March 23 and May 11, 1907, respectively.

Among the social workers were Edward T. Devine, general secretary of the Charity Organization Society and professor of social economy at Columbia University, which was to become a stronghold of inquiry into lending activities; Ernest P. Bicknell, general superintendent of the Chicago Bureau of Charities, which would offer key support in the passage of lending legislation in Illinois within a few years; Samuel McCune Lindsay, director of the New York School of Philanthropy, already interested in lending problems; W. Frank Persons; and Frank Tucker, vice-president of the Provident Loan Society.

Educators endorsing the Foundation included luminaries from Yale to Wisconsin with professors such as Simon Patten of the University of Pennsylvania stating: "My joy in the Sage Foundation is a double one. I am glad that social work is to be made efficient and the poor are to be aided, but I am also glad that the tone of the universities can be elevated, their work made definite, and that young men will go out with higher and clearer ideals." There is no question that the spectacular news of the Foundation's establishment was to lead many people into the field of social work.

Of course there was the inevitable spoilsport, even for so worthy a cause. A well-known teacher and writer of the period, Franklin H. Giddings, chafing over the current tendency of jurists like Oliver Wendell Holmes, Louis D. Brandeis and Roscoe Pound to stretch the law, wrote in another periodical: "Bearing in mind the ingenuity of judicial reasoning, it would seem to be entirely possible that so far as the law of the case is concerned, the income of the Sage Fund could one of these days be devoted to the propagation of either anarchism or socialism, free trade or protection, neo-Malthusianism or the patriarchal family." [9]

Notwithstanding this blow, the reception of the Foundation was auspicious and it immediately enjoyed a national reputation of the highest order which it was never to lose. There was something appealing about the elevation of social work through the new Foundation. The popular President in the White House was a Harvard man who not only read books but wrote books, who sniffed at businessmen and their activities with patrician disdain and reminded all young Americans that each person owed a duty to his country to participate in works of good deeds.

V

The new Foundation was authorized in its charter to investigate the causes of adverse social conditions, to suggest how these conditions might be remedied or ameliorated, and to put into operation means to that end. In retrospect, one can see how harmoniously the reform loan law program would fit into this pattern. On the other hand, the Foundation could also establish new agencies necessary to carry out its conclusions, or contribute to the resources of existing agencies. In this alternative, one can also see how a quite different approach could be determined for lending problems and, in fact, was followed at first. Finally, the Foundation was authorized to go into business itself, in semi-philanthropic enterprises. Since the Foundation had to live on its income or expire, these investments of capital funds would be limited to one-half the total and would be expected to yield an income of no less than a charitable 3%, one-half the traditional 6%. Here again the Foundation was to apply the alternative to lending problems and would actually establish its own lending agency.

Loans to the oppressed, however, were far from the minds of the original trustees, or at least far at the bottom of the list. In fact the original list of suggestions prepared by Mr. de Forest, who was certainly in command at that time, was as follows:

1. Tenements in the city and small houses in the suburbs—for the working classes on a business basis, or for semi-dependent families on a semi-charitable basis.
2. Lodging houses for women, comparable to the Mills Hotel for men.
3. "Neighborhood charity buildings" in New York City.
4. Retail stores, to sell the necessaries of life "to the poorer classes" at cost plus a reasonable profit of say 6%.

5. Industrial insurance for the working classes, at cost plus a reasonable profit of say 6%.
6. Tuberculosis sanatoria in the country, providing opportunities for the patients to earn something.
7. Convalescent homes.
8. Management, maintenance, and possibly establishment, of children's playgrounds in cities.
9. Industrial education.
10. A great exhibition building in New York.[10]

What a naïve program this seems to Americans of only sixty years later. But what a different world, too. Our Congress now considers laws whereby even rent will be paid for lower income people in an affluent society, while in de Forest's day, tenement safety laws were a bold reform. We are all familiar with the changes in manners, clothes and technology in these sixty years, but we tend to forget how completely reversed the role of government has become in the field of public welfare.

Governor Charles Evans Hughes signed a special bill in the New York legislature on April 11, 1907, and the Foundation began its operations. The variety of the early efforts of the Foundation indicates its vitality and reminds us that even when it was active in loan legislation, this activity represented but a very minor part of its program.

One of the first major efforts was on balance a failure. In spite of the cautious attitude to be expected from such sound Trustees, they were anxious to experiment with the idea of a "philanthropic investment," and hit upon the construction of inexpensive suburban homes for New York wage-earners, as an "investment for social betterment." Early in 1909 land was bought in Forest Hills and the Sage Foundation Homes Company was incorporated for the purpose of creating a suburban community that would be a classic example of intelligent town planning for others to follow. The idea was to provide healthful and attractive homes and to demonstrate that quiet, peaceful streets and pleasant thoroughfares were economically practical as well as socially desirable.

Forest Hills Gardens contained about 200 acres. A development company financed by the Foundation offered moderately-priced, attractive homes on easier payment terms than were possible to get anywhere else, five to ten per cent down, a fifty per cent mortgage from a title company, and the balance in ten years of monthly payments to the Homes Company. Aside from such prophetic terms for the home-building industry, the project had its disadvantages. Concerned with beauty and harmony, the architects seemed to have upgraded the project to one where only the middle class, which really didn't need that much betterment, would be expected to live. In an excess of romanticism, Grosvenor Atterbury, the designer, produced a mock Tudor village straight out of a Hollywood movie set. Roofs with niches for archers, Tudor gables and half-timbers, towers and turrets sprung up amidst the handsome landscaping. An Inn on Station Square completed the make-believe, and by 1917 the community was solidly established. There were shops around the Square, and the West Side Tennis Club was around the corner. There were activity clubs for both men and women. Beginning in 1914, July Fourth celebrations ended with dancing in the Square in the evening. On Sundays the community attended a church donated by Mrs. Sage, and not surprisingly there was an active Audubon Society for the bird-watchers.

Unfortunately over $4,000,000 had been invested in the Gardens by 1914, offset by the ten year mortgages to some extent as well as the investment in the Inn. Bearing in mind the value of the dollar at the time, the residents were getting a bargain, but the yield to the Foundation was far below what could be expected from good railroad bonds and the annual income of the Foundation dropped from $460,000 to $260,000 between 1908 and 1917. Considering that at a meeting in 1907 Mrs. Rice, one of the Trustees, found her minutes regarding a grant of $25,000 for an investigation of the standard of living, as proposed by the New York State Conference of Charities and Correction, "positively terrifying" (it should have read $2,500), we can imagine the second thoughts on the Forest Hills project.

In February 1922, after painfully seeing their income on the investment not even approaching three per cent, the Trustees sold their interest in the Sage Foundation Homes Company to John M. Demarest, vice-president and manager of the property, and some of his friends who were enjoying their residence there. The books were finally balanced with a capital loss of $350,000, but at least they felt assured that Mr. Demarest and his associates could be trusted to maintain the character of the place. Unfortunately, they had to foreclose on the new owners in the 1930 depression and more losses were suffered. In 1965, the newspapers noted that the old Forest Hills Inn, with its 98 apartments and 146 transient hotel rooms, had been sold for the fourth time since being built by the Russell Sage Foundation in 1910. The purchase price was $1,500,000, including a $1 million mortgage to be assumed by the new owner, fittingly enough Claudius C. Phillipe, formerly vice-president of the Waldorf Astoria.[11]

VI

The Foundation, like its namesake, was not to be burned twice and it avoided such projects from then on, with the result that by 1947 it could report cumulative income of nearly $21,000,000, of which $9,000,000 was distributed in grants and $12,000,000 in research and other direct works of the various departments. Its capital had been increased to $15,000,000 by an additional $5,000,000 gift from Mrs. Sage when she died in 1918 and is intact today.

Meanwhile, the Foundation carried on its basic work of research and publication through a staff of its own and grants to other agencies. By 1913, it was comfortably established in a building erected at the corner of Twenty-Second Street and Lexington Avenue. The building this time was reminiscent of Florence, Italy and looked much like the home of a Medici prince, perhaps correctly comparing the era of the Medici with America's Gilded Age.

The early 1900's, however, had firmly turned its back on the substance if not the form of the Gilded Age, and the Foundation began striking out in important pioneering directions. Substantial appropriations were made to each of the four existing schools for the training of social workers, including The New York School for Philanthropy, which is now The New York School for Social Work. The funds were designated for "investigations to be made for the Foundation subject to the discretion of the director," and the results were to be far-reaching for the lending industry.

Meanwhile, investigations were launched into the conditions of work for women and children in the canneries of New York, supplementing the work of the Consumers' League of New York City. Other investigations were initiated into child labor in southern mills and factories; into workmen's compensation insurance; and into the plight of backward children in the public schools. Funds and personnel were devoted towards extending the growth of the Charity Organization Societies and public playgrounds. From time to time in the Foundation's experience, an initial concern for a movement would come under the direction of a particularly able man or woman who would turn it into a major break-through on the basis of his or her own skill coupled with the Foundation's resources. Such an example was the development of the playground and recreation movement in America under the leadership of Dr. Luther H. Gulick, who was director of physical training in the New York schools and so greatly impressed Mr. de Forest and Mr. Glenn that the

Foundation appropriated $25,000 for "national playground extension" with Dr. Gulick as the guiding force. If a major Foundation project proved to be worthwhile, it would be set up as a Department, with a separate budget and staff, and carried on for as long as needed to launch the movement on its own. This idea of planting a seed, nourishing it and moving on has been similarly used by the Society of Friends and has served as a criterion for recent philanthropies such as the Ford Foundation's Fund for the Republic.

Among the new Departments of the Foundation were the Charity Organization Society Department, which became the clearing house for social work, the Recreation Department under Dr. Gulick, the Child-Helping Department and the Women's Work Department. This last Department, which eventually became the Department of Industrial Studies, was made to order for the talents of Miss Mary van Kleeck, who displayed formidable investigative and propaganda ability of the type most productive for the Foundation's work. Wading into the conditions of women in the bookbinding trade, she wrote a strong report that was used by Louis D. Brandeis to defend the constitutionality of New York's new law prohibiting night work for women in factories. Conditions in millinery work, artificial flowers and among Italian immigrant female workers were also explored and surveyed in depth under the direction of Miss van Kleeck, who became an international authority on industrial investigations, unemployment and the touchy subject of collective bargaining. From the period when the *New York Times* was reporting that Miss van Kleeck's investigation of female working conditions "angered the town officials of Newburgh, New York" in 1913, she could be counted on to move boldly and to make news.[12] The backbone displayed by Glenn and his Trustees in defending Miss van Kleeck augured well for the criticisms they would endure in the lending field. Miss van Kleeck was to state in 1917 about her interest in labor:

The Foundation is concerned with the labor movement from the viewpoint neither of employers nor of workers, but as representing the public interest. The public interest may sometimes square with the interest of employers. Sometimes it may be in conflict with the interests of both. Conflicts are inevitable but the important thing is that employers, workers and the public should understand the facts and know the tendencies involved in action. The Foundation has tried to describe the facts, and its investigators have sought not to influence the conclusions, but to help to establish the habit of making facts, rather than prejudice or self-interest, the basis for conclusions.[13]

Such probity and detachment made the Foundation a force to be reckoned with when private interests clashed with public needs.

This capacity for in-fighting was also to be decisive in the halls of state legislatures where the remedial laws for most reforms had to be passed. From the very start the Foundation was immensely practical in this respect, reflecting the tough-minded experience of men like de Forest and Glenn. An omen of future legislative activity was revealed by a call for the Foundation's services in October 1907, only seven months after it had been founded. President Theodore Roosevelt was about to announce the admittance of the former Oklahoma Territory as America's forty-sixth state. Looking forward to the first session of the state legislature, Miss Kate Barnard, the outstanding social worker of the Territory, announced her candidacy for the elective position of State Commissioner of Charities and Correction, as that unkind alliance of welfare and punishment was usually called in those days. She wrote an impassioned letter to Mr. Glenn, pleading that he use "a small portion of Mr. Sage's millions . . . in securing ideal laws for a new state" by sending some of the recognized authorities on social legislation to help in the preparation of fundamental measures. The Trustees approved Mr. Glenn's suggestion that a modest appropriation be made, and he asked Hastings M. Hart, a staff member, to go to Oklahoma to confer with Miss Barnard. He also inveigled his friends from the National Conference of Charities and Correction, the New York Prison Association and the National Child Labor Committee to go to help her, having first been reassured by Oklahoma Senator Robert L. Owen that she was all right and "knew a lot about her work." Glenn's formidable staff, in consultation with Miss Barnard and local experts, drew bills for compulsory education, control of child labor, and state systems for the care and treatment of criminals, feeble-minded and insane, all of which were passed by the legislature. It is pleasing to note that this paragon of social workers led her ticket by several thousand votes and, according to Mr. Hart, had a phenomenal hold in the new state—"she has the legislators following her like a flock of sheep." Unfortunately, an adequate small loan law wasn't thrown in the hopper because there was none to throw, and the new state suffered from loan sharks for years to come.

III

THE MAN FROM
LIVERMORE FALLS

On January 1, 1900, seventeen year old Arthur H. Ham joined 76 million Americans in greeting the twentieth century. Only about 3,000 of his fellow countrymen could claim the distinction of living in Livermore Falls, Maine, on that date, but those who did were quite happy about it.

A small Maine town at the turn of the century inevitably recalls the innocent, pastoral, horse-clopping charm of a Currier and Ives print. Its citizens, on the other hand, were likely to be strong-willed, wry, independent Yankees of notable stubbornness and capacity for decision. On at least two counts, therefore, heredity and environment, Arthur Ham could be said to be well prepared to make his mark in the world. In the next seventeen years, he would quite unexpectedly become the country's leading authority on "small loans," as consumer finance was then known. As the first Director of the Department of Remedial Loans for the Russell Sage Foundation, he would also make the decisions that would spell life or death—reform legislation or elimination—

for the business that was to become a giant in the American credit system.

In 1900, however, Arthur Ham was content doing odd jobs around town, having graduated from Livermore Falls High School two years before at age fifteen. Common sense indicated this was too young for college. Besides, as the son of the town druggist, there was plenty for him to do in Livermore Falls as the sharply defined New England seasons rolled by.

There was no question about his going to college. He was bright and the family pharmacy on Main Street was fast becoming one of the most attractive and up-to-date pharmacies in the whole state. It was just a matter of time before he would enroll at the place he had set his heart upon, Bowdoin College, founded in 1794 in Brunswick, Maine. Being an intellectual young man, thoughts of college no doubt directed his mind tentatively towards those two catchwords of the day, heredity and environment. They were words that typified a good deal of the questioning and self-examination that was being done in turn-of-the-century America. They were certain to be echoed in the adult world. We can imagine their recurrence in the soft voices on the front porch of the comfortable Ham house on the tree-lined street, as the long summer evenings and his eighteenth birthday drew near.

For a true understanding of the social, intellectual and political atmosphere that produced the "progressive reform movement" of the early 1900's, these Darwinian concepts of heredity and environment provide a convenient point of departure. As in all fields of human endeavor, good or bad, ideas precede action, even if it takes a century or so to sort out the ideas and relate them to their consequences. In the spirit of leisurely and deliberate hindsight, therefore, we may profitably examine the stage and a good deal of the script that attended Arthur Ham's world.

In the realm of ideas, one can start with Charles Darwin deciding to sign on Her Majesty's Ship *Beagle* as ship's naturalist in

1837 hoping to unravel that mystery of mysteries, the origin of species. When Darwin's epochal book of that title was published in 1859, it accelerated a revolution in intellectual history. As with the equally important works of Freud and Marx, people discussed the heady implications without reading the involved technical works themselves. Every thinking American at the dawn of the twentieth century was a Darwinist of sorts, just as much as he was a Republican, Democrat, or, for a brief million vote fling in the 1890's, a Populist. The reason for this was that Darwinism led straight to religion, economics and politics. In fairness to Darwin, he would gladly have confined the consequences of his work to biology, and he saw with some dismay the popularizers such as T. H. Huxley and Herbert Spencer fashion "Darwinism" into supports for current beliefs and prejudices.

Briefly, Darwin started with the idea that there was a "struggle for existence" behind the veil of history which resulted in some organic and animal forms surviving while others became extinct as the dodo. Obviously, the surviving ones were endowed with special qualities that enabled them at least to get to the available food supply. In a homely illustration that any Maine farmer could appreciate, it was pointed out that the runt of a litter of suckling pigs was going to lose out in the struggle for the sow's milk. Thus that cruel phrase "survival of the fittest" was endowed with scientific authority and entered the treasury of the world's clichés.

In the process of surviving, the organisms best equipped tended to procreate young that were equally adept in the scramble for living, so that after many generations, a new species evolved. This process of evolution reflected the workings of "natural selection," a third key Darwinian phrase, and one that plant and animal breeders had long recognized through observation and experiment.

Most of us are familiar with the religious upheaval that this doctrine planted in the Garden of Eden. It persisted as late as 1925, with that fallen hero, William Jennings Bryan, thrice defeated candidate for the Presidency, babbling about his preference for the Rock of Ages over the age of rocks, under the merciless goading of Clarence Darrow during the trial of Scopes, the Tennessee school teacher who taught evolution.

II

In 1896, however, Bryan was a phenomenon in full sunburst on the American scene. The handsome thirty-six year old Congressman from Nebraska captured the Democratic nomination with his electrifying speech on, of all things, the gold standard: "You shall not press down upon the brow of labor this crown of thorns; you shall not crucify mankind upon a cross of gold."

It is difficult to believe that anything so abstract as the free coinage of silver versus the gold standard could gain a Presidential nomination. Bryan's obsessive eloquence not only carried the Democratic nomination but also won him the endorsement of the Populist party, which represented the first great protest or reform movement in American history and happened to identify the gold standard with the monied interests.

Bryan's outlook was essentially conservative compared with the "radical" Populist wave of protest that had won James B. Weaver 1,041,028 votes in the prior election of 1892. He was liberal and exciting enough, however, to steal the Populists' thunder in 1896 and as a result to end their hopes of becoming an important third party. These new allies of the Democrats were mainly farmers who had risen in indignation against what they considered to be the devouring, un-American industrialism which followed the Civil War and the blatant, corrupt forces of business and finance which they felt were dominating the nation. To top it all, not only were these farmers of the plains and the south caught in the depression of 1893, but also their status as the heroes of an older America, where they were the yeomen tillers of the soil, was vanishing under mortgages, deflation and the emigration of their sons to the despised, mushrooming cities.

The Boy Orator leaped into the campaign with fantastic energy, stumping the nation and mesmerizing unforgettably audiences exceeding 5,000,000 people. He made a foray into New England where the smug students at Yale booed him off the stand but the opposition was more impressed by the endorsements he had received from all the Indian tribes. Mark Hanna, the Republican political boss, felt obliged to raise vast campaign funds from the business and financial community to give his candidate, William McKinley, the most lavish propaganda machine ever mounted in America—over one hundred million pamphlets and tracts to supplement the fierce attacks on Bryan in the overwhelmingly Republican press.

The Republicans need not have pulled out so many stops. Bryan was defeated by 600,000 votes, the largest defeat since Greeley by Grant in 1872. The plain fact of the matter was that the nation was ready for reform but was not ready to accept it from "below." Middle class America did not cotton to the uncouth, unbridled forces of protest in spite of the glaring weaknesses in the distribution of power and wealth in the country. The native optimism of a country still vital and growing resisted the winds of change until they would arrive under more respectable auspices. In Maine, not one county was carried by Bryan.

III

Yet reform was in the air and for leading responsible citizens like the Ham family, the disturbing influences of the calls for reform were not taken lightly. As a trustee of the Library Association, Arthur Ham's father, Joseph Gardner Ham, was well

49

read in the literature of protest that flooded the country, books questioning the system that seemed to hold so many illusions after such great designs. There was not only *The Origin of Species* to mull about, but take, for example, Henry George's *Progress and Poverty*. Published in 1879, its sales still climbing over the 2,000,000 mark, the very title suggested a national sickness of want amidst wasted opportunities.

Henry George's "single-tax on land" proposals as a cure for the sickness were less important than his startling diagnosis of an *economic* interpretation of American life, and here we return to Charles Darwin, whom George used to buttress his "reform" point of view. For George, the differences between individuals were not ordained as inevitable: "The influence of heredity, which is now the fashion to rate so highly, is as nothing compared with the influences which mold the man after he comes into the world." Similarly, George applied his Reform Darwinism to the doctrines of the prominent minister Henry Ward Beecher, whose statement "God has intended the great to be great and the little to be little" must have been hard for even Deacon Joseph Ham, treasurer of the First Baptist Church, tenor in the choir and sometime superintendent of the Sunday School, to digest. "Such a gratuitous attribution to the laws of God," wrote George, was simply "interpreting Christianity in a way that made it possible for the rich Christian to bend on Sundays in a nicely upholstered pew . . . without any feeling of responsibility for the squalid misery that is festering but a square away." Other conservative concepts in the realms of law, philosophy and politics were unsparingly exposed as "rationalizations of economic interests" by the growing legions of Reform Darwinists. In summary, there were no absolute, unyielding conditions. The very history of change proved that social problems were amenable to reform. Even the law, stated Oliver Wendell Holmes in 1881, must reflect "the felt necessities of the times."

The Conservative Darwinists, however, were still securely

entrenched in their strongholds of wealth, power and majority opinion. Another Sunday School teacher, John D. Rockefeller, could explain to his Sunday School class that the development of the Standard Oil Trust was "merely a survival of the fittest . . . This is not an evil tendency in business, it is merely the working out of a law of nature and of God." Darwin's most brilliant exponent, Herbert Spencer, had come to America on a lecture tour in 1882 and received triumphal acclaim as he reassured the leaders of American opinion that society was just another evolution of the fittest and that poverty and corruption, while highly regrettable, must evolve away through the centuries rather than be submitted to unworkable social legislation. This was the scientific analysis and "scientific" was a catchword of the times, especially appropriated by both sides of the debate.

Reform . . . laws reflecting social needs . . . the scientific way . . . all to be stored in the subconscious of a boy in Maine at the start of a brand new century. But life is only part passive—there is also the time for action. Forget Bryan, the champion of free silver. How about William Jennings Bryan mounted on a beautiful black horse off to free Cuba? The Spanish-American War had only lasted ten months in 1898 but what an exciting, satisfactory little war it was! Cuba had been freed from Spanish tyranny and Teddy Roosevelt had led that furious charge up the hill. Best of all, there was the glorious performance of the U.S. Navy with Commodore Dewey laconically directing Mr. Gridley to fire when ready and thus avenge the sinking of the *Maine*. The odd jobs were over for Arthur Ham, the small town lost its hold. Twelve days after his eighteenth birthday, on July 13, 1900, he went to Boston and enlisted in the U.S. Navy. He shipped out from the Charleston Navy Yard in Boston on the *U.S.S. Hartford* en route to the newly acquired Phillipines and points East and was not to see the United States again for four years.

As he gazed into the ocean we can surmise that this young

New Englander must have wondered what course the future would hold for him. Perhaps it would be the sea. After all, his mother's father, Captain Joseph Chandler, who used to live in nearby Portland, was a retired sea captain. All New Englanders had thrilled to the story of Richard Henry Dana, who had spent two years before the mast. The gem of sea stories, however, was Herman Melville's *Moby Dick*, that epic treatise on whaling and on the moral struggles of life itself. *Moby Dick*, the white whale, engaged in mortal combat with Captain Ahab. Moby Dick, the personification of evil, or was the obsessed Ahab the evil one? As he squinted his eyes into the salt spray, he saw no whales on the horizon, but there were sharks, silent, fascinating, elusive.

IV

THE IMPULSE TO REFORM

Arthur Ham returned to Livermore Falls after his youthful service in the Navy in July, 1904, and prepared to enter Bowdoin in the autumn of that year. He was somewhat older than the other freshmen and no doubt was considered a sophisticated world traveller by his awed classmates.

Bowdoin, one of America's oldest colleges, was named after James Bowdoin, a leading supporter of the Revolutionary Movement as a member of the Massachusetts Council and later one of the first Governors of Massachusetts. An example of that fine flowering of the eighteenth century which produced enlightened men of both action and intellect, he also took a great interest in natural philosophy. He presented various papers before the American Academy of Arts and Sciences, and served as president of the Academy from 1780 to 1790. Bowdoin College was founded in 1794 and named in his honor.

Not all colleges sustained the inquiring mind of the eighteenth century, however, and for the most part they formed a link in the nineteenth century of what Eric Goldman in his book on reform movements, *Rendezvous with Destiny*, calls "the steel chain of ideas." These ideas tended to support the status quo and to discourage reform; they were the ideas we have previously seen enlisting Darwin's survival theories on their side. In the 1870's through 1890's the respectable, opinion-making classes had given almost unqualified support to the conservative side of most issues. Editors, ministers, and professors time and again preached the great truths of *laissez-faire* and deplored Bryan, labor unions and social reformers in the same breath. They may have raised their voices against corruption from time to time, but their outlook was distinctly unfriendly towards any changes in the system in spite of cracks such as the severe depression of 1873 to 1879, or the massive Pullman strike of 1894.

When Grover Cleveland became the first Democratic President following the Civil War, in 1884, he had illustrated the prevailing concepts with a veto of a $10,000 appropriation by Congress for drought-stricken farmers. "Though the people support the Government," he said, "the Government should not support the people."

One of the most interesting breaks in the wall of standpatism that marked the end of the century occurred in the colleges. It is hard to believe that professors before 1870 had little broad public influence in the first place, until we note that the percentage of college graduates was minor and that the colleges themselves, unlike European colleges, generally lacked national or international reputations.

This began to change with the sudden emergence of the modern American university in the last years of the century. The small number of denominational colleges were now accompanied by large universities with great libraries, laboratories, graduate and professional schools and better paid professors. Of course the huge endowments for all this came largely from the fortunes of men whose world would eventually be exposed to relentless academic criticism, but the great millionaires cheerfully

54

continued to immortalize themselves by donations to educational institutions. Meanwhile, the state universities were burgeoning and in Wisconsin, for example, the progressive La Follette had formed the first prototype of a "brain trust" in politics by enlisting the guidance and advice of professors at the state university in Madison.

This does not mean that the universities or their students were providing, or were in a position to provide, any hotbed of reform. In fact, an honor roll of professors dismissed for ideas unfavorably received by a solid front of conservative trustees soon developed, finally leading to the defensive formation of the American Association of University Professors in 1915. There was enough bold thinking, however, to give professors and the universities their rightful claim for recognition in the affairs of the times. After all, this was still considered a "scientific" age and the opinions of educators began to count highly in the halls of the state legislatures. Some of the professors would soon be lending valuable respectability to the perplexing anti-thrift concepts of the new small loans and sales financing industries.

Another factor in the conversion of the professors was the large proportion of academics who were going to Europe for their Ph.D.'s, because of the great reputations of the universities on the other side of the Atlantic. Those who went to Oxford and Cambridge found in England an upper class with a large section already committed to reform and intellectuals who displayed their typical British nonconformity by going so far as to join with Beatrice and Sidney Webb in Fabian Socialism. Most of the Ph.D. candidates went to Germany, however, which was considered the very fountain of academic distinction at that time. The leading German scholars emphasized the new "historical" approach which viewed the development of institutions as a continuous evolution largely subject to environmental influences. As far as social legislation was concerned, Bismarck, Germany's "Iron Chancellor," appropriated some of the socialists' thunder by handing out a series of startling benefits in the 1880's, including compulsory insurance against sickness and accidents, old-age insurance and other items of social security. These German-trained American professors included the first president and most of the key professors of Johns Hopkins University, another of the provocative centers of the times and closely connected with the Sage Foundation.

The social scientists in the faculties of the universities were among those most excited by the prospects of reform. If reform legislation were to mark the new age, then they would be called upon as never before to become expert witnesses and even technicians of change. For once, their laboratories were to be arenas of applied rather than theoretical science. The development of regulative and humane legislation would call upon the skills of lawyers, economists, sociologists and political scientists, and they responded to their new status enthusiastically, as we have noted in their salute to the new Foundation.

In addition to Wisconsin and Johns Hopkins, the three other universities most generally associated with reform ideas at the turn of the century were Columbia University, in the heart of New York with its reminder of festering slums, the University of Chicago, so handsomely endowed by John D. Rockefeller that it captured a lion's share of the brightest and most free-thinking faculty men and another open-minded state university, Washington, in the far west. None of the universities escaped the ferment. Although Harvard, Yale and Princeton were late-comers, they more than made up for lost time by placing two scholarly reformers, Theodore Roosevelt and Woodrow Wilson, the latter an ex-professor, in the White House within a dozen years. Bowdoin, in the quietness of Maine, could not remain untouched.

II

Arthur Ham was a brilliant scholar at Bowdoin, graduating *magna cum laude* with an A.B. degree in 1908. He was a member of Phi Beta Kappa.

He had wide extra-curricular interests and seems to have been the ideal gentleman, scholar and athlete. The records list him as being a member of the Glee Club and the Chapel Choir for each of his first three years, a member of the varsity tennis team for his last three years and captain of the team as a senior. He was the sophomore class president, a finalist in the Class of 1868 prize-speaking contest, and was an assistant in economics.

As an economics specialist, Ham probably thought in terms of making his mark in the business world. His father not only had a thriving pharmacy but was also president of a paper company. When the Livermore Trust and Banking Company was established, the elder Ham was elected a trustee and secretary and served the bank for sixteen years. In addition, he was for years treasurer of the Androscoggin County Agricultural Society. With such a secure background in the affairs of his community, Arthur Ham must have considered deeply the economic and social problems of his times.

America was actually in a period of prosperity during most of Ham's college years, to be interrupted only by the panic of 1907, an opportunity which Russell Sage had missed by only one year. Strangely enough, the farmers, who were the class that had seemed to miss out most completely in the expansion after the Civil War, had come back strongly. Having supported Bryan as their savior in 1896, they were pleasantly surprised to see prosperity by 1898 under the conservative McKinley. Foreign crop failures enlarged the farmer's market and sent his prices upwards. At the same time, huge new gold discoveries in Alaska, South Africa and Australia inflated the currency supply more rapidly than would have occurred if silver had been favored, thus making farm mortgages easier to repay. A round of business expansion and the demand of the fast-growing city populations for food completed his prosperity. America had once again bounced back with a typical unplanned solution to a crisis, reflecting the great resources and vigor of the richly endowed country. The increasing middle class now looked for new ways to enjoy itself, watching baseball, the new national pastime, football and boxing, while travelling Chautauqua companies and circuses entertained the rural population. The greatest fad of all was bicycling, with ten million Americans riding the new, low safety-wheel bicycle by 1900. In the same year, 3,000,000 records were bought by the public to play on their improved Edison phonographs. The automobile industry produced only 4,000 vehicles in 1900. By 1910, Henry Ford had begun the principles of mass production and lower prices, producing 18,000 cars, but the full effects of the automobile age, which would also usher in the consumer credit age, were beyond the comprehension of even the most imaginative thinkers.

The quality of a nation's conscience, however, is often reflected by what it will do in a period of prosperity rather than a period of crisis to advance the public good. Just as President Johnson's Great Society and war on poverty were conceived in a period of record prosperity, so was the progressive impulse to make America better for all Americans conceived in the relative prosperity of the early 1900's.

The term "progressive" is used to refer to the bi-partisan reform movement dominated by the "liberal" wings of the middle and upper classes in the early 1900's. It was neither a Republican nor a Democratic movement, although Theodore Roosevelt appropriated the name Progressive for his splinter Republican "Bull Moose" party in the election of 1912, which placed a Democratic progressive, Woodrow Wilson, in the White House. It is easily distinguished from the Populist movement, which was largely agriculturist, rural and touched with a radical, hysterical quality that caused it to be shunned by middle class America and abhorred by upper class America. The progressives were basically urban, middle class and upper class Americans who for a variety of reasons produced a morally based movement which sought remedies for those aspects of industrialized America which they sensed were wrong. The Republican followers of La Follette in Wisconsin were progressives of still another stripe, more advanced in their demands for reforms and representing a basically rural state. In 1905, Governor Robert M. La Follette hammered through his legislature an industrial commission—the first of its kind in the nation—to regulate health and safety conditions in the factories. A direct primary for all nominations was legislated, and La Follette and his professors passed more than a hundred other laws reaching into corrupt practices, public utility controls, education and conservation.

III

A hero in his home state, Robert La Follette was elected Senator and embarked for Washington in 1906 to bring the "Wisconsin Idea" to the federal government. By 1910 this idea would already have resulted in progressive legislation in most of the states, particularly in New York, California, New Jersey, Michigan, Iowa, North Carolina and Texas.

One of the characteristics of progressivism was the youth of its leaders, a factor that must have excited the college students in Arthur Ham's day just as the election of John F. Kennedy quickened their pulses in the 1960's. The preceding reformers, the Populists, were neither intellectual nor youthful in their leadership, many of them being silver-haired veterans of monetary reform crusades who wearily turned their hopes over to the young "prairie avenger," William Jennings Bryan. In William Allen White's *Autobiography*, the "Sage of Emporia" speaks of the hundreds of thousands of young men in their twenties, thirties and forties who felt a sense of the inequities and frustrations of American society and provided manpower and votes to bring about reform. Arriving in Washington, Senator La Follette found a President who had become, upon McKinley's assassination in 1901, the youngest President in history at age forty-three. The new Senator himself had just passed fifty and was something of an elder statesman of the movement. William Allen White further describes the progressives as a movement of little businessmen, professional men, successful farmers, engineers and enlightened country editors such as himself. Alfred D. Chandler, Jr., a more recent historian, made an actual research project into the backgrounds and status of 260 leaders of Roosevelt's Bull Moose Progressives in the 1912 election and came up with 95 businessmen, 25 lawyers, 36 editors, nineteen college professors, seven authors, six professional social workers and a scattering of men in several professions.[1] Interestingly enough, there were no labor union leaders or representatives of the salaried-executive class. A movement that included social workers in its leadership must certainly have captured the interest of the new Russell Sage Foundation and the people who would make it their life's work.

Movements are brought to life by individuals, however, and to review the 1900's without concentrating on the phenomenon of Theodore Roosevelt would miss the point as well as a good part of the excitement. Roosevelt, like William Allen White, had started out as a conservative interested in clean government but opposed to social legislation. As they matured, each became an advocate of reform legislation and the rebalancing of the power structure in the country. The difference was that Roosevelt, an aristocrat, represented the "patricians" of reform, the upper class leaders who from time to time make a permanent impression on American life, usually chastising the class that nurtured them, but generally recognizing, in their own conservative way, that timely reforms are a much better alternative than

60

drastic change, even for the privileged. By 1900, he had served a popular term as Governor of New York, having learned the effectiveness of reform as a source of votes when he ran third behind Henry George in the New York Mayoralty election of 1886. He was the ideal man to lend ultimate respectability to the progressive movement since his impulse to reform was solidly tempered by an impulse not to go too far. It was still with some misgivings that the Republican bosses matched him as a running mate with McKinley against the magnetic Bryan in 1896 and with more concern that they saw him suddenly become President in 1901.

Roosevelt left a permanent imprint on national policy as the strongest president since Abraham Lincoln. A good deal of his success rested on expanding the progressive doctrines of executive leadership and its corollary, effective regulation under the policing of strong administrators. This type of thinking had a direct bearing on the future theory of the reform legislation that would create the consumer finance business, namely a sound law which provided for regulation through strong supervision.

Typical of Roosevelt's use of executive leadership was his prodding of Congress to forbid railroad rebates, strengthen the Interstate Commerce Commission, pass a meat-inspection act and a pure food and drug law, bring the federal government into the workmen's compensation field and withdraw vast acreages of land for conservation purposes. Lashing out at the "malefactors of great wealth," Roosevelt put new teeth in the Sherman Antitrust Law, making it clear, however, that his purpose was to regulate corporate growth and not to destroy it. When the Supreme Court upheld in 1904 the government's prosecution of the Northern Securities Company railroad combination as a restraint of trade, Roosevelt earned a reputation as a "trust buster" which heightened progressive enthusiasm for the colorful President even though in fact not much had changed in that particular area. What had changed was the atmosphere in Washington which made it clear that the government considered itself to be a force in the economy with which business interests must reckon. A further startling example of executive leadership was Roosevelt's assumption of the position of arbiter in the anthracite coal strike in 1902, when he called both strikers and operators to the White House and forced the arrogant operators to settle by the exertion of his own position and personality. The concept of regulation by a neutral executive was firmly launched in American government during Roosevelt's administration. One happy result was that a new generation of men of talent and integrity decided to follow the crusading President into the service of both the federal and state governments.

IV

Still another factor contributed to the crusading progressivism of the 1900's, which was to include reform loan legislation in its wake, and that was the journalism of the era. There occurred in the early 1900's a tremendous vogue for sensational, fact-packed exposé journalism in the mass circulation magazines which have since been labelled "muckraking" articles. The term muckraking was applied to the magazines in a petulant moment by Roosevelt himself, comparing them in an uncomplimentary manner to the rakers of muck in Bunyan's *Pilgrim's Progress*. Actually, Roosevelt wrote in the same vein himself and was an excellent muckraker. He had contributed articles to these magazines including one for the champion of all, *McClure's*, entitled—one wonders whether Arthur Ham read it—"Reform through Social Work," in March 1901. In *McClure's, Collier's, Everybody's, Harper's Weekly, Munsey's* and other magazines, some of the best writers in the country whipped up the interest and emotions of millions of readers about items of corruption and chicanery in the halls of business, politics and other American institutions. S. S. McClure had sent Lincoln Steffens on a tour of American cities resulting in a series called *The Shame of the Cities,* which kept people on edge to see which metropolis was next on the seamy list. Ida Tarbell wrote a devastating history of the Standard Oil Company with facts so carefully checked that the usual libel suit was not forthcoming. In all, at the height of the muckraking movement, ten journals were publishing about three million magazines a week featuring articles of exposure. *Harper's Weekly* ran a series on loan sharks in 1908 with titles such as "The Lures of the Loan Shark" and "Parasites of the Poor" [2] in which the villainy of the sharks and their legal subterfuges were outlined with detective's thoroughness and skill to be emulated by district attorneys and the Russell Sage Foundation people within a short time. The difference was that the muckraking articles were all exposures of the loan sharks. There was yet no interest in a remedy or a solution for the social problem involved. The muckraking magazines ran out of ideas within a few years and began to lose their worried advertisers as well, but this type of literature, in addition to books like Upton Sinclair's *The Jungle,* about the meat-packing industry, and Frank Norris' *The Octopus,* about railroad corruption, played a most important part in the reform movement.

The newspapers of the time were equally sensational and competitive. The immensely rapid shift of the population from country to city had greatly enlarged newspaper circulation. In 1877 there were only 574 daily newspapers in the country; by 1909 there were over 2,600. The circulation had increased from 2,800,000 to 24,000,000 in this period, an effect on communications comparable in magnitude to our introduction of television. These newspapers were read by city dwellers who often felt detached and anonymous in their sprawling city habitats away from either the town or the country of their birth. The editors quickly learned to offer them gossip, human interest stories, interviews and crusades in their ruthless scrambles for circulation. Dominated by men like Joseph Pulitzer and William Randolph

Hearst, the papers even created events to report, sending the reporter Nellie Bly around the world or helping to stir up a war with Spain, thus creating enough personal publicity for the rough-riding Teddy Roosevelt to guarantee his eventual ascendancy to the White House. In a fascinating way this ability to carry a crusade into the newspapers was of tremendous importance in the Sage Foundation's success in fighting the loan sharks. Strangely enough, a great deal of support was forthcoming from newspaper men, particularly the reporters and city editors, who, like the railroad workers, had a great predilection for using the services of the sharks, reflecting some occupational characteristics not yet analysed.[3]

A similar development in the progressive story worthy of mention is the growth of the "consumer" as a special interest group in addition to the usual interests of the farmer, the businessman and the laborer. The new laws regulating the sale of certain foods and drugs, for example, were consumer protection laws of a pioneering nature. It was in this era that politicians began to feel the pressures of the city-dwelling, magazine-and-newspaper-reading clerk, laborer, businessman or housewife, all equally indignant over rising prices, monopolies, false advertising and other harassments affecting their daily bread. There were already Consumers' Leagues in existence in many large cities and times were propitious for concern over other revealed consumer needs such as the borrowing of money.

V

While Americans rode their bicycles and played their phonographs, at least 1,700,000 children under the age of sixteen were employed in factories and fields. In the factories, mines and on the railroads, the accident rate was higher than in any other industrial nation in the world. In 1907, an average of twelve railroad men were killed every week. In the rapidly expanding industrial system, little was done to prevent occupational diseases such as phosphorous and lead poisoning. The masses of immigrants that had passed into America were easily exploited. Although conditions were greatly improved over the appalling standards of mid-century America, wages were more often than not at subsistence levels and the city tenements were crammed with people working in their own sweatshops. Seven-eighths of the country's income and wealth belonged to the top one-eighth in a system pledged to provide opportunity for all.

Yet a nation which fought a war over slavery could also be expected to have a resurgence of national conscience, and this moral quality was to be the distinctive ingredient of the progressive movement. The tone of the movement was almost evangelical and its leaders often thought of themselves as crusaders, readily admitting they were picking up civic responsibilities their own fathers had neglected. Woodrow Wilson, who carried the progressive movement to its peak before it expired under the exigencies of World War I, was often thought of as a preacher in the White House.

America's background, of course, is highly endowed with morality, tracing its high-minded lineage through the Puritan fathers to the social justice of the Judaic-Christian tradition. Our lapses are as periodic as our peaks, however, and the resurgence of morality in the 1900's was an actual felt phenomenon. "One could hear virtue cracking and crushing all around," wrote Walter Rauschenbusch, a New York minister who preached the social gospel, ran a church in New York's "Hell's Kitchen" and wrote a book called *Christianity and the Social Crisis* in 1907 which made its readers blush to think how Henry Ward Beecher had been venerated not so long ago. Father John Augustus Ryan joined in the fight for social justice under the authority of Pope Leo XIII's encyclical *Rerum Novarum*, which deplored the fact that "a small number of very rich men have been able to lay upon the masses of the poor a yoke little better than slavery itself." European influences were eagerly absorbed by an America which had cast aside its isolationism for a questionable imperialism in the Spanish-American war and would soon fight for the world's democracy in 1917. England, our waiting ally, had already had its turn-of-the-century social justice or reform movement. Englishmen like William Morris and John Ruskin, who glorified working with one's own hands, also had emphasized the morality of social reform and had a wide following in America. Almost every prominent English reformer had visited the United States and many of the progressive leaders had visited and studied in England. Toynbee Hall, the first of the settlement houses in England, had been started in a wave of upper class conscience pangs by Arnold Toynbee, uncle of the historian, in the 1880's in the Whitechapel section of London. Young Jane Addams had worked at Toynbee Hall and in 1899 she returned to the United States to establish Hull House in Chicago, which soon had imitators in Boston and New York. The Salvation Army, a direct import from England, had 3,000 officers and 20,000 privates in America by 1900. The doers of good were reinforced particularly by the legions of newly emancipated women who did not yet have the vote but were taking other matters into their own hands. Typical of the upper class progressive women who worked in the settlement houses of New York as a social worker before her marriage in 1905 was Theodore Roosevelt's niece Eleanor. In summary, the progressive movement was essentially morally directed. Its actual reforms now hold a minor place in the cumulative total of America's reforms since the Civil War. They are outweighed by the practical, necessity-ridden, experimental changes that Franklin D. Roosevelt was required to usher in after the catastrophic depression of the 1930's, but their record is a bright one in America's history.

VI

Such was the background of the times and influences bearing down upon Arthur Ham while he attended Bowdoin College. There is no reason to think that upon graduation he felt the impulse to reform as his own destiny, or even that he accepted all the premises of the progressive movement. We can assume one fact, however, and that is the world was too exciting, there was too much to learn about and see before he could decide whether or not to return to the small town way of life. The same adventurous spirit that had led him to the sea directed him to the biggest city of all to pursue his education.

V

NEW YORK, NEW YORK

Let us imagine a parade of 200,000 men, sixteen abreast, in close formation, reaching the Washington Arch on Fifth Avenue to 130th Street, a distance of six and one-half miles. In the front ranks are 2,500 firemen, then 2,000 other city employees, 500 letter carriers, 75,000 clerks of railroads, insurance companies, and public service corporations, 75,000 employees from large mercantile houses, with school teachers, professional and business men, and others totalling 50,000 more . . .

Of all the splendid sights in New York, nothing matches a parade. A parade of such dimensions, however, would be a rare occasion, even on St. Patrick's Day. The description goes on:

If you will just imagine a parade of this size and character, you will get an idea of the loan shark evil in New York.[1]

The narrator was Arthur H. Ham, still in his twenties, addressing the Merchants' Association of New York City in 1911. He spoke as the Director of the new Department of Remedial Loans of the Russell Sage Foundation. In his dramatic presentation,

68

styled on the muckrakers themselves, the crusading young executive was giving a preview of the vigor and imagination with which he intended to stalk the loan shark and net him. He had found by chance an assignment calling for all of his skills and resources and he had plunged eagerly into the field which would engage him for most of the rest of his working life. He was to become the country's leading expert and authority on small loans and would make decisions that could spell life or death for the future of the loan industry.

II

Arthur Ham had enrolled in the graduate school of Columbia University after graduating from Bowdoin College in 1908. The New York of his day was a city of violent contrasts, with only a few blocks separating the richest and the poorest people of America, the palatial homes of Fifth Avenue and the slums of Mulberry Street and Hell's Kitchen. The city had made considerable progress in alleviating its worst problem, housing, since the crusading reporter Jacob A. Riis had written his memorable book *How the Other Half Lives,* in 1890, forcing tenement reform under the leadership of stalwart citizens like Robert de Forest. It could not keep up with the tremendous influx of immigrants from southern and eastern Europe, however, and of the city's three and one-half million population, two-thirds lived in tenements which for the most part were substandard. In the single year of 1905, over 1,250,000 of this new type of immigrant had passed through Ellis Island into the promised land. Most of them decided to stay on in the great metropolis which they enriched with their labor and ambition. The city grew and prospered, with its trolleys, skyscrapers, great stores and the thundering Manhattan Elevated Railroad—Russell Sage's legacy—careening over Sixth Avenue and pumping dividends into the Russell Sage Foundation. Some of the Foundation's income had been used to provide grants for fellowships in the Bureau of Research at the New York School of Philanthropy, which was closely allied with Columbia. Here occurred one of those accidents of life which so often affect history.

The Foundation had provided the school with a large list of subjects on which it thought research projects would be desirable. Making appropriations to other agencies was a quick way for the new Foundation to get started in its endeavors while building up its own staff and projects, and these grants were among the first to be made. The list was submitted to two graduate studdents at Columbia, selected for the fellowships, Clarence W. Wassam in 1907 and Arthur Ham in 1908. Wassam chose *The Salary Loan Business in New York City,* which he published under the imprint of the Russell Sage Foundation in 1908 as part of his requirement for his Ph.D. degree at Columbia. Ham, for no apparent reason, chose *The Chattel Loan Business,* the business of lending on personal security rather than wage-assignments, to supplement Wassam's study.

We know why the Foundation was interested in the loan problem. It reflected very definitely Robert de Forest's acquaintance with the problem from his connection with the Provident Loan Society and, of course, W. F. Persons had been concerned with it as a social worker and as screener of Mrs. Sage's 60,000 letters. What fortuitous event led Ham to choose his subject is a matter of conjecture. Certainly in his experience in Livermore Falls, loan sharks were non-existent. His father, secretary of the bank, would be interested in loans, but not small loans, which were definitely a big city specialty. At any rate, Arthur Ham recognized the topic would be a fertile field to explore and he spent three months in the preparation of his paper.

Naturally his first move would be to review Wassam's research which had already been completed. Wassam is one of the unsung heroes of the reform loan movement, being so completely overshadowed by Ham who made it his career. Yet Wassam's study was by far the more thorough and important one and of particular significance because he arrived at pioneering conclusions and recommendations to which Ham also subscribed.

III

Clarence Wassam was born in the town of Hudson, Black Hawk County, Iowa on October 23, 1877. He attended the Iowa State Normal School at Cedar Falls, Iowa for four years, graduating with the degree of Master of Didactics in 1900. He taught in the public schools of Hudson, Iowa for one year, then went to the State University of Iowa in Iowa City where he did special work in Political Economy and Sociology, receiving a Bachelor of Philosophy degree in 1903 and a Master of Arts degree in 1904. He held a scholarship in economics for the year 1903-1904 and a fellowship in economics for the year 1904-1905 in the State University's School of Political and Social Science. After a teaching stint at the University of Iowa, he applied for one of the Sage fellowships at the New York School of Philanthropy and came to New York and Columbia to spend the fellowship towards obtaining his Ph.D. degree.

His paper on the salary loan business, which was much more important than the chattel loan business in New York City at that time, is a remarkable combination of research, investigation and presentation, far surpassing Ham's more superficial follow-up on the chattel loan business. One could speculate that here was the man who would be well-equipped to make loan history as agent of the Foundation. Apparently he did not have any interest in this direction, or more likely was seen by the Sage officials as not having the particular propaganda and executive talents of Ham. At any rate, although Wassam and Ham are quoted in all the loan company activist literature from then on as a kind of academic team whose "scientific" research proved beyond a doubt the necessity of fair legislation, Wassam, the true academic, vanished from the hurly-burly of New York to return to the teaching world. In the fall of 1908, with his tidy little booklet in his valise, he returned to the University of Iowa faculty and stayed there until 1928. During these years he lectured extensively all over the Iowa region, specialising in lyceum and commencement addresses before educational groups. In the summer for seventeen years he lectured on the Chautauqua circuits covering practically every state in the country. This was the period when the Foundation officials were hammering away at the state legislatures to pass regulatory laws but Wassam evidently had closed that chapter in his life, although he would have made an expert witness. In 1928, he joined the faculty of Florida State University in Gainseville but poor health forced his return to Iowa City where he died in June 1931 at the age of fifty-four.

Wassam was only thirty-one when he wrote his salary loan paper. The following section from his introduction indicates the vision and maturity the young mid-westerner brought to bear upon his study:

The business man when he secures a loan from his bank finds that the strong arm of the law has so regulated the banking business that the borrower is reasonably well protected. He also finds that there is no special disgrace connected with a loan secured by a mortgage on his real estate or on his business. His friends consider that he is speculating and is prosperous. The maxim that "One never becomes rich until he is in debt" is considered sound in the business world. A very different condition of affairs exists when a man is compelled to borrow money for purposes of consumption. There is a reason for this difference. The one man used the money he borrowed as an investment, while the other man borrowed as a last resort to maintain his economic independence.

The man who loans money to the latter type of borrower is very likely to be considered cruel and unreasonable if he attempts to collect his debt when the borrower is unable to pay. The very fact that it is necessary for an individual to borrow to meet living expenses is evidence that it will be difficult for him to meet his obligations. This condition of affairs naturally increases the risk of the loan, for which there should be a reasonable return. The position of the borrower is uncertain and the amount of the loan is small, and both of these considerations require a higher rate of interest. It is therefore evident that in order to conduct a business in which a small loan is made to salaried employees secured by an assignment of wages, it is necessary to charge a higher rate of interest than the ordinary legal one. These facts are often overlooked by the ordinary individual and when a money lender charges more than the legal rate he is immediately marked as a usurer. This popular opinion is reflected in the laws of the several states, practically all of which provide for a general usury law, but very few make any exception as to the amount of the loan or the nature of the security offered. The bill recently introduced in the House of Representatives at Albany by Representative Herrick from the Borough of Manhattan, New York City, is a good illustration of this type of legislation. It provides that to charge more than 6 per cent *per annum* upon small loans secured by salary or household furniture shall be a misdemeanor.

The presence of a very definite economic need, and the absence of legislative protection to any organization which would legitimately fill such a need, has resulted in the development of the salary money lenders, commonly known as "loan sharks." Their operations are very extensive and they do a large business in practically all of the important cities of the United States. They either openly ignore the law or evade the spirit of it by some scheme of administration cleverly devised and charge a rate of interest which is believed to be not only sufficient to pay for the additional risk which they take, but adequate to secure enormous profits for those engaged in the business.[2]

Wassam's approach to his subject was pure investigation. He kept records of interviews with one hundred and thirty-two borrowers, some of whom were personal acquaintances. He interviewed the managers of twelve different offices to get the facts on how they conducted their business. Since the business thrived on secrecy at the time and had already become the object of intermittent hues and cries from some of the newspapers and the district attorneys' offices, Wassam must have been a particularly disarming man to gain their confidence. Perhaps it was because he convinced them that he would present both sides of the story or that he held out a glimmer of legislation that would protect them as well as the borrowers. At any rate, he not only got his facts and loan papers, all of which he printed in the appendices of his treatise, but he also hinted at some kind of ingenious inside information tactics by stating: "The relation between the writer and owner of two large offices and the manager of five important offices was such that a considerable amount of information from their point of view was secured." [3]

Wassam's illustrations of how these loans were made calls attention to the fact that not factory workers but salaried men were the major clientele of loan sharks in those days as well as the participants in Arthur Ham's parade. The emergence of the need to borrow on the part of the consumer is often discussed as a by-product of America's new industrialism after the Civil War which created a wage-earning class that desperately required loans to meet emergencies. This is not particularly borne out by the available statistics which indicate the lenders themselves preferred to do business with the frayed and genteel middle class and civil servant class which just couldn't live on their meager incomes. The non-competitive field was too much of a monopoly for the lenders to go all the way down the ladder and deal with the immigrants and the more precariously employed wage-earners if they could help it. Even the lenders who lent on chattels such as furniture or wagons and horses dealt with a similar group of customers, including many rooming-house keepers and small businessmen.

The idea that such respectable people were handling their affairs so poorly as to get into debt created a real obstacle in the efforts to get public approval for the concept of the business as a public necessity. Newspapers such as the *New York Times* never lost an opportunity to criticize the borrowers as well as the lenders on such a premise and some of this attitude carried over into the Sage Foundation's first approach. The semi-philanthropic loan agencies of which the Foundation approved, such as the Provident Loan Society, took a paternalistic attitude toward their borrowers and made attempts to limit borrowing to loans for good purposes.

The salary loan business, however, by its very nature encouraged loans for the races or other sporting instincts of this so-called Victorian Age. First of all, it was easier to make a salary loan than a chattel loan. The lender only had to verify the employment, a task made particularly easy when the fireman, policeman or letter carrier walked in, whereas the chattel lender had to undergo expensive, time-consuming credit and character checking, since his loan was not made on a wage-assignment. The salary lender preferred the wage-assignment for other reasons, including the fact that the claim on the borrower's wages was almost guaranteed security for repayment, as this was an age when employers believed strongly in the sanctity of contracts. This included, incidentally, the rights of a bakery proprietor and his bakers to contract for the bakers to work more than ten hours a day or sixty a week, in spite of a New York State law to the contrary, according to a famous Supreme Court decision (*Lochner* v. *New York*, 1905). The decision caused Oliver Wendell Holmes to look down his patrician nose and register a vigorous dissenting opinion.

If the borrower decided to fight the lender's wage-assignment, there was the equally effective threat of using the assignment in the first place, as the employers to a man would generally fire an employee who dared show such irresponsibility in his financial affairs. In addition, this wage-assignment, tied as it was to the weekly or bi-weekly pay check, was made to order to create chronic, repeat borrowing, as often no planned retirement of the principal was provided for and the borrower could be counted upon to renew his loan over and over for a fee. A final

75

argument in favor of the salary loan rested upon the fact that in case the matter was brought to court as a usurious transaction, the ingenious lender would claim that it was not a loan of money but a purchase of salary, like the purchase of any other commodity, and Wassam exhibited the bill of sale that was taken for that purpose as well as the wage-assignment itself. The New York salary lenders felt so confident about their technique that they even violated their usual tactic of beating a strategic retreat when attorneys or employers demanded settlements for borrowers by taking the case of *Thompson* v. *Erie Railroad* right up to a victory in the Appellate Division in Brooklyn, only to find the judgment reversed in the Court of Appeals when Walter S. Hilborn, a Foundation attorney, argued a similar case successfully for the borrower several years after Wassam's analysis.[4]

Wassam pointed out what must be considered the height of impunity regarding the salary lenders' attitude by quoting the following from the *Montreal Star* of March 3, 1908, concerning one of the most enterprising of New York's salary lenders, D. H. Tolman, who was soon to acquire fame as the "King of the Loan Sharks":

Word was recently sent out by Mr. A. Bienvenue, of the city licensing department that the money-lenders would have to pay the sum of $200 a year under by-law 362 which so provides.

When the notification was sent to his (D. H. Tolman's) office here it was forwarded to him in Brooklyn, for, of course, it could not be handed to him in Montreal. In due course the following answer was received by Mr. Bienvenue:

Auditing Department,
D. H. TOLMAN
Room 515
367 Fulton Street,
Brooklyn, N. Y., Feb. 26th, 1908.
Mr. A. Bienvenue, Supt. of Licenses, Montreal:

Dear Sir.—Replying to yours of 24th, would say you seem to be under the impression that my office in your city now does a money-lending business, WHICH IT DOES NOT DO. We have done no loaning business in Canada for about two years. We simply buy time. That is if a man wants to sell a week's or a month's future wages we buy the same, just as we would so much growing crop of wheat or apples on the trees, or any other commodity, for future use. WE TAKE NO NOTES WHATSOEVER, THERE-FORE NO INTEREST. Consequently we are not liable for any money-lending license whatever. I am, however, perfectly willing to pay my business tax, same as any one else does, any time, in proportion to my rent, and, I don't think that you should try to enforce any license that I am not liable for, or in any way to annoy my employees or to cable at my expense, as I wish to do the proper thing and obey the laws at all times.

Yours very truly,
D. H. TOLMAN

Mr. Tolman is invited to come to Montreal and discuss the question with the city attorney.[5]

Wassam thoroughly reviewed the ineffectual regulations re-garding wage-assignments in the various states, but he concen-trated on conditions in New York. He noted that there had been the first of a long series of prosecutions of salary lenders by the New York County District Attorney in 1903-1904. This resulted in the closing of practically all of the offices in New York City for the simple reason that the District Attorney, Mr. Jerome, decided to ask the courts to regard violations as mis-demeanors in conformity with the law. By an amendment to the Penal Code in 1904, however, salary loans were excluded from criminal prosecution, and back the lenders came to re-open their offices, welcomed by generally friendly courts. Their only new legal problem was that the law of 1904 provided the employer would have to be notified within three days after the assignment of wages had been made for the assignment to be effective. The

77

wily lenders, who seemed to have a hydra-headed ability to counter every obstacle, had the borrower sign a power of attorney to the lender's attorney who in turn would stand in the wings as a dummy ready to sign the bill of sale regarding the salary assignment within three days' time of its later service upon the employer. *Thompson* v. *Erie Railroad* referred to such a case.

Another device used to circumvent any regulation at all by the state of New York was the practice of a lender named H. A. Courtright, who used a broker to negotiate the loan for a fee in New York, while payments were made by mail to Courtright's office in Providence, which had issued the check. The use of the "broker" concept persisted wherever evasion of loan laws was tried, until the Uniform Small Loan Law's sophisticated and all-embracing language nipped the subterfuge once and for all. The heritage of this device lived on in the naming of the first national trade association of the lenders, which was short-sightedly called The American Association of Small Loan Brokers.

IV

One of the most difficult facts to realize about the loan business of the pre-regulation days is the small size of the loans. The salary loans of the period were generally in the $10 to $40 range and the chattel loans averaged only about twice that amount. Even allowing for a four to one inflation of the 1900 dollar, one can see that the dollars involved were small and if a lender were to cover his overhead and make a profit commensurate with his risk, the rates would be extremely high, which they were. The average salary loan office analyzed by Wassam was estimated to have only $10,000 out in loans but the annual rate of interest was of course in the 120% to 240% or more range.

Wassam detailed the usual cases of harsh collections and other disasters to be expected from an underground business, and even devoted a section to the rather amiable advertising which the lenders used. In his discussions of personnel, one is fascinated to find that the typical loan office manager in a New York salary loan office was a woman. According to Wassam, one worried manager told him: "We never give our rates to anyone until we make the loan and we never permit anyone to see the papers the customers sign. We must be very careful about our business or we might all get put in jail like the girls did a few years ago when the District Attorney drove all the salary loan offices out of New York City." Wassam further noted:

The offices are almost exclusively in charge of women and girls. Several reasons are given for this situation, a very important consideration being that it is cheaper. Another important reason is that D. H. Tolman, who owns offices in sixty-three different cities, has made it is his custom for several years to hire young women and in so doing they have learned the business. The result has been that in nearly every case when a new loan office has been opened in the city the owner has secured the services of one of Tolman's experienced managers. This has been a source of much trouble to Mr. Tolman, who has tried several plans to keep his employees from leaving him and working for a competitor. He insists as a condition of employment that each new employee sign an agreement that she will not reveal the secrets of his business and will not enter the employ of any individual doing a similar business for a period of two years after the termination of her contract with him. The contract is extremely binding and is so worded that the salary is considered compensation for services rendered and for keeping the aforesaid agreement. Some have suggested that the women managers are employed in order to avoid friction with angry customers. It would be very difficult indeed for the customers to refrain from physical violence if they were treated by a man as they are often treated by the women managers, although it must be said that the women in charge of some of the offices are most courteous.[6]

One gets the impression of a rather un-gallant Mr. Tolman letting his girls run unnecessary risks but certainly not assigning them outside collection work. We find, however, that both the salary loan offices and the chattel loan offices relied strongly on a female employee called the "bawlerout" whose job was to go to the place of employment of the delinquent borrower and bawl him out in front of all his colleagues for not paying his bills. One of the most unbelievable mementoes of the loan shark age is an actual novel called *The Bawlerout* written by one Forrest Halsey and published in 1912. The bawlerout is employed in the loan office of a man named Charker. She falls in love with a hapless bank clerk who works for the Tobacco National Bank for eighteen dollars a week and, like any good bank clerk might, falls into Charker's clutches. Meanwhile, a high class gentleman named Brice has been trying to get a loan from Charker and Company but they suspect his references and turn him down. The bawlerout, a Miss Sullivan, portrayed by the author as a kind of Irish Gibson Girl with flaring nostrils and a silver voice that strikes terror in the hearts of slow-payers, meanwhile has been fired for bawling out the Tobacco National Bank President instead of his cowering clerk. Brice tells Miss Sullivan that he is really a person who intends to set up an agency to lend money at reasonable rates and in connection with it offer legal aid to help the victims of the sharks. The problem is first to find out who Charker is, as he operates invisibly. Miss Sullivan ingeniously discovers that Charker is none other than Mr. Bendis, President of the Tobacco National Bank, who is also embezzling his own bank's trust accounts. Charker is apprehended, Miss Sullivan marries the bank clerk and Mr. Brice, elegantly attired in a silk topper and cape, sets out to establish his semi-philanthropic loan agency.

V

Wassam's business was a serious one, however, and *The Bawlerout* would have remained in literary limbo had not Col. Frank Hodson, founder of Beneficial Finance Co., deemed it worthy of inclusion in a bibliography of loan subjects he was personally distributing from 1919 on, in which he described *The Bawlerout* as a "Sociological Convincing Study of the Loan Shark Evil Carried Through the Medium of a Pretty Love Story." [7] Wassam's less romantic summary of his study came to these conclusions:

1. So many people in large cities had to spend their entire income for the bare necessities of life, there would constantly be cases where a loan to be repaid in small instalments was an absolute necessity.
2. The present underground business resulted in evasion of the law and exploitation of the borrowers.
3. Legislation, more semi-philanthropic lending agencies and publicity to drive out the loan sharks were needed.
4. The legislation should recognize the lending of small sums as a special type of lending which should have close regulation and a rate permitting a fair profit.
5. "The evils in the present system should be remedied, the poor who are compelled to borrow in time of need should be protected from the unjust charges of the money lender, but care should be taken not to destroy the present system until something better has been developed to take its place." [8]

To that end, he appended an actual draft of a law covering both salary and chattel loans, prepared by Dr. Samuel McCune Lindsay, Professor of Social Legislation at Columbia and Frank Tucker, vice-president of the Provident Loan Society. The bill was an admirable one in many respects, providing for regulation, licensing, elimination of extra charges and the power of the Superintendent of Banks in New York to determine and establish reasonable rates of interest for each type of loan. The law, of course, never passed and was just one more in a series of frustrating efforts at legislation which would await the full-time leadership of the Russell Sage Foundation before progress could be made. Wassam, however, deserves particular praise for his brilliant far-seeing conclusions which must have encouraged the Foundation officials to keep loan legislation high on their list of works for "social betterment." He demonstrated himself to be a thorough and ingenious investigator, even going so far as to borrow from Courtright personally and then to sue Courtright to invalidate the usurious transaction.[9] He set the style for the formidable arraying of facts and figures that would be the tradition in all future discussions of lending and he inspired Arthur Ham to complete and round out his study of conditions in New York City.

VI

Arthur Ham's report on the chattel loan business was distinguished in its own right. He established that the chattel loan companies also produced distressing results among borrowers who in his opinion were generally more deserving and needful of small loans than the salary borrowers. He deplored the fact that a remedy by legislation seemed presently unobtainable and agreed with Wassam that the laws were continually punctured by evasions, reviewing several techniques of the chattel lenders in that respect such as obtaining receipts for extending cash in full, regardless of deductions. At that stage, he concluded that philanthropic competition was the most practicable remedy, offering the cities of Cincinnati and Baltimore as cases in point. He noted that chattel loan companies could incorporate and charge two per cent a month under the New York law but pointed out that most of them didn't bother to incorporate because they didn't want the accompanying supervision and felt they couldn't operate at 24% a year anyway. Somewhat despairingly, he stated that lenders were having little difficulty in evading the law by devices that made proof of usury almost impossible, even though, in the case of chattel loans, the penalty was both a fine and imprisonment.

He did not see much hope in Wassam's prescription of publicity, either, stating that aside from bringing the plight of a few borrowers and their experiences to the public attention and perhaps slowing down the lenders, the publicity was soon forgotten and conditions resumed their former status. On the other hand, he expressed optimism in laws plus competition, especially the competition of semi-philanthropic companies. This attitude was repeated by Professor Samuel McCune Lindsay who in the foreword to the paper stated the case for both competition and legislation but warned that "legislation can make an effective contribution if for merely repressive measures it will substitute discretionary action based on contemporary knowledge." An important consensus was building up between social workers and professors that repressive legislation was not the answer.

Ham reported that only three of New York's forty chattel loan companies were within the law, and, like Wassam, he collected advertising and walked into the offices to apply for loans himself. The typical loan was $50 for eight weeks, for a charge of $15, which he stated averaged about 100% a year. In a short time, he would be calculating these charges more accurately, this case, for example, being at least 360% per annum. Some of the subterfuges were ingenious as usual. One lender required the borrower to buy a worthless oil painting at a price sufficient to sign up the loan at 6% per annum. Others required tie-in sales of life insurance. Another required the borrower to sell his furniture and "lease it back," but generally obtaining a receipt for more money than the borrower received was considered adequate. Ham's range could not be confined to New York alone, however, and in a preview of the national point of view he would soon take, he included in his report a mass of information from Philadelphia, where so many unemployed people were losing their household furniture to chattel loan companies in 1907 that the sheriffs raided the offices of a number of concerns and seized their records. Excessive charges and collection practices were the same as found in New York but the durable lenders would not die easily. "The campaign conducted by the Philadelphia Department of Public Safety seriously affected the receipts of the loan companies for the time being," he wrote, "but it cannot be said that the campaign was productive of any lasting results for as soon as the activity of the Department waned, business returned to its former basis. Not only are the old companies continuing to operate as we have said, but new companies of the same sort are known to have entered the field." [10]

In a section entitled "What the Philanthropic Companies are Doing," however, Ham felt himself to be on more optimistic ground, and it was obvious that he thought a proliferation of these limited profit, low-rate companies would solve the problem by out-competing the high-rate lenders who so easily flouted the law. Baltimore, he noted, had once been considered one of the best "loan towns" in the East. The law even encouraged loan sharks by allowing 6% plus almost unlimited charges for drawing papers, and the penalty for charging more than 6% was simply the return of the excessive interest. It was a lender's paradise, but into this paradise stepped the Reverend Maltbie B. Babcock in 1897 to gather capital of $75,000 and start The Loan Association of Baltimore, a chattel loan company which would operate at 6% plus the least charges possible and when it found out what these were, would ask the legislature to make those charges the maximum, which it did in 1902. By 1907, reported Ham, the two largest commercial loan firms had been driven out of the city and the others were practically inactive. "The experience shows that much can be accomplished by legislation, but that more can be afforded by lending money at low rates, and that such a business is a fair-paying safe investment for capital." [11] He noted a similar program at St. Bartholomew's Loan Association in New York and a handful of others making chattel loans. "The experience of these companies proves that 1% per month business may be profitable," [12] was Ham's tentative conclusion, with a well-considered use of the subjunctive tense, since he would repudiate the statement soon enough when he had more facts.

Several financial statements of semi-philanthropic firms were appended to his report. They were certainly not a fair basis for establishing the income and expense for a commercial enterprise but they were the *only* financial statements available in the entire field. They were the beginning of an informed, impartial approach to the costs of lending money in small sums and as such would prove to be invaluable guidelines for future legislation. This legislation would be based on a chattel type of commercial lending rather than the less constructive and easily exploited salary loan. The chattel idea provided a most uniquely suitable security. It required the lender to rely on character and credit as well as security. The security stayed in the possession of the borrower who yet felt a compulsion to protect it by paying his obligation. The basic, helpful relationship between borrower and lender was possible as against the sheer odds in the lender's favor represented by the salary loan. Finally, the chattel loan was more suitable for encouraging a liquidation of the loan over a period of time as against the shorter term salary loan. This reluctance to encourage orderly liquidation was one of the severest indictments of the whole unregulated loan industry in the first place.

For a twenty-six year old graduate student, Ham had made a good start. Mr. de Forest and Mr. Glenn thought so, too, and they hired Arthur Ham right out of college as the Foundation's agent to promote the work of the newly formed National Federation of Remedial Loan Associations, an association of fourteen chattel loan companies of a semi-philanthropic nature.

VI

AN OLD PROFESSION

When Arthur Ham became a staff member of the Foundation on August 1, 1909, his assignment was "to make a study of the Remedial Loan Associations of the country, to give advice to societies already established as to methods of work and to give advice to those who wish to know about the formation of new societies." [1]

Note the emphasis on "study" in Ham's original assignment. In keeping with the intellectual, scientific approach to reform, rather than the pragmatic, emergency-laden trial and error method of say, the New Deal period, the reformer of the early 1900's laid great emphasis on first, study and then laws based on these studies. In the literature of the loan legislation propagandists, over and over again reference is made to the recommendations of the most eminent "students" of the lending industry. This cover of intellectual detachment provided a most unique opportunity for the men of the ivory tower to work with the men of business and politics. An additional reason, of course, that made such a liaison possible was the fact that this earlier generation of tower inmates, unlike their successors, had a most congenial respect for the profit motive. Even their semi-philanthropic lending agencies were based on "philanthropy plus six per cent" and one may recall Robert de Forest's first list of tentative projects for the Foundation, which included retail stores and industrial insurance for the poorer classes "at cost plus a reasonable profit of say 6%."

Arthur Ham was to become the leading student as well as authority on the lending business. In his Foundation files, which rest unclassified and unsorted in the stacks of the Library of Congress, there is ample evidence of the wide-ranging interests of the historian and economist as well as the busy department director promoting semi-philanthropic lending agencies, commercial lending agencies and credit unions. For example, his files include photostats of the first unregulated lenders' ads which appeared in the Chicago newspapers in 1869, correspondence with students writing papers on usury and other aspects of lending, even correspondence with ministers and rabbis about the theology of interest. It remained for Professor Louis N. Robinson and Rolf Nugent, Ham's successor after Leon Henderson, to publish in 1935 the Foundation's *Regulation of the Small Loan Business*, which was the first definitive history, but Ham's research and activities are reflected in its pages. This Foundation book also owes a great deal to the brilliant Leon Henderson, who similarly supplied background and insight to Evans Clark's pioneering *Financing the Consumer*, which was published under credit union auspices in 1930.

II

Joining this company of students of lending, what do we find as antecedents for today's billions of dollars in consumer credit, including five billion dollars now held by the consumer finance industry? Depending on how far back one wishes to delve, the story is as old as money. In fact, the lending of money is one of the world's oldest professions, which probably accounts for the recurring skepticism about its virtue.

In the earliest days of primitive societies, lending was purely philanthropic, almost a duty, as tribes owning communal property could hardly conceive of charging anything for the use of such property. To the extent that primitive property was privately owned, it was not through the acquisitive instinct which mankind was to develop soon enough, but because the property had an animistic, or spiritual relationship, with the owner. A far-fetched example from a far-fetched age would be a ball player's lucky bat.

In time, man sought additional problems to those involved in the hunting of game and the protection of his wife and children. He became a land-owner, particularly in those regions, such as islands or desert areas, where land was limited. Here began the opportunity to offer something of value for loans, namely security, and the story of lending begins. At the same time, those who did not have land to borrow on had conceived of the idea of offering themselves in servitude to secure loans. It did not take much ingenuity to substitute the concept of paying interest to replace personal servitude as recompense to the lender.

Leviticus and Deuteronomy offer ample evidence of a rather highly developed property concept in the tribes of Israel over three thousand years ago. Many of the provisions of the Mosaic Code refer to protection of private property in case of damage or theft by others, and Leviticus refers to debtors who have sold themselves into servitude. The idea of interest, however, was resisted if not forbidden in laws calling for loans without interest to the poor and the cancellation of all debts every seventh year. The ancient Chinese, incidentally, developed a more favorable custom for the lender, calling for the repayment of all debts on every New Year's Day.

In practice, the taking of interest certainly existed in Biblical times, since many kings and prophets of Israel thundered against it. Having ceased their wanderings and established cities in the land of Canaan, the Israelites began to trade and trade begot interest in spite of the Mosaic Code. Meanwhile, the records show that ancient Babylonia and Assyria had far exceeded the Israelites as traders, and in these countries interest-taking was common practice, at rates of 20 to 360 per cent a year. The enlightened Babylonian Code of Hammurabi waived interest in case of flood or drought, credited the work of slaves taken as security towards the interest payment, and limited the period of servitude for debt. Hammurabi's Code preceded and influenced the Mosaic Code of the Bible, being produced in Hammurabi's reign, around 1704-1662 B.C. Cyrus Gordon, the noted scholar of antiquity at Brandeis University, calls Hammurabi's Code, discovered in cuneiform on a seven foot black diorite stone column by French archaeologists in 1901, "the apex of legal codification prior to Roman Law." He points out that the Assyrians and Babylonians of Hammurabi's time, known as Akkadians, were extremely advanced in business and law. It is his theory that the Akkadians, from about 2,000 B.C. on, devised the capitalist idea of interest for a loan of capital in a world that had previously known only barter. He traces the word for "capital" in Babylonian, *quaqqadum*, also meaning "head," to similar words in Hebrew, Aramaic, Egyptian, Greek and Latin, each meaning "capital" and "head." [2] Our word capitalism thus traces back in Latin and Greek to the Mesopotamian businessmen who devised the idea of interest as a return for capital and exported the idea to the shores of the Eastern Mediterranean. The Code establishes the rate of interest at 20% maximum and provides for the forfeiture of principal in case of overcharge. [3]

III

Leaping into western civilization, we find that Solon, the Athenian lawgiver whose name became standard for enlightened lawmakers, decreed about 594 B.C. the abolition of all debts secured by land, and the freeing of all enslaved debtors. Interest persisted at high rates in Ancient Greece, however, as well as in its successor in influence, Rome. Gibbon, in his *History of the Decline and Fall of the Roman Empire*, notes that interest was regulated and even abolished in Rome from time to time, but that non-paying debtors were still subject to imprisonment, slavery or even dismemberment under early Roman law. Interest protection extended only to Roman citizens, and the rulers of the western world thought nothing of imposing harsh interest terms on subjugated nations. Even in dealing with his fellow citizens, the Roman businessman soon learned to evade the usury laws. For example, a lender against ships' cargoes could add a handsome premium for the peril of shipwreck and additional lesser or trivial risks. The practice of tie-in charges thus has a notable genealogy which survived in the small loan field until the Russell Sage Foundation finally spelled out the idea of a single charge for interest *and* expenses.

Christianity and Mohammedanism, owing much to Judaism, were deeply influenced by the provisions of the Mosaic Code regarding usury. The early Christian Church took a stand against interest which the Medieval Church fathers, influenced by Aristotle, who labelled money "barren," as well as by Moses, deemed to be sufficient reason for prohibiting interest altogether. For over one thousand years the controversy would rage. In a series of edicts, interest was declared a punishable offense by bishops in 789, subject to excommunication in 1179, and its prohibition superseding all civil laws to the contrary in 1311. It goes without saying that the rich and the trading classes found devices to circumvent these canon laws even during the height of the Church's power in the Middle Ages.

In fact, the Church's attitude towards interest was far too complex to infer that it single-mindedly, or even successfully, prohibited interest throughout the Middle Ages and then suddenly permitted it when the growth of trade and banking in Europe made such a concept obsolete. On the record, the modern Church finally approved of interest through official pronouncements, some of them as late as 1836, but it already had made far-reaching compromises in its position even during the height of its power. There is no question about the vehemence of the official position of the Medieval Church. It had branded usury a mortal sin, a sin that was particularly reprehensible because it was tinged with avarice. Its peak of condemnation, the excommunication edict of 1179, was the most powerful deterrent it could possibly level at any practice. The medieval poet Dante, reflecting the official attitude of his times, assigned usurers to one of the most uncomfortable compartments of a Hell that was all too vivid and real to his readers. Yet usurers abounded and in 1208, an exasperated Pope Innocent III remarked that if the usurers were to be barred from the Church, the Church might as well be closed.[4]

The problem was partially one of semantics, as is so often the case. The Church's position was an ethical position aimed at all kinds of business extortion, not just those connected with the lending of money. The term usurer itself was generally used to refer to all profiteers, and any kind of unfair bargain would be classed as usurious. This elastic interpretation of the word was the practice of laymen as well as of ecclesiastical theorists of the time. Not only the taking of interest was deemed to be usury, but also the raising of prices by a monopolist or the excessive profits of a middle-man. Indeed, any kind of grossly material dealings and bargainings were considered by the all-embracing Church as within its province and subject to condemnation as usury in an age which did not venerate profits. In the later debate in the Commons on the issue of interest in 1571, a proponent of interest states the case: "It stands doubtful what usury is; we have no true definition of it."[5] After the law permitting interest was passed, some liberal English divines had no trouble in going along with the concept of regulated interest as unsinful and necessary for trade. On the other hand, the concentration on interest as the worst form of usury persisted in the minds of the majority of the clergy and the sixteenth century was flooded with sermons and tracts against it.

Meanwhile the prohibition of interest hardly prevented the development of banking in Italy itself. Not only were money lenders' tents a necessary adjunct to the great market fairs of the medieval period but lords and kings required loans as well as merchants. In Florence, by the mid-thirteenth century, there were eighty bankers serving the dukes, counts and princes who ran Italy's flourishing city-states. Banking families such as the Bardi and Frescobaldi lent money with interest openly stated, or with special benefits and concessions to be received in lieu of interest. Edward III (1327-1377) heard his English churchmen rail against the sin of usury, but when he needed more money for his wars with France, he borrowed heavily from the Italian banking families at 42% a year and even put up the Crown jewels for security. Incidentally, he repudiated his debts to the Italians in 1339.

Even more startling is the involvement of the Church itself in usury. As one of the richest institutions in Europe and an international political force as well, its financial affairs were exceedingly intricate. It employed banking families as its fiscal agents to journey as far as Greenland to collect its tribute. When the Pope taxed an English monastery, a Florentine banker would present the bill, often lending the money to the monastery and collecting later against the monastery's harvest or wool crop. "The whole world knoweth that usury is held in detestation in the Old and New Testament," complained Bishop Grosseteste in 1253, "yet now the lord Pope's merchants or money-changers practice usury openly in London . . ." [6] At times, the Church itself had to borrow from the Italian bankers and paid interest, disguised or otherwise, further enmeshing itself in the practice it condemned. In the irony of history, the Church, caught up in social changes it could not comprehend, and fighting to maintain its fading authority in temporal affairs, had singled out interest as a practice to prohibit long after it was incapable of being prohibited.

IV

One of the first breaks in the Church's official stand was the establishment of charitable lending agencies for the poor and necessitous, generally without interest or with low scales of interest sanctioned by the local bishops. After a few abortive attempts at such institutions in France and England in the early part of the fourteenth century, Italy produced the first charitable loan organizations to achieve prominence, institutions which exist to the present day. Known as *monti di pietà,* or "funds of charity," these charitable pawnshops were established in Perugia and other cities in the second half of the fifteenth century. The Franciscans, a high-minded order more acquainted with poverty than others, since its followers took the vows of poverty, were leaders in this movement. The actual running of the pawnshops was placed in the hands of municipal officials who served on a joint board of management with the clergy. The laymen on the board soon recognized the need for interest and papal sanction was obtained for limited charges on these loans. This created a storm of protest from the rival Dominican order. Upon appeal to the Lateran Council, the verdict was rendered in favor of low interest rates with an additional proviso that those who opposed them were now subject to excommunication themselves. The movement then spread rapidly and 589 such institutions were reported by 1896.

In France, a similar movement made slow headway because of opposition to the charging of interest, but in 1777 *monts de piété* were established by royal decree. The Paris institution, owned by the French government, has offices throughout the city and is probably Europe's largest pawnbroking establishment. *Monts de piété* are now run by municipalities throughout France as well as in Italy, reflecting a European solution to loan problems never followed in America. Incidentally, the Stavisky scandal in France, which touched off violence between rightists and leftists in 1934, centered around the *mont de piété* in the city of Bayonne, for which Stavisky, a shady promoter closely connected with important men in the government, had sponsored a fraudulent bond issue.

In England, this type of lending agency never made progress, particularly because of its relations with the Church from which Henry VIII was to separate in 1534. Having made himself independent of Rome, it was an easy step for Henry VIII to end the church-influenced law against interest-taking by a short-lived act of 1545. Prior to that time, Jews, who were exempt from canon law and whose Mosaic Code was conveniently interpreted as not applying to Gentiles, had received special charters from the authorities to lend money at interest during the twelfth and thirteenth centuries. Their role has been romanticised in fiction by the character of Isaac of York, Rebecca's father in Walter Scott's *Ivanhoe*. When the Jews were temporarily banished from England in 1290, Lombards from Italy, papal agents and some Englishmen themselves found ways to disguise their interest-taking and supplied the demand for loans. Henry VIII's act of 1545 permitted interest at 10%, which rate was gradually reduced through the eighteenth century, setting the stage for a complete counteraction which repealed interest limits altogether in the nineteenth century. Borrowers of small sums, meanwhile, had to pay more than the earlier interest limits. As usual, the British moneylender, as the non-banking lender of small loans was called, perfected devices for evasion, such as having the borrower agree to pay the lender a lifetime "annuity" in addition to interest which annuity the lender obligingly cancelled when the loan was repaid. English pawnbrokers, however, were exempted from the usury limits in a series of laws starting in 1757. This exemption represented one of the first passages of laws based on the validity of a special rate of interest for a class of loans, a concept essential to the eventual constitutionality of the American laws. Ironically, when the English usury laws were later repealed, leaving rates wide open, the pawnbrokers objected that their formerly privileged status, which allowed a 20% annual rate on loans of £10 or less, was now discriminatory, and they received some relief.[7] These constant changes in attitudes and practices in relation to lending and interest illustrate the great service the Russell Sage Foundation would be supplying as a clearing house on all matters related to a complex field.

V

Before approaching America's colonial period, a postscript is in order on the story of England's lusty Henry VIII. Within two years after he had permitted the taking of interest, Henry VIII was dead. Only seven years later, in 1552, the Anglican Church, still committed to the idea that interest was unholy, succeeded in having the Parliament of the boy King Edward VI prohibit interest all over again as a "vyce most odyous and detestable as in divers places of the hollie Scripture it is evident to be seen." [8] In 1571, during the reign of Elizabeth I, Parliament permitted interest up to 10% once more. The wily Queen was more concerned with England's greatness as a trading nation than with her reputation as the keeper of that much faith. Besides, the rising commercialism of the times and the need for public loans had already made the twenty year prohibition an anachronism.

R. H. Tawney, in his *Religion and the Rise of Capitalism*, sees the intense debates in the House of Commons over the Usury Bill of 1571 as a decisive step in the changing relationship between the Church and the individual, leading to the final denial of the Church's official authority in civil and business affairs altogether. He also agrees with Max Weber, author of the famous *The Protestant Ethic and the Spirit of Capitalism,* that although bishops would no longer influence business, the spirit of Protestantism would exert its influence in its own subtle way. Protestantism, especially in its Calvinist form, would be an essential factor in the growth of capitalism and the rehabilitation of its partner interest. Calvin himself condoned interest, stating it was necessary to consider both the terms of the loan and the position of borrower and lender before it should be considered usury. The new Protestant ethic saw morality and godliness in hard work and thrift, which encouraged producers to plough back their profits and create new capital rather than consume their wealth in waste and luxury. More than that, idleness bred mischief and every hour and every opportunity should be utilized. Driving a hard bargain was but a step away as a new virtue and in time most Protestant theologians would find it possible to reject the medieval Catholic doctrine of a "just price" for merchandise or labor. These stern theologians and their hard-working capitalists would find it much easier and more profitable to accept the more modern notions of free competition and a free market. Thus, the Protestant ethic met and reshaped the thousand year old interest controversy in full stride, giving tremendous impetus to the borrowing of money. The same Protestant ethic, with its austere concept of thrift, was in turn destined to come into conflict with the unimaginable consumer credit development, as we shall later see, illustrating that nothing is so certain as change.

VII

EARLY LENDING IN AMERICA

On the American scene, the British experience is significant since American institutions naturally would reflect English laws and traditions more than those of the Continent. In 1713, the latest of the British laws reducing the maximum rate from Henry VIII's original 10% to a low 5% was enacted. This was known as the Statute of Anne, in honor of the Queen who had no more interest in interest rates than in the handsome furniture also associated with her name. The thirteen American colonies, with the exception of New Hampshire, also followed such English statutes and established their own maximum interest rates, taking care, however, to make them just enough higher than 5% to attract British investment in the Colonies.

The Colonial merchants and importers meanwhile relied heavily on credit from their British suppliers rather than on bank credit. They were accustomed to receiving rather long credit terms from the English as their means of payment often depended upon proceeds from the sale of goods and produce they received as barter for the English goods in the first place. Seeing America placed in the position of a debtor nation did not please Thomas

Jefferson, one of the founding fathers. Commenting on the continuous debts of the Virginia tobacco growers to the British merchants of tobacco, he complained that "these debts had become hereditary from father to son for many generations, so that the planters were a species of property annexed to certain mercantile houses in London." [1] In 1787, Jefferson, heavily immersed in debt himself, wrote: "The maxim of buying nothing without the money in our pocket to pay for it would make of our country one of the happiest on earth . . . I look forward to the abolition of all credit as the only other remedy. I have seen with pleasure the exaggerations of our want of faith with which the London papers teem. It is indeed a strong medicine for sensible minds, but it is a medicine. It will prevent their crediting us abroad, in which case we cannot be credited at home." [2]

Jefferson to the contrary, the infant republic flourished by using credit and would become the world's greatest exponent of it. On the consumer credit side, one would have expected Benjamin Franklin, the well-known apostle of thrift, to echo Jefferson. In a paper on *Consumer Credit in Philadelphia*, Professor Wilbur C. Plummer, an authority on consumer credit, took the trouble to look into the records of the Historical Society of Pennsylvania and discovered one of those unexpected truths which seem to be the rule about historical myths. The many-sided Franklin penned dozens of homilies such as "Save and Have," and "A Penny Saved Is a Penny Earned." Yet he extended credit liberally as a printer and bookseller, and took the usual leisurely time to pay his own accounts in the various shops of Philadelphia. Franklin also made several small loans, mainly to relatives, which he recorded neatly in his books. One of these entries is of special interest to the historian because of the information it gives about the type of security taken. On November 26, 1763, Benjamin Franklin lent £50 to Anthony Armbruster and secured the loan with a "mortgage" on Armbruster's printing materials. This proves that the chattel mortgage, so common in today's financing, was in use at that time.[3]

This predisposition to make loans and extend credit contradicts Franklin's statement to his good friend, Dr. Benjamin Rush, that credit produced idleness and vice and that he wished all debts were irrecoverable under the law.[4] Actually Franklin was a debtor or creditor all of his life. He started in business by borrowing. He tells in his *Autobiography* that he called off certain marriage plans because the parents were unwilling to give him a dowry large enough to pay off his printing house debts, and he even had the temerity to suggest to his prospective in-laws that they could raise the funds by mortgaging their house. Finally, although his will reveals the great man had a substantial share of uncollectable bad debts on his books, he struck a blow for the cause of small loans by establishing the first philanthropic loan funds.

When he died in 1790, it was found that by a codicil to his will Franklin had made unusual bequests to the cities of Boston and Philadelphia.[5] Two loan funds of £1,000 each were established to be used for loans "to such young married artificers under the age of twenty-five years as have served an apprenticeship . . . and faithfully fulfilled the duties required in their indentures." The loans were to be payable in annual instalments of not less than one-tenth of the principal, were to be secured by two endorsements, and were not to exceed £60 nor to be less than £15 in amount. The selectmen and certain ministers of the oldest Boston churches were to administer the fund in Boston and the Philadelphia fund was to be managed by the Corporation of the city.

The author of *Poor Richard's Almanac* detailed in his will the ultimate distribution of the funds, assuming all loans were repaid and the 5% interest was continuously compounded. At the end of the first 100 years, £131,000 from the Boston fund was to be used for fortifications, bridges and other public improvements.

An equal sum in Philadelphia was to be used for such items as making the Schuylkill river navigable. In 1990, the remainder of each fund would be exactly £4,061,000. The Philadelphia fund was then to be divided equally between Philadelphia and Pennsylvania, and the Boston fund between Boston and Massachusetts.

Assuming the old philosopher was not indulging in a huge posthumous joke on posterity, he might have known from his own uncollectable debts that it just wouldn't work this way. By the end of August 1791, the Boston £1,000 had been lent to 27 married young men. In 1800 the report was "91 loans had been made of which 50 at least had been repaid in whole or in part by sureties and on four of these are balances which cannot be collected." So it went until in 1836 the fund more or less terminated.[6]

The Philadelphian artificers were no more responsible than the Bostonians and that fund also had a premature retirement. From time to time, the early loan business propagandist literature would refer to the Franklin funds as a kind of original loan establishment in America, even drawing a comparison between the $300 loan limit of the first Uniform Small Loan Laws and Franklin's £60 maximum loan, but of course the relationships are completely tenuous. The Franklin funds, though they produced no oaks from their acorns, are still a charming antecedent of consumer finance.

II

The American Revolution severed the ties with the mother country as far as interest theories and lending institutions were concerned and from that point on America would write its own story with typical American institutions.

Still one more development in the English experience would be of significance. By 1787, a little over two hundred years after interest was legally permitted, one of the leading philosophers of the day, Jeremy Bentham, had published his *Letters in Defense of Usury*. The young philosopher's theory was not against the ethics of limiting interest. His argument was purely economic; for example, the usury laws made it easy for the old established business enterprises to get money, but new enterprises, because they were not established, could not get loans because the risk was too great for the rate permitted. In addition, as a disciple of Adam Smith, Bentham pushed Smith's ideas of *laissez-faire* to their logical conclusion, that every man was the best judge of his own interest, and that it was desirable from the point of view of the public good that borrower and lender should determine the rate of interest between themselves. Actually Bentham was a high-minded man devoted to the utilitarian principle of the "greatest happiness of the greatest number," and it is an interesting development in the history of ideas that he should reach such a conclusion. Of course, the possibility of the poor being exploited did not enter his mind. He was propounding a logical economic fact which he thought would produce more economic good than the artificial limitation heretofore advanced as an ethical concept. Similarly, Blackstone, the leading historian of the law in the eighteenth century, had stated the case against too low a rate as inviting evasion: "Without some profit allowed by law, there will be but few lenders, and those principally bad men who will break the law and make a profit, and then will endeavour to indemnify themselves from the danger of the penalty by making that profit exorbitant." [7] This type of thinking, probably compounded by the flight of capital from a country with a 5% interest rate, resulted in Parliament exempting promissory notes and certain bills of exchange from the usury laws in 1833 and 1837, and in 1854 repealing the usury laws altogether.

A direct influence was produced in one American state, Massachusetts, which illustrates the basic business disadvantage, rather than the ethical consideration, that the English must have felt about their former limitations. In 1834, over two hundred Boston businessmen, who claimed they experienced severe trading difficulties from the existing usury laws, signed a petition to the Massachusetts legislature urging their repeal. Although their concern must have been to put themselves in a better merchants' position, their catalog of methods of evasion rings a familiar bell:

> We would respectfully direct the attention of the Legislature to the numerous modes that have been devised for evading the laws; modes of transacting business, which, besides being circuitous and inconvenient, and besides taking away the sanction and protection of the law from those who engage in them, leaving no security but what is termed honor, this increasing the risk, and of course the premium paid. Besides these evils, which are loss of time, money, comfort and security, produce a fearful disregard of the laws, and establish a precedent of the utmost danger, while they tend to throw pecuniary negotiations in the hands of unprincipled and dangerous men. We need not specify the various methods by which the law is now evaded, and by which interest *above six per cent is taken,* in defiance of law, under the various names of "premium," "exchange," and "commission," for these are matters of notoriety, and need only be alluded to in order to secure the attention of the Legislature. So long as our laws remain unchanged, it is vain to hope for a better state of things.[8]

It took thirty-three years for the request to register and in 1867, Massachusetts repealed its usury law. In addition, Maine, Colorado and New Hampshire followed suit, but all of these states eventually established maximum rates for small loans as well.

A young man in Illinois about the time of the Massachusetts petition was giving thoughts to the matter while poling a flatboat on the Sangamo river. Abraham Lincoln, age 23, decided to run for his first elective office, in the hope of becoming a representative in the Illinois General Assembly, as the lower house was called. In March 1832, he distributed handbills setting forth his platform. No copies of the handbill are known to exist, but the speech was reprinted in the *Sangamo Journal* on March 15, 1832. In it, Abraham Lincoln advocates making the Sangamo river navigable by certain improvements rather than undertake the great cost of a publicly-owned railroad through the county. He states he knows the river well as "in the month of March 1831, in company with others, I commenced the building of a flatboat on the Sangamo, and finished and took her out in the course of the spring." His second plank in his modest platform relates to interest:

It appears that the practice of loaning money at exorbitant rates of interest has already been opened for discussion, so I suppose I may enter upon it without claiming the honor, or risking the danger, which may await its first explorer. It seems as though we are never to have an end to this baneful and corroding system, acting almost as prejudiced to the general interests of the community as a direct tax of several thousand dollars annually laid on each county for the benefit of a few individuals only, unless there be a law made setting a limit to the rates of usury. A law for this purpose, I am of the opinion, may be made without materially injuring any class of people. In cases of extreme necessity there could always be means found to cheat the law, while in all other cases it would have its intended effect. I would not favor the passage of a law on this subject which might be very easily evaded. Let it be such that the labor and difficulty of evading it could only be justified in cases of the greatest necessity.[9]

There we have it—honest Abe advocating cheating! The man who had studied his Blackstone at night was searching for a way to regulate interest and yet not let the regulation prohibit a necessary transaction at a higher rate. In his own groping way, he foresaw the necessity of flexible loan laws, such as the Uniform Small Loan Law that would finally come to Illinois in 1917.

III

Lincoln correctly noted that America's usury limits in the various states were easily evaded under the general technique of "note-shaving," the practice of deducting one expense or another from the proceeds of a note bearing the maximum permitted rate. With an eye to weakening the statutes deliberately, most states required only the forfeiture of interest rather than loss of principal or treble damages in case of usury. As a result, high interest rates generally prevailed, particularly in the western states where land speculation was rampant. In time, competition among banks and stricter law enforcement, along with the treatment of small loans as a special class with rigidly enforced maximum rates, would solve America's interest problems. This would not be accomplished, however, until a great deal of unnecessary hardship had been suffered not only by consumers but farmers as well.

When Lincoln was a young man, country people had a lively antagonism for city people, one of the reasons being that they associated bankers, loan sharks and land sharks all as one conspiracy against them. Farm magazines of the period abound in warnings to country people about the danger in store for them. In *The Cultivator* of November 1838, a farmer is given a list of things not to do, including:

A farmer should shun the doors of a bank as he would the approach of a plague or cholera; banks are for traders and men of speculation, and theirs is a business with which farmers have little to do.

In *The Unjust Usurer—a Tale of the Prairie*, the *Prairie Farmer* in 1860 ended on the following note:

This is no imaginative sketch, but a stern reality. It shows the danger of getting into debt, of the sure ruin that will arise from accumulating interest, and the tender mercies of land-sharks and unjust usurers.

These quotations, from an article by Paul H. Johnstone, in *"Farmers in a Changing World,"* published in the U. S. Department of Agriculture Yearbook for 1940,[10] are among the first American references to the usage of the word "shark" in this context. The lender at high rates of small sums to the city dweller had not yet appeared on the scene but he was ready to take his bow.

VIII

GROWTH OF
UNREGULATED LENDING

The lender of small sums not only had to await the development of the city with its tendency to keep its dwellers in a state of precarious financial balance, but he had to await also the development of a class of wage or salary earners with enough margin above the bare necessities to be able to repay the lender, whether legal or illegal. In other words, the borrower had to have the capacity to handle a credit transaction.

The average annual earnings of the American worker in 1900 were about $500 a year. This was low enough, even allowing for the value of the dollar, but the other factor that kept the worker in constant financial fear was the unsteadiness of employment. According to the census of 1900, 6.5 million workers were idle during some part of the year, and of these nearly 2 million were out of work at least one-third of the year. There was real poverty in the America of the 1900's. It was at its worst in the big city slums and the grim industrial towns. Obviously, the lenders were not going to lend to the poverty class, but in such conditions the lower middle class was close to insecurity and want as well. These were the conditions, of course, that were striking at the American conscience and would soon involve the whole country in a momentum for reform and sharing of responsibility from the White House down that is today's commonplace understanding.

With borrowers available, the lender still would want a reasonable security device if he were going to specialize in small sums. He found this, as we have noted, in the wage-assignment, which in many states made the salary loan possible. In addition, the chattel technique, a breakthrough of the pawnbroking concept by the simple expedient of deciding to leave the chattel in the borrower's hands, had come into use. Thus prepared, the first professional lenders of small sums in America are believed to have started business in Chicago and other mid-western cities about 1870.[1] Filling a need but aware that their loans were basically illegal, the early lenders endowed their transactions with secrecy, a practice which suited the embarrassed borrowers as well. As the lenders found their services to be profitable, in spite of setbacks in the 1893 depression, and the demand for their services practically unlimited, they rather intrepidly began to advertise publicly for business. By the 1880's, ten to thirteen loan companies were advertising regularly in the *Chicago Tribune* and beginning to specialize in loans on furniture, specifying the furniture would be "without removal" from the borrower's possession. A further development in the advertising was to emphasize the confidential nature of the transaction, which proved to be an advantage after all. An example of the exuberant, confident approach of the early lenders' advertising would be the following from the *Tribune* of November 23, 1890, which seems to be typical except for the doubtful upper loan limits mentioned, since the average loan was about $50:

Any amount of money from $20 to $10,000 to loan on furniture, pianos, teams, etc.

The property to remain in your undisturbed possession.

At a lower rate of interest than you get elsewhere. Everybody who wants money call and see us.

We are just as happy to make you a $25 loan as one for $2,500; we will give you plenty of time to pay the money back; in fact we let you make the payments to suit yourself; as we do not ask for references or make inquiries of your neighbors the transaction is sure to be private; no fear of losing your goods as we loan money for the interest and not to get the goods; we take up loans from other loan men; if you now have a loan on your goods call and get our rates.[2]

Without attempting to pass judgment on the activities or charges of these lenders at this point, one must admit the new business caught on with amazing rapidity. Boston was also an early lenders' city, as were St. Louis, Kansas City, Cleveland, Detroit, Indianapolis and Philadelphia. Frank J. Mackey, the founder of the chain of offices which eventually became Household Finance Corporation, began to make chattel loans in a small room adjacent to a jewelry store in which he was a partner in Milwaukee in 1878 and by 1890 he had fourteen branches in major cities from Omaha to Newark.[3] By 1900, almost every large city in America had its loan companies, all operating illegally as to the rate of interest and with interest rates covering a high and wide range reflecting the lack of regulation. Some were specialists in chattel loans, others in salary loans. Their competition for business was aggressive and lively. By 1890, the *New York World* was running dozens of ads from companies of the type Arthur Ham and Clarence Wassam were to analyze after the turn of the century.

The spread of the business from city to city was largely due to the development of chain lending, something of a remarkable achievement in that era of American business technique when the A & P had only 200 stores. Frank J. Mackey, as noted, was one of the first to expand his chattel loan business into a chain of offices. The chains specializing in salary loans, however, were much more rapid in adding units, probably because of their smaller sized offices and simpler loan techniques. John Mulholland, who opened a salary loan office in Kansas City about 1893, soon had more than 100 offices scattered throughout the country and is reported to have sold a million dollars worth of stock from his New York office alone.[4] Daniel H. Tolman appears to have started his sixty-odd offices in the East about the same time and Wassam was to write of him in 1908: "It is the belief of a number of employees of D. H. Tolman that he began the business of loaning on salaries a few years ago with practically no capital and today he is many times a millionaire with offices in all the principal cities of the United States and Canada." [5]

Commenting on the ability of some of these early lenders to run their businesses profitably in spite of obvious handicaps, Robinson and Nugent, in *Regulation of the Small Loan Business*, astutely observe that they developed a knowledge of human nature of the type acquired by politicians in "playing upon the fears, passions, and motives that govern men." [6] There is no question that Tolman's "girl bawlerouts" were a fantastic move in this direction, especially considering his respectability-ridden clientele of clerks and civil servants. Yet there is something curiously modern about D. H. Tolman's following instructions to his managers, about 1900:

The foundation and success of our business depends upon getting accurate and reliable reports. The proper time to find out about a customer is before we part with our money and managers can save fully three-fourths of their labor of running after delinquents and fully three-fourths of these losses by "skips" (Borrowers who have moved without notice to the lender) and "out of works" by making proper investigations in the start.

Managers should not refuse to loan customers again *who do pay* simply because they have had some unpleasant words or from any prejudice as they are in part what constitute our good business; our losses come from those who may treat you nicely but who never pay.[7]

Since the pre-regulated business did not reveal its figures and for the most part worked on its own capital, the actual extent it reached before legislation can only be estimated. Arthur Ham estimated in 1911 that in every city of 30,000 or more population, one lender would be found for every five to ten thousand people. The Department of Public Welfare in Chicago reported 139 active loan offices in Chicago in 1916. Some figures that have become available recently indicate that the Mackey chain had $3,000,000 outstanding in loans in 1908.[8] Considering that the average loan in those days was possibly under $50, approximately 60,000 customers were involved. Yet even for the most ethical of the pre-regulation lenders, the rising tide of public opinion and anti-loan shark crusades were so strong that by 1911, outstandings had dropped to $1,000,000 and Mr. Mackey strongly considered closing his business.[9]

The files of the Russell Sage Foundation, the early reports of Ham and Wassam and similar investigations in other cities, particularly Philadelphia in 1893 and Atlanta in 1904, prove beyond a doubt that the unregulated lenders for the most part were unconscionably exploiting the public. The fact that their losses were small and that their services met a tremendous demand testified to their absolute necessity, but the business by its very nature carried the seeds of its own destruction. Being immensely profitable, commensurate with the risk and public stigma attached to it, the business was bound to attract more and more marginal entrants and to produce sharper and sharper practices. Being illegal, it was certain to be legislated out of existence sooner or later in an age capable of much more important reforms. From the hindsight of history, nothing could have been so lucky for those early lenders who survived and eagerly "reformed" than the discipline of legislation and regulation. It was lucky for the public, too, as even the loans of the unregulated lenders were better than no loans at all, and countless emergencies and hardships must have been solved by these loans in spite of their excessive charges.

IX

FIGHTING THE LOAN SHARKS

The National Federation of Remedial Loan Associations was founded in Buffalo in June 1909. The representatives of the fourteen original members met under the auspices of the National Conference of Charities and Correction, now the National Conference of Social Work, which indicates how closely these remedial lending agencies were associated with social workers. The guiding forces in forming the organization were Frank Tucker, manager of the Provident Loan Society and a good friend of Robert W. de Forest, and W. N. Finley, who was managing the Reverend Babcock's The Chattel Loan Association of Baltimore.

These institutions were already formidably successful at the time. Ham immediately went into action and made his office temporarily in the Provident headquarters under Mr. Tucker's direction. Within a year he had aroused interest in a number of cities and helped organize several new loan associations operating at limited profit rates, generally 1% to 2% a month. His work was soon rewarded by the Foundation naming him the first Director of the Department of Remedial Loans in October 1910. From 1910 through 1917, when he went into the War Savings

Division of the Treasury Department, he promoted remedial loan associations, fought the loan sharks, helped develop credit unions and negotiated a program for commercial lending agencies which led to the first small loan laws.

Since his initial efforts were in the remedial loan field, a review of the largest of all, the Provident Loan Society, would be in order. In 1894 a report of the New York Charity Organization Society recommended the establishment of a semi-philanthropic pawnbroking agency to be organized by investors who would receive only a limited return on their capital, any profits to be reinvested or to result in lower rates for the borrowers. James Speyer, a New York banker whose family has given among other things an animal hospital to the City of New York, had just returned from Europe where his imagination was kindled by the *monts de piété* in France. Through the efforts of Mr. Speyer and that good citizen Robert W. de Forest, a blue ribbon panel of bankers and businessmen, including Jacob H. Schiff and Seth Low, furnished the initial capital of $40,000 and quickly ushered the new organization through a special enabling act of the New York state legislature.

These bankers playing pawnbrokers had their time of troubles —the depression of 1893 lingered on, lawsuits appeared and capital ran out—but with such a Board of Trustees and a great demand for their services, they soon were eminently successful, opening fourteen branches throughout New York. On the way, they also suffered a substantial embezzlement, which brings to mind the demise of England's first and only venture of this type. In that paradoxical land whose tilts with lending and interest we have already observed, almost every financial foible has been experienced, in spite of visions of conservative men with bowler hats and umbrellas. This particular one was a companion in time to the "South Sea Bubble," in which the schemers contracted successfully to take over England's entire national debt in 1720 (it was only £51,000,000, consisting of annual payments due to

"annuitants" of the government) in return for trading concessions in the South Seas. They quickly ran the stock up from
£128 per share to £1,000 per share, then watched it collapse like
a bubble as a result of fraud and trade that never materialized.[1]
Against such a background of finance, a giant pawnbroking organization, The Charitable Corporation, had been granted a special charter in 1707 for what its name implies. It was a swindle
on a grand scale. The directors gambled wildly with the shareholders' money and in the end the common council of the City
of London petitioned Parliament to dissolve the concern in 1731
when its principal officers disappeared, leaving £30,000 of the
original £600,000 of capital and abandoning the borrowers to less
charitable pawnbrokers.[2] Its story is admittedly a digression. Yet
it affords additional satisfaction to note that American remedial
loan societies have been the essence of probity and the Provident
remains today an expanding and serviceable institution dominating the New York pawnbroking business, its loans and other
assets in excess of $10,800,000 and its capital and retained profits
over $9,000,000, reputedly the largest agency in the world lend-
ing money on pledges. It had the benefit not only of Frank
Tucker to direct it, but Arthur Ham himself became its executive vice-president in 1918 and stayed on for a quarter-century,
still maintaining an advisory relationship with the Foundation's
Department of Remedial Loans. In 1930, the Provident's loans
exceeded $20,000,000, a reminder of a sad chapter in the coun-
try's economic history.

II

In the long run the remedial loan association movement was to
lose its impetus and for the most part leave the business, especially
after the aggressive regulated companies entered the field. The
idea that the remedial associations would tame the loan sharks by
competition was of course fanciful as the associations could not

possibly cover the field adequately and borrowers then as now do not necessarily nor even generally seek the lowest cost lender. The partnership of the Foundation with these lenders was, however, of the utmost importance in the eventual joining of forces that achieved the model loan laws. First of all, the national publicity about the remedial associations gave the public insight into the reality of the situation whereby even a semi-philanthropic institution could not make loans at anywhere near the traditional 6%. In addition, the caliber of the boards comprising these associations added dignity to the business of lending in small sums. In Boston, for example, the first of the remedial associations in the country, the Collateral Loan Company, incorporated in 1859, and the Workingmen's Loan Association, incorporated in 1888, included on their boards a Cabot, a Sears and a descendant of a signer of the Declaration of Independence, Robert Treat Paine.[3] For this reason, shortly after his daughter married an ambitious young businessman named Joseph P. Kennedy in 1914, Mayor "Honey Fitz" Fitzgerald designated his new son-in-law as the city appointed director of the Collateral Loan Company. "Do you know a better way to meet people like the Saltonstalls?" Kennedy is said to have remarked at the time.[4]

These Boston companies, like most of the other remedial associations, were not pawnshops but actual lenders on chattels which remained in the custody of the borrower. The Collateral Loan Company, incidentally, had 105,099 customers on its books in 1911, totalling only $1,211,800—an average of less than $15 each![5] Thus, the remedial associations developed a group of informed, influential people who gradually became committed to the idea that repressive legislation was no solution to the small loan problem. As businessmen, regardless of their limited profit intentions, the managers and boards of these companies experienced the costs and risks of lending, and were not likely to expect the impossible from commercial agencies. Under the inspiration of Arthur Ham, they regarded themselves as involved in a larger mission than their own companies. They felt they were actually running experimental workshops for a rapidly expanding, socially significant business, always on the lookout to expose and drive out the loan shark but also committed to finding an ultimate and fair solution, as called for in the widely circulated Wassam and Ham studies. In fact, some of them later participated vigorously in campaigns for the Uniform Small Loan Law,[6] a remarkably altruistic position since they were advocating the creation of higher rate companies which they realized would very likely replace their own services. Meanwhile, Ham was largely responsible for their national program and policies. He developed a standard accounting and office procedure system, framed model forms for financial statements and incorporation, and assisted in the training of new managers as needed. Even a philanthropic loan association had to have special enabling laws to charge more than the usual 6%, and in promoting these organizations throughout the country, Ham received valuable legislative experience. He also acted unofficially as the Federation's executive secretary and from 1909 through 1918 edited the proceedings of the annual meetings which the Foundation published.

The Foundation's policy provided for investments in worthwhile organizations so long as they gave indications of being able to provide a modestly philanthropic 3% return. Ham recognized that there was a need for more chattel loan companies in New York and apparently the Provident Loan Society was not a candidate. He preferred a separate company that would be a specialist in furniture loans, anyway, as he thought it would serve as a laboratory where he could get the facts about income and expenses. In January 1911, he convinced the Trustees of the Foundation to invest in the chattel loan business and they voted to subscribe $100,000, on condition that outsiders would put up another $100,000. This was accomplished and the Chattel Loan Society began business on February 19, 1912, with a capital of $200,000. Mr. de Forest was elected president; Pierre Jay, former

Bank Commissioner of Massachusetts, treasurer; Ham, secretary, and several Provident trustees joined the board. The first dividend of 3% was paid in 1915; 4% to 6% was paid in later years. In January 1925, the Society was sold to "commercial interests," according to the Foundation's history, for a profit.[7] The buyer was Household Finance Corporation, which continued to run the Chattel Loan Society at the low rates then permitted in the hope that some day an adequate loan rate would be established in New York, which finally occured in 1932. Household had early become an active proponent of regulation and was highly esteemed by the Foundation. Not to be outdone by its competitor, Beneficial Finance Co. subsequently purchased the venerable Workingmen's Loan Association of Boston, when the latter's directors also decided that "philanthropy plus 6%" was no longer necessary in the small loan field.

III

Ham's office was apparently a whirlwind of activity in those early days of his directorship. With his network of remedial loan associations and his own talent for publicity, public interest in the loan business was maintained at a high pitch in the press and among the social workers and their publications. In his first report to the Federation in 1910, he said he was "carrying on active correspondence with interested people in 85 cities located in 30 states." [8] Actually he operated on two fronts, first as leader of the remedial loan association movement and secondly as foe of the New York loan sharks. At this point he was convinced that an airtight 2% a month law, along with the quick expansion of the remedial companies, which had grown from 14 to 21 in the first year of the Federation, was the answer to the social problem that engaged him. He was not then particularly interested in converting the unregulated lenders unless they met his terms. In fact, he was undoubtedly highly chagrined at the tough, effective opposition they were giving him at every turn. From their point of view, 2% a month was as bad as being put out of business and they fought back accordingly.

Ham presented his cause to the National Conference of Charities and Correction in 1911 and plans were established to have local Charity Organization Societies organize institutions in their home cities that would drive the loan sharks out of business or force them to conform. By 1912, the young organizer began to realize that the unexpected combination of powerful lenders and legislators who found even 2% a month a difficult concept to accept was gaining the upper hand, in spite of the rapid growth of new remedial associations. In his report to the Federation for that year, he hardly covered his impatience:

I have little to report in the matter of remedial loan legislation enacted. That we are preparing the way, through study and the dissemination of information for satisfactory legislation in the future, is shown by the fact that an increasing number of bills that were introduced, though failed of passage, contained many of the provisions which we have advocated as essential to adequate legislation.[9]

To add to his frustration, in some of the new states where the rate was established on a remedial loan basis, the bill had been so altered that the unregulated lenders found easy loopholes. "We found that the loan shark had discovered a way of escaping even before the bill was signed," reported the remedial association member from Detroit to the 1912 Federation meeting.[10] It was obvious that the Federation did not then regard the complete elimination of the elusive loan shark as "repressive legislation" so long as an enabling law for remedial companies was on hand. In his home state of New York, Ham gained some satisfaction by drafting an amendment to the chattel loan law, signed by Governor Charles Evans Hughes in 1910, which gave the Superintendent of Banks the kind of effective supervisory powers Ham thought necessary for a model law. This law, which still limited interest to 2% a month and in addition possessed a highly unique limitation on the lenders' profits, regardless of the interest rate, was a good remedial loan law. It found few takers, however, who would join the Chattel Loan Society to do business on such terms.

IV

At this point Ham carried the fight directly to the subjects of the Wassam and Ham reports. After all, he was not interested in merely leading a study group and it was intolerable that in his own city the loan sharks flourished. If they could not be eradicated here, how could the Federation make progress elsewhere? Ham's department quickly became the leader of an out and out war. Borrowers flocked to his office with tales of exploitation and were advised of their legal rights and to refuse to pay. The support of the Legal Aid Society was enlisted to defend some of the victims and on occasion Ham's office even furnished bond for bail when the courts held against the reluctant borrower.[11] In a great many cases, the lenders made settlements with borrowers but they were not giving up their business by any means. This was not the first time they had been engaged in battle in New York with a crusading press or an ambitious district attorney. It was the first time, however, that they were pitted against a full-time, non-political adversary who was so relentless in his knowledge and determination.

We have noted that District Attorney Jerome had a brief success with salary lenders on misdemeanor charges in 1904, which the lenders apparently quickly terminated by lobbying through an exemption from such a penalty in the same year. Still another District Attorney in a long line of loan shark fighters that would extend all the way to Thomas E. Dewey in the 1930's entered the lists, and that was Franklin Brooks. Although the Russell Sage Foundation publications surprisingly do not mention him at all he certainly deserves recognition. In the *System* magazine of February 1913, a businessman's magazine of the day which featured, in typical Theodore Roosevelt language, the "players of the great game," Brooks is honored as the man who "knows more of loan sharks and their ways than any other man in America." [12] Brooks in 1913 was under an appointment as assistant district attorney for the purpose of fighting the loan sharks, according to this article. He had already spent five years pursuing them, his interest having started when a young relative borrowed $50 from a lender and found he still owed the same amount a year later after having paid $50 in charges. Brooks was elected to the state legislature and pushed through a bill in 1913 called the Brooks-Levy bill which in many ways was a model bill. In proposing his bill he had stated:

In the destruction of the usurious loan business, several men who do a business of making small loans in bank-like fashion, supplying a needed demand for the poor at a reasonable rate of interest, have also been driven out of business. As a result the supply of funds to the poor in times of need have been practically shut off. . . . It now remains for the construction of a legitimate business of making small loans to the worthy poor in times of financial distress, under proper protection, alike to the borrower and lender which can only be done through proper legislation at the coming session of the Legislature. . . . I have no sympathy for the borrower who makes a loan and, failing to pay it back or pays but part of it, seeks to get the money lender in the clutches of the criminal law, because it is so framed that merely to charge more than the legal rate of interest constitutes in itself a misdemeanor. Such a borrower is on a par with the money lender who has already received three or four times the amount of his loan and is still demanding more, and through the means of fraudulently secured documents and agreements is threatening to take away the borrower's household furniture or tie up his salary.

These abuses on both sides should be eliminated and the business of making small loans should be legitimate, and properly safeguarded, alike for the borrower and the money lender, all of which demands further or supplementary legislation in Albany this year.[13]

Somehow, the bill was passed, having received favorable support editorially from the *New York Globe* and a few employer organizations. Mr. Brooks then accepted the district attorney appointment and proceeded to try to help make his own law work. According to *System*, he had handled more than one thousand cases of usury in the past five months. An even more important part of his work was "a correspondence course (without fees) which he has maintained with officials and organizations all over the United States who want to know how to handle the men who prey on pay envelopes." [14]

The Brooks law established the position of supervisor, put salary lenders and chattel lenders in the same boat, provided for licensing and a maximum charge of 3% per month on loans of $50 or less, 2½% on loans between $50 and $100, and 2% on loans of $100 to $200, plus an additional charge of small fees starting at $1.00 for a loan of $25 or less. Other exemplary features included limiting the collection on wage-assignments to 10% of the monthly wages. Remedial loan associations were exempted from its provisions.

Yet the law lasted less than a year and the supervisor was never appointed. Who was behind the opposition to this apparently desirable law? The answer is undoubtedly Arthur Ham and the Sage Foundation. The act was criticized strongly for allowing too high rates for licensees [15] and Ham introduced a new bill in the New York legislature in 1914 which replaced the Brooks law with some superior licensing and supervision procedures but still limited the charges to 2% a month plus a fee of $2 on loans to $50 and $1 on loans above $50 to $200. The limitation on profits was maintained but capped at 12%. One can easily see how firmly committed Ham was to the remedial idea at that time and how unlikely it appeared that any effort would eventually be made to "reform" the present lenders against whom he was crusading full steam ahead. The great power of the Foundation had been clearly illustrated and at this point the *rapprochement* with the unregulated lenders of a few years later seemed unlikely.

Meanwhile Ham urged the District Attorney to appoint Walter S. Hilborn as assistant district attorney to prosecute the loan sharks,[16] probably desiring for the post a person more favorably oriented towards his program. Hilborn had won distinction in 1913 for defending Gimbel Brothers against the legal actions of salary lenders after Gimbel Brothers had followed both Brooks' and the Foundation's advice to resist attachments. He was conversant with all the devices employed to evade existing laws and assumed his post in January 1914. Hilborn was also thoroughly committed to the remedial loan idea and drew no distinctions between good and bad loan sharks as Brooks had done. In fact, in a private report to the District Attorney at the conclusion of his first year's work, Hilborn noted among the illegal devices:

The simplest and most obviously illegal was the device of charging the rates authorized by the Brooks-Levy Bill although the lender was not licensed and no supervisor had been appointed. The charges there made were, for a loan of $50, 3% per month and an examination fee of $1.50. . . .[17]

Inevitably the inference would be made that Brooks represented loan shark interests in his attempts to give them a fair deal, which a few of them, as in the above case, apparently found acceptable, and Hilborn recalls such a feeling.[18] It is true that Brooks' bill had inadequacies, such as no limitation on the repeating of fees, but these surely could have been amended to provide a better commercial lending law, had not such a consideration been premature. In Massachusetts, Supervisor of Small Loans E. Gerry Brown, who was also to cross swords with Ham on rates, commented in his annual report for the year 1913 that the short-lived New York law had been at too *low* a rate and that "the district attorney who secured its passage bravely admitted that in practice it was bad public policy" [19] in that respect.

This was not Brooks' first attempt at constructive legislation. In the summer of 1911, another Brooks law was passed by the New York State legislature and went into effect September 1, 1911, aimed at the salary lender. It contained three notable features. First, it put into legislation the recent Appellate Division of the Supreme Court decision that before an assignment of wages of an employee could be valid a copy must be given to the employer within three days of the time the loan was made. Knowing that the lenders were evading this by obtaining a power of attorney to insert the date of assignment at the lenders' convenience, Brooks' law stipulated that the date of the loan would be deemed to be the date on which the money was received by the borrower. Second, data about the lending concerns' principals was required and third, 18% per annum was fixed as the maximum rate.[20] In commenting on this bill, which was apparently so short-lived or innocuous that the Foundation's otherwise comprehensive *Small Loan Legislation* by Gallert, Hilborn and May does not even include it, Ham noted in the *Survey* of October 11, 1911: ". . . the brief history of the Brooks Act adds to the testimony that 18% a year is too low a rate on which to conduct a salary loan business. The result is that conscientious companies are driven out of business and unscrupulous concerns comprising most of those in the field easily evade the law, which carries no enforcing clauses." [21]

Thus Brooks was criticised first for too low a rate and a few years later for too high a rate. In view of the fact that both Ham and Hilborn were to support a 3½% bill in just a few years more, Franklin Brooks should be accorded in these pages at least some belated praise for his valuable contributions.

V

The newspapers had been giving Ham hearty cooperation in his crusade from the very beginning. In the summer of 1911, the *New York Globe* devoted several columns daily to reports of developments and invited the borrowers to report their complaints. The paper engaged a firm of attorneys to assist the "victims" and capitalized on the news for a period of three months. During that time, their lawyers settled 300 cases for people who had been in the clutches—as the word inevitably was used—of the loan companies for periods up to five years. The total principal borrowed by these 300 persons was $8,290. The interest they had agreed to pay for this money for three months was $3,744, or 180%, the paper reported, understating it by one-half. The paper's attorneys were able to effect settlements in practically all cases from the harrassed lenders for principal plus six per cent. The paper's report, incidentally, stated that nearly all of the loans were for burial expenses and doctors' fees, which it noted contradicted the popular opinion that a person who borrowed on his salary was either a profligate or a spendthrift.[22]

It was but another step for Ham to persuade the newspapers to match their convictions with their pocketbooks and cease taking the sharks' advertising. By 1912, the leading newspapers of the city were refusing to accept such advertising, with the exception of the *New York World*. The *World* was Jay Gould's old newspaper, which Gould and Russell Sage had deliberately used to run down the reputations of rival companies so they could buy their stocks at bargain prices. The owner was now the upright Joseph Pulitzer whose paper was running 66 column inches in December 1910 as the loan sharks' favorite advertising medium, but even he cut them out completely on May 5, 1914.[23] With a nod of encouragement from Ham and his august associates at the Foundation, landlords suddenly became unwilling to renew their leases with the lenders.

Leaving no stones unturned, Ham carried his fight to the large employers. He persuaded Raymond B. Fosdick, then Commissioner of Accounts of the City of New York, to investigate the loan business as it applied to city employees. The report confirmed some of the conclusions he and Wassam had drawn from their earlier studies and resulted in the city refusing to honor the lenders' claims. Following up a proposal he had made in 1910 to the Retail Dry Goods Association, Ham succeeded in rounding up a conference of the leading department store employers who listened to his graphic address about the parade of borrowers and were then persuaded to adopt resolutions not to make assignments of salary a ground for discharge, to fight illegal claims by moneylenders in the courts and "to urge the organization of co-operative savings and loan associations within their own establishments." [24] This last item reflected Ham's new interest in promoting credit unions, which had only recently come on the scene in Massachusetts. Meanwhile, he never lost an opportunity to speak before such audiences as the Legal Aid Societies and the Academy of Political Science, or to write articles for newspapers and magazines.

VI

On top of all this, Ham developed still another barb for the loan shark. He wrote a script for a movie and negotiated with the Edison Company to produce it in 1912.

The Great Train Robbery, the first motion picture to tell a connected story, had only appeared in 1903, but Ham was ready to use the new medium to advance his cause. In his files, we find correspondence with the Edison Company in New York in which the story idea is negotiated through his secretary for $25. In August 1912, the Edison Company is asked to include "produced in cooperation with the Russell Sage Foundation Division of Remedial Loans" in the official title. The story line sold to Edison includes the following:

The debt is subsequently settled by the district attorney, just in the nick of time, for when they arrive at the house, the loan shark is taking the furniture away. The last act shows him out of the clutches of the loan shark, the child well, his debts paid . . ." [25]

The film was actually released to commercial theaters on October 5, 1912, with the title *The Usurer's Grip* and the brochure accompanying it states in part:

A clerk, on account of the illness of his child, finds himself in great need of money. He happens to see in the morning paper an alluring advertisement of a loan company offering confidential loans without security at low rates. He goes to the loan company and finds that for a loan of $25 for six months he is compelled to mortgage his furniture and repay $45 in six monthly instalments of $7.50. On account of his necessity he finally agrees to pay these ruinous rates. At great sacrifice the first few payments are made regularly but he soon gets behind, and after repeated threats the loan company sends to his place of business an agent known as a "bawlerout," who in loud tones and in the presence of his fellow-clerks demands the overdue payments, denouncing him as a liar and a cheat. His employer, hearing the uproar, enters the room, and finding out that he has a loan with a loan company, discharges him. The employer little realizes that in doing this he is playing into the loan shark's hands—for it is this fear of disapproval or discharge which compels many men to pay extortionate and illegal rates of interest to usurers.

The picture was reviewed in the *Moving Picture World* of October 5, 1912 as a serious feature film. It was termed "a conception of the highest order, pregnant with consequence and intrinsic meaning, a social phenomenon of deep interest presented in a way that will reach human hearts by the millions." The reviewer also presented a bouquet to the memory of Russel

Sage himself: "Sage in name and sagacious in action, the great financier laid the foundation of a noble beneficence named for him and formulated by Mrs. Sage and her advisors." [26]

Perhaps encouraged by these efforts, Ham also worked on the outline of a literary series on the loan shark which was fortunately neither published nor completed. The outline of *The Green-Backed Peril* is not only amusing but indicates that the symbolised antagonist was a constant preoccupation in the mind of the young executive: I. *In the Maw of the Thing.* II. *In the Thing's Den.* III. *On the Trail of the Thing.*[27]

All in all, Ham felt a sense of progress to offset the legislative stalemates he was meeting. In the social workers' magazine, *Survey*, of November 30, 1912, Arthur Ham, age 29, reviewed the situation with satisfaction, meanwhile gallantly paying his respects to Franklin Brooks.

HARD TIMES FOR THE LOAN SHARKS

The loan sharks in New York are facing a distressing situation. Advised by eminent counsel that their schemes for evading the statutes were proof against attack; firmly entrenched with long leases in reputable office buildings; their alluring and misleading advertisements gladly accepted by powerful newspapers; using the courts and the attitude of short-sighted employers as effective instruments in enforcing their outrageous demands, they have for years reaped an abundant harvest of dollars wrung from unfortunate victims. In no city has so much effort been made to check their extortionate practices as in New York, and it is apparent that the effort is now bringing results, for the situation is undergoing a marked change.

The courts recently have ruled that the laws of the state render any person who exacts more than the legal rate of interest on salary or chattel loans liable to fine and imprisonment; that such laws are constitutional; that a greater charge than the legal rate of interest may not be covered by exacting attorney's fees, commissions or by any other device or pretext; that a judgment obtained by confession on a usurious loan may be reopened and reversed with costs imposed on the lender; that usurious loans are void as to both principal and interest and if usury has actually been paid the borrower may recover twice the excess paid in all transactions within a period of two years.

To make matters worse many employers have discontinued their practices of discharging men who have borrowed and are refusing to recognize illegal assignments of wages. Owners of office buildings are evicting their loan shark tenants, and with the exception of the *World* the daily papers are refusing to print their advertisements.

The district attorney has established a usury bureau under the charge of Franklin Brooks, who, as the result of complaints received, has raided many offices and carried off to court proprietors, safes, books and papers in common patrol wagons—it used to be the custom for the loan shark to ride to court in his limousine accompanied by his secretary and counsel. Sixteen of the elect have been held by the magistrates for trial by the Court of Special Sessions during this month, and although they are represented by able attorneys some of whom are influential members of the legislature and high in party councils, it is thought that they can not be saved from real punishment for their insatiable greed and lawless practices.

Strangest of all to relate, the despairing, cringing borrowers have been reading the newspapers and have sought advice from those who have been studying the problem. Men who signed notes, assignments confessions of judgment, powers of attorney and chattel mortgages in blank without daring to inquire their nature, who have paid interest at 300 and 500 per cent per annum only to find the original debt had increased, who have borrowed from one loan shark to pay another and have been overwhelmingly grateful for a few days' extension on their monotonous payments now have the temerity to notify their taskmasters that they will pay no more, daring them to proceed against them.

This anomalous state of affairs has caused consternation in the loan shark camp. Many offices have been closed, some are refusing to make loans even to old customers while the majority are quite willing to discount their outstanding claims when offered principal and legal interest. Those who thrive on the adversities of others are themselves getting a touch of hard times.

It is hoped that the district attorney will not be satisfied with a good beginning but will continue his efforts until his part in the campaign has been fully done.

It has been observed frequently that there exists a well-defined demand for small loans to deserving people. It must be said therefore that no amount of publicity or enforcement will bring results of permanent value unless deserving borrowers are afforded adequate facilities for obtaining loans at reasonable rates.[28]

Neither the New York laws of 1913 and 1914 nor the tireless efforts of Ham were to administer the *coup de grace* to the loan shark. The incident that really set the stage for Walter S. Hilborn to be able to report the expiration of the shark by the end of 1914 was the sentencing to prison at the end of 1913 of D. H. Tolman, "King of the Loan Sharks."

X

MR. TOLMAN GOES TO JAIL

"For the attack on the loan shark to be a success," Walter Hilborn wrote in his personal report to the District Attorney for the year 1914, "he must feel the majesty of the law both in his pocket and in his person—he must feel it impossible to collect principal or interest on his illegal loan and he must suffer imprisonment if he persists in his illegal conduct." [1]

We have already noted that District Attorney Jerome put some of Tolman's girls in jail but these were overnight stands suffered by employees in the line of duty. In Philadelphia in 1911 more than 40 moneylenders were indicted, but little was accomplished as the Pennsylvania law offered no clear method of prosecution. In Atlanta in the same year the grand jury returned 146 indictments against loan sharks and reported evidence that justices of the peace were acting in collusion with moneylenders but no sentences were served. In a dozen other cities in the 1900-1911 period, crusades and even raids were undertaken but there was a standard result of punishment short of imprisonment. The lenders themselves employed eminent counsel and generally were able to plead a legal defense. In most states they proceeded on the theory that they might lose their interest or at worst their principal.

In some cases the defendant lenders were dealt with leniently by judges who sensed they were the victims of a social problem as well as the exploiters of borrowers who had come to them voluntarily, with no other place to turn. Court appearances usually found the lender to be the plaintiff rather than the defendant, at any rate, and the lender often would bring his cases only before magistrates who were on the lender's payroll or who depended on his flow of cases for court fees which were the basis of their income. In 1912 a city magistrate in Baltimore was tried on the charge of conspiracy to defraud. It was found that he had been acting in collusion with a loan shark company and a six months' jail sentence was imposed. In the same year in Philadelphia a lender was imprisoned by a federal court but the charge was using the mails to defraud. Therefore the distinction of being the first lender to go to jail in a local court goes to Lawrence Murphy, a "millionaire Milwaukee usurer" who was sentenced in January 1912 to 90 days in jail.[2] Invariably the same offense had brought no more than a fine in Milwaukee, where this possibility was considered one of the costs of doing business. No doubt consternation hit the ranks of the lenders but Milwaukee was not New York.

II

On October 10, 1913 the New York papers reported that Tolman, King of the Loan Sharks, had been convicted and sentenced to six months in prison. On the previous August 1, Tolman had suffered a $1,000 fine and was placed on three years' probation in Trenton, New Jersey. Twelve hours later Tolman was arrested in New York on the same charge and undoubtedly resigned himself to another fine. The complainant,

one Carl Schick, who earned $12 a week as a clerk, had bor-
rowed $10 for $15 from Tolman to buy his father and mother
a golden anniversary present.[3]

All the ingredients were on hand—Tolman the king actually
sentenced and Schick borrowing for as nonsensical a reason as
was possible in 1913.

The *New York Times* was quick to comment editorially:

VICTIMS OF THEIR OWN FOLLY

When Tolman, king of the loan sharks in this part of the country,
was fined $1,000 a few weeks ago, it doubtless gave him some pain,
but the diminution of such profits as his was trivial, and of course he
went right ahead doing what he calls business. Now he has been
sentenced to six months in prison, and that is different— or will be,
after he has exhausted such possibilities as the law provides too
kindly and in such large quantities for men as resourceful as he.

This conviction, naturally, will be highly satisfactory to all who
reprehend the merciless and unscrupulous exploitation of poverty
and improvidence, but the case on which it was founded illustrates
the fact that while a Tolman cannot be too much despised, his
victims are often if not usually people whose woes are the result
of their folly rather than of their need.

From this particular debtor the loan shark tried to extort $5 as
interest on a $10 loan for three months. But the man borrowed the
money, not because he really had to have it, but because he wanted
to give his father a golden wedding present. Such a gift, for those
who can afford it, is highly commendable, and many a much worse
use of money can be imagined, but the father would have been
better honored if the son had shown more sense.

Only in instances comparatively rare is application made to these
villainous usurers for reasons desperate enough to justify resort to
them for their so dangerous aid, and in one way or another they
will probably continue their thievish trade till the possession of
wisdom is considerably commoner than it is now.[4]

Much bigger news was to follow. On December 24, 1913 the headlines noted "HIS PARDON PLEA BACKED BY $500,-000." [5] Tolman actually was behind bars on Hart's Island. His lawyer, former United States Senator Charles A. Towne, had gone to Albany to request a pardon for his client from Governor Glynn as a Christmas gift. On behalf of his client, Towne offered to surrender to the Governor $500,000 of usurious notes, reserving the right to sue only for the principal and the legal interest. Meanwhile Tolman had told reporters that he had grown wealthy in the salary loan business but had decided to retire because of the hard life he was leading as a result of the wave of prosecutions in many states. Governor Glynn refused to act until after Christmas in spite of Tolman's friends actually bringing the $500,000 of notes to Albany on December 24 and offering to burn them in the Executive Chambers if the Governor would issue the pardon.

On December 26, the news took a dramatic turn. Elmer E. Tolman, the son and business successor of D. H. Tolman, offered to surrender without reservation $500,000 in notes from 25,000 borrowers and in addition close as many of his places of business as possible by January 1, and all of them by May 1, 1914. The Governor remarked that this was not enough.[6] E. E. Tolman then made it clear that he meant to cancel the entire $500,000 worth of debts, to forever relieve the borrowers from paying at all! [7] On December 26 and 27, 1913 the *Times* took up the case again in its editorial columns, practically warning the Governor it would not stand for any leniency on his part. The papers dropped the subject on December 28 with a final item to the effect that E. E. Tolman had just been arrested in Washington, D.C. on a loan shark charge.

Ham and his fellow workers at the Foundation must have sensed that the illegal lenders would surely now be leaving New York, especially with the able Walter Hilborn in the district attorney's office. Hilborn prosecuted every type of evasion in

1914, even crossing state lines with deadly efficiency. Hilborn reported:

The moneylenders having been driven out of the state of New York, one of them attempted to do business from the state of Massachusetts. One of them, the London Finance Company, under the management of Jacob Brodie, attempted to do business from Massachusetts under a Massachusetts license. The London Finance Company sent to civil service employees printed application blanks and published in the New York press application blanks. The Massachusetts Supervisor permitted a charge of not only 3% a month authorized by the Statute, but an additional "paper" charge of 10%. Numerous complaints were made by the borrower, but it was obviously impossible to institute any prosecution because no person within the State participated in the lending. On the default of the borrower judgments were entered in New York state upon confessions. At my suggestion the Legal Aid Society moved to vacate such confessions. The Supreme Court at Special Term, in New York County, vacated the judgments and orders were affirmed in the Appellate Division. In addition representations were made to the Supervisor of Small Loans in Massachusetts of the activities of the London Finance Company, and upon his inaction representations were made by persons interested in the small loans situation to the Governor, who thereupon removed the Supervisor. As a result of these activities the London Finance Company ceased to make loans in New York County.[8]

They made an invincible team. Ham's background and motives we have already analyzed. Hilborn was a Bostonian, a product of Harvard and Harvard Law, and a former clerk in the Boston office of Louis D. Brandeis, the highly successful corporation lawyer who had become so dedicated to progressive reforms he thought he had little chance for the Supreme Court position to which Woodrow Wilson would appoint him in 1916. Leon Henderson feels that whereas Ham was motivated by a New England conscience, Hilborn's devotion to service throughout his life reflected the traditions of the Jewish prophets with their penchant for social justice.[9] Just as Brandeis joined his Yankee friend Oliver Wendell Holmes on the Supreme Court Bench, so did Hilborn join Ham in the work of the Russell Sage Foundation.

An ominous note can be read in a small news item of December 26, 1914 adjacent to the story of Tolman's offer to burn the notes in the Executive Chambers of the Governor:

Special to The New York Times
WASHINGTON, Dec. 24.—Prints of a peace cartoon handsomely framed were sent by Andrew Carnegie as Christmas gifts to Secretary William Jennings Bryan, Secretary L. M. Garrison and Secretary Josephus Daniels. The cartoon represents a soldier going to war, while his little child asks if he is going away to kill the father of some other child.

Secretary Garrison was asked to comment on the gift.

"Yes, it is a very handsome frame," he said.

Secretary Daniels was also asked to comment.

"I am glad that Mr. Carnegie was good enough to remember me at Christmas," was his response.

Secretary Bryan's cartoon is at the State Department, awaiting Mr. Bryan's return from Florida.[10]

Some of the friends with whom this story begins thus were still weaving their portion of the loom of history. Most of the pattern as always was beyond prediction. The events of consumer finance would now turn quickly towards major legislation as the war approached. In fact, had this legislation not been accomplished so quickly within the next few years, it might not have happened at all.

XI

THE BEGINNINGS OF
EFFECTIVE LEGISLATION

The single most important date after the establishment of the
Department of Remedial Loans of the Russell Sage Foundation
in October 1910, with Ham as its director, was the establishment
of the American Association of Small Loan Brokers on April
19, 1916. Its object, in the words of its chairman addressing the
National Federation of Remedial Loan Associations in 1917, was
to "standardize, dignify and police the small loan business." "We
are as much opposed to loan sharks or unfair and oppressive
moneylenders," he said, "as is the National Federation." [1]

Before this significant *entente cordiale* between the better or
at least wiser lenders and the Foundation took place, Ham had
stepped beyond the enactment of remedial, lower-rate laws and
into the area of laws designed to encourage commercial interests
to dominate the field. In 1913, under his influence, the Committee on Legislation of the National Federation of Remedial
Loan Associations presented to its convention a proposed satisfactory law that defined an adequate interest rate as "3% per

month without additional fees of any character" as well as providing for effective supervision. The opposition of the commercial lenders to this rate was just as determined and unanimous as it was to the previous standards of 2% plus small fees.[2] It is a tribute to Ham's patience and foresight that he did not succumb to abandoning the commercial lenders altogether to their fate in favor of promoting remedial associations and credit unions, in which he had also become extremely active. On the other hand, the charges of even the least objectionable lenders far exceeded 3% a month at that time. Few if any of them could foresee how greatly their volume, size of loans and operating efficiency would be increased through the advantages of regulation. Most of them preferred their present devils to the tune of a reformer, though no doubt Mr. Tolman's experience was a constant nightmare.

In the light of this background, Ham's entry into the legislative arena in New Jersey for a 3% bill in 1914 is most significant. Ham not only drafted the bill but marched right in and led the campaign for its passage in the best lobbying tradition. In effect, it was the first modern bill. In 1916 the State Commissioner of Banking and Insurance characterized it as "the most important piece of financial legislation ever enacted in New Jersey."[3] This also marked a change in the Foundation's policy, as it now became an active advocate of regulatory bills for commercial agencies and a watchdog for the subversion or weakening of these bills through innocent-looking amendments.

Charles M. Egan had been elected to the New Jersey State Senate on the issue of bringing in effective legislation for the loan business. He joined forces with the Jersey City Chamber of Commerce's Anti-Loan Shark Committee, the Foundation and the Newark Provident Loan Society and, as a result, on March 23, 1914, Ham's draft of the law was passed. According to the records, "the lenders fought its passage to the last ditch."[4] Several saw the light soon afterwards, however, and Beneficial

Finance, which approved of the law, opened its first office in Newark that very year. Of those lenders most willing to accept legislation, of course, the chattel lenders rather than the troublesome salary lenders were the most prominent.

Another milestone of early legislation was the Lloyd Act in Ohio. Following a statewide clamor the Ohio Governor called a special session of the legislature in 1914 to improve the loan law. The New Jersey legislation was used as a model and this time a leading group of lenders joined the forces of reform. At the last moment, however, a fee proposal caused Ham resolutely to withdraw his support and without his support the bill failed to pass. In the 1915 session a compromise was reached and another satisfactory piece of legislation for the times was added to Ham's tally sheet. By now he was an experienced in-fighter and a nationally known and respected authority in one of the most discussed state legislative activities of all time. Probably no other business, except public utilities, has had such widespread and continuous attention in the state legislatures of this country. From 1904 to 1933 alone, 1,078 bills relating to small loans were introduced.[5]

The Pennsylvania experience is of great interest as it compressed within a few years a most energetic period of trial and error involving the courts, the Foundation, the press, the legislature, social agencies and conflicting groups of lenders themselves. As always, the publicity of abuses preceded the reform and we have already noted the Philadelphia detectives and their spectacular raids in 1911. In 1913, three leading bills, among many anti-loan shark bills, were introduced by Representatives Cox, Wildman and Walnut. Each bill had its own special approach towards providing a reasonable rate and protection for the borrower, but Walnut's bill contained the blessings of Ham with its flat 3% a month and other New Jersey precedents. The battleground in Pennsylvania was unique as here all the chain lenders happened to have offices and the outcome was watched with great interest. As Ham had learned, he not only had to overcome the unreconstructed lenders, but also the minds of legislators and the well-meaning public who objected to 3% a month by its very sound. Thus, the Cox bill was passed having disguised its higher than 3% rate through the use of fees. The legislature had balked at Walnut's undisguised 3% a month.

The Cox Act of 1913 made use of the brokerage concept and claimed it did not come into conflict with the established rate of interest in the state. It therefore made no attempt to establish a separate classification for small loans, which is an essential provision for the constitutionality of all laws permitting a special rate of interest. A young attorney named Frank R. Hubachek, counsel for Frank J. Mackey's interests, found the Cox Act was unsatisfactory on many scores and a target for his keen legal mind on the point of constitutionality. He therefore boldly initiated test cases against the law of his fellow lenders whose distinguished counsel included the future Senator George Wharton Pepper. After two years of litigation, the Pennsylvania Supreme Court declared the Cox Act unconstitutional in 1915.

Hubachek had a replacement bill ready for immediate introduction in the legislature. He had modelled it on the Foundation's proposals but included some moderate fees which the Mackey chain, with its widespread experience throughout the country, still thought necessary for its margin of profit. He gained the approval of the Remedial Loan Association of Philadelphia, the majority of the lenders and some social agencies, but could only get a reluctant acquiescence from Ham because of the fees. The bill was passed in 1915 and the opposition soon tested its constitutionality in the courts. The opposition lost the case although it was represented by the future United States Supreme Court Justice Owen J. Roberts.

Cox himself had introduced the new bill prepared by Hubachek but there was still resistance from the salary lenders. This group was on its last legs in Pennsylvania, however, as they were bearing the brunt of continuous attack by social agencies and the press, which was beginning to distinguish between the salary lender and the more ethical secured lender. For example, newspapers would not take the advertisements of the salary lenders and employers were urged not to honor their wage-assignments.

Obviously, the results in states such as New Jersey, Ohio and Pennsylvania were driving home to the better lenders that regulation was inevitable and should at least be welcomed provisionally, particularly with Arthur Ham and his National Federation showing signs of accepting higher rates. If Ham could look upward, the commercial lenders could afford to look downward. The times were propitious for a reconciliation before everyone's attention would be diverted, perhaps irrevocably, by the approaching war.

II

In this day and age of 15,000 trade associations and their continual conventions, it is surprising to note that there were less than 800 associations in 1914. Except for an occasional round of discreet price-fixing, most businessmen were too independent to want to share techniques and product information. Of all businesses the loan chains were among the most secretive and their decision to join forces in 1916 reflects not only their precarious position but a flash of good sense. Of course, they had a model to go by in having seen the effectiveness of the National Federation of Remedial Loan Associations. The legislative battles in states such as Ohio, New Jersey, Pennsylvania, Maryland and Indiana had produced organizations which stayed in effect after the laws were passed. It was a natural sequence of events for Clarence Hodson of Beneficial Loan Society to send out invitations to the lenders in these five states to meet in Philadelphia on April 19, 1916 to organize a national association which was named the American Association of Small Loan Brokers. Within a few years it would drop the word "brokers" as a hangover from more complicated days and become the American Industrial Licensed Lenders Association. Its name kept changing with the times and today it is the National Consumer Finance Association. Arthur Ham, representing the Russell Sage Foundation and the National Federation of Remedial Loan Associations, attended the second day of this first meeting and, according to the records, commended its aims and wished it well.

Within six months, in October 1916, committees from both the American and the Remedial Associations met in New York and agreed to form a law that could be endorsed as a uniform regulatory law. By this time the remedial movement was losing momentum. Only five new associations had been organized by Ham after 1914, compared with 24 in the years 1910-1914, as a result of the increased number of states under regulation and the aggressive growth of the regulated companies. In fact, at this New York meeting, remedial members were authorized to join the state associations affiliated with the American Association. They still enjoyed an élite status, however, and for years their speakers would be featured at American Association meetings.

The impatient Mr. Hodson had already taken a hand at drafting a model law and had presented it to an Atlantic City meeting of the lenders on September 8, 1916. In the beginning of an ancient and honorable rivalry between Beneficial and Household, the Hubachek forces found a number of objections including excess verbiage in the Hodson version and the Hubachek draft was selected by the Association to be submitted to the Russell Sage Foundation for approval. A subcommittee consisting of L. C. Harbison, Chairman, J. H. Aufderheide, C. H. Watts, Clarence Hodson and E. P. East was authorized to meet with Arthur Ham and Walter S. Hilborn in New York on November 27. F. R. Hubachek was also present representing the Association Committee.

At this historic meeting, only the rate of interest was a subject of controversy. Ham and Hilborn had experienced nothing but trouble with fees and resisted the 3% plus moderate fees presented by the lenders. Several lenders with experience in New Jersey were brought in to testify that 3% without fees might work in the larger cities but never in smaller communities or for smaller loans. After all these years of study, experiment and outright warfare, neither side was going to be intransigent and a compromise was sought. The Association asked for 4% a month. Ham and Hilborn settled for 3½% a month and prepared to re-draft the bill. The conference had taken three full days and produced a model bill still known as the Uniform Small Loan Law. At the end of the conference, the following agreement was made:

At a conference held in New York City, November 29, 1916, attended by Mr. A. H. Ham, of the Russell Sage Foundation, and Messrs. L. C. Harbison, E. P. East, J. H. Aufderheide, C. H. Watts, a committee representing the American Association of Small Loan Brokers, the general form of uniform law regulating small loans was approved (Colonel Clarence Hodson, a member of the committee, was not present, but approved.) It was understood that all those present will do whatever they can to secure the passage of this law in Illinois, Indiana, California, and in other states in which satisfactory legislation is not now in effect.

It was understood that this law is not to be introduced or its passage advocated in any state not enumerated above without due notice to all interested and ample opportunities for correspondence or conference. It was understood that in some states changes to this law may be advocated in order to make it conform to local laws or conditions, but none of those present at this conference or those whom they represent will advocate any change in the provisions of this law governing the rate of interest, the collection of fees or the regulation or supervision to be exercised by state officials without due notice to all parties interested and an opportunity for conference, and in no event until the present form shall have been energetically urged for passage in a number of states and given a fair test in any states in which it may be enacted.[6]

The model bill, bearing the approval of the Association, the National Federation and the Russell Sage Foundation was quickly introduced in 1917 in the legislatures of California, Illinois, Indiana and Ham's own state, Maine. In every case, its reception was stormy, but failure was recorded only in California, where it missed by a few votes in the House after passing in the Senate.

Illinois, the cradle-state of unregulated lending, witnessed a particularly hard core of resistance on the part of lenders who preferred things as they were. To get an idea of Ham's talent in mustering forces, the bill was endorsed by the Chicago Association of Commerce, the Department of Public Welfare of Chicago, Commercial Club of Chicago, Industrial Club of Chicago, Committee on Local and State Charities of the Chicago City Club, United Charities of Chicago, and the Illinois Committee on Social Legislation, representing 42 local social agencies. Clarence Hodson circulated his own booklet in which his inimitable prose style pulled no punches:

Of course, a certain type of money-lenders are fighting this bill tooth and toe-nail.

They are ready to do anything under Heaven, fair or otherwise, to defeat it.

Why?

Simply because they can't evade the proposed law like they do the present one.

If they run afoul of the courts under present conditions about the worst thing that can happen to them is that they lose their usurious interest. In any event they get the principal back.

But under the new law, they will have to go to jail if they violate the law's provisions.

Illinois jails are not very lovely places.

Even the most heartless loan shark who squeezes his damnable gains from his victims drop by drop would rather conduct his business decently than board at the expense of the public for six months as this bill provides.[7]

Professor Eubank's article was reprinted from the *Journal of the American Institute of Criminal Law and Criminology* in support of the bill. In his article he quotes from the confidential handbook of D. H. Tolman which had somehow reached his hands:

Do not get timid on account of kicks by customers. Do not allow too much sympathy, when they come around with hard luck tales . . . We need managers with bull-dog determination. Get some attorney who will sell you his legal letter-heads and then write your customers upon them . . .[8]

Of course, the professor did not mention that the realistic Mr. Tolman had served his penance four years ago and that most of his determined managers were young women. Another colorful participant was baseball's future czar, Kenesaw Mountain Landis, who as a federal court judge wrote to Senator Austin:

The great bulk of loans are small in amount and extend for a short time, in view of which it is my considered judgment that a 3½% per month rate is a just rate. At all events, it is better than 20% a month, which, unless you gentlemen do something, will continue to be exacted. A law, to be effective, must absolutely prohibit any other or additional charge beyond the statutory rate, and must provide for a prison penalty. I do not want to appear to be interfering in legislative matters, but my observation of a great multitude of heartbreaks induces me to submit to you the above.[9]

The newspapers gave substantial editorial support and this campaign produced one of the greatest anti-loan shark cartoons of all time, the *Chicago Examiner's* cartoon of March 26, 1917 by Harry Murphy, entitled "PASS THE LOAN-SHARK

BILL!" On a raft in a sea of sharks, an embattled family man, a club in his hand and his desperate wife and children at his feet, prepares to go down fighting. The man bears an unmistakable likeness to Abraham Lincoln, who had given thought to the subject back in 1832.

III

With assurance that "the loan shark evil was in a fair way to be eliminated," Ham, in the latter part of 1917 submitted a memorandum to the National War Savings Committee calling attention to the need for a plan for purchasing Liberty Bonds on the instalment plan and making several other suggestions to increase their sales. He became as a result manager of the War Savings Bureau of New York City and within a short time had organized about 9,000 group-savings societies for bond purchases throughout the city. His work in New York was used as an example by the National War Savings Committee and Ham was called to Washington. He severed his connection with the Foundation on October 15, 1918 and after the war returned to the Provident Loan Society. He stayed on, however, as a guide and consultant to the Department of Remedial Loans and also became a trustee of the Foundation.

The close relationship of the Foundation with the newly regulated industry is illustrated in two significant addresses to the Association at its annual conventions of 1921 and 1922, the first by Arthur Ham and the second by Walter S. Hilborn.

Hilborn and his partner, David J. Gallert, were retained to represent the Foundation in connection with small loan legislation as needed. Although Hilborn was appointed acting director in 1920, he still gave only part of his time to the Foundation. Between 1918-1925, Hilborn appeared before legislative committees in a dozen or more states supporting bills acceptable to the Foundation. In addition he participated in revisions of

145

the drafts of the Uniform Small Loan Law, in collaboration with the American Association, in 1918, 1919 and 1923. The most important change was the draft of 1923, whose new Section 16 expressly brought "purchases of wages" within the scope of the act. This was occasioned by the necessity to stem the activities of those durable salary buyers who still managed to evade the law by maintaining the fiction that their transactions were not loans. In a fine statement of the history and intent of small loan legislation as promoted by the Foundation, Hilborn noted that as of 1922 nineteen states representing a majority of the population had adopted the Uniform Small Loan Laws since 1916, when "the small conference held in the city of New York changed the small loan history of the United States." His speech was entitled "The Philosophy of the Uniform Small Loan Law."

Reviewing the Foundation's three choices of repression, remedial loan societies or commercial enterprise under regulation, he noted that the remedial associations now numbered only thirty and were not adequate to meet the needs of all borrowers. He also noted with regret that the 3½% rate was overdue in New York and Massachusetts. Incidentally, in a statement that was soon to be an anachronism, Hilborn justified the 3½% rate because the lender, among other reasons, had only his own capital to use. Actually, a great revolution in financing the lender through banks and other sources was about to appear. It was this additional source of money, increasing the return on capital, which eventually enabled the lender to survive at far lower rates than 3½%. Hilborn, however, would have been the first to acknowledge that change was inevitable. For the time being, he was reviewing the history of an important six years and he concluded with these wise words:

The student of the small loan field has met the practical man of affairs in the small loan business, and together they have devised a law which admirably fits the situation.

146

The commercial lenders operating under the Small Loan Law have made their business a recognized, honorable, commercial venture.[10]

The rest of the convention featured the delivery of a paper on credit unions by Miss Caro Coombs of the Russell Sage Foundation, which quite impartially had been actively working, particularly under Ham's early guidance, in promoting the movement, especially in New York State. A representative of a remedial loan association in Philadelphia gained the only newspaper headlines, however, with a speech against secrecy in family loans. He warned his colleagues against loans to husbands without their wives. The *New York Times* thereupon editorialized that between husbands and wives there should be no secrets, failing to note in its coverage that New York still had an inadequate small loan law.[11]

Arthur Ham's speech, "The Trend and Progress of the Movement to Improve Small Loan Conditions," was delivered a year earlier at the 1921 meeting of the American Association in Harrisburg, Pennsylvania. Ham, then only 39 years old, pointed out that the first real attempt to make any kind of a serious and exhaustive study of the subject was the financing and publication of the investigations by Wassam and himself. Adopting a rather scolding tone for the occasion, Ham said of the remedial societies:

These societies were expected to provide such competition as would result in an improvement of the methods commonly employed by moneylenders and to afford an object lesson that would attract reputable capital into the business. It was never expected or hoped that the remedial loan societies would so grow in strength as to monopolize the field. They were intended as experimental agencies —an object lesson—a stabilizing force. I know that the Division was looked upon by the loan men as an enemy of the business; that it was believed to be seeking to drive out the money-lender and monopolise the field for the remedial loan societies. It was even stated that the Foundation was seeking in the small loan field a profitable way of investing its endowment. Nothing could be farther from the truth, and the loan men were slow to realize it.

We found that usury, like profiteering, is readily denounced but not so easily defined or prevented. We found ourselves between two groups or forces; one representing the belief that all loans, no matter how small or upon what security made, should be limited in interest to the ordinary banking rate; the other representing the belief that competition untrammelled by law or regulation could be trusted to establish interest rates, and that rates so fixed were bound to be fair and reasonable. The first group consisted of a large part of the public which had any opinion on the subject whatever, and its views were frequently and forcefully voiced by newspaper editors, legislators and would-be reformers.

In commenting on the first group's contention that loans should be made at the banking rate of 6% per annum, Ham commented sarcastically:

Of course I know that we still have a chain of loan agencies organized "to lend to workingmen on their character at 6% per annum," which are accomplishing "remarkable sociological results."

He was referring to the Morris Plan companies which had started in 1910. These companies and their imitators had been multiplying and had become formidable opponents of the Uniform Small Loan Law.

Their charges of course were more than 6% per annum, since a savings certificate had to be purchased in instalments to extinguish the loan at maturity. Actually, the rate was an effective 18 to 20% a year, and since at least two endorsers were required, they hardly solved the loan problem although they certainly supplied a useful service at lower rates than were otherwise available. Yet, by posing as "6% companies," in order to avoid usury charges among other reasons, they often made it difficult for the advocates of loan legislation to make a convincing case for a higher rate. As a result they were not on particularly friendly terms with the Russell Sage Foundation which insisted that they reveal their true rates. Ham continued:

To educate the public to a realization that the evil was inherent in the methods pursued, which were more or less a product of the laws in force, was not an easy task. Our facts and motives were first questioned. The conscientious objectors received able succor from the loan men themselves, who, perhaps not unnaturally, felt constrained to oppose us strenuously as they had opposed previous interference from any quarter. If we had been able to convince the loan men of our good faith, the story would not have been so long in the writing. But gradually, as a result of speeches, articles, motion pictures and meetings, defense of borrowers, arrests and prosecutions, and every available means of propaganda, we began to secure results . . . One by one the barriers were forced down and the striking fact is that in the short space of five years this bill is now a law, either in toto or in large part, in nearly half the states of the Union, and has fulfilled our hopes and expectations. Its constitutionality has been definitely established. It is being ably administered by state officials who have come to have an appreciation of the importance of the business, a respect for the licensed lenders and a realization of the earnestness and sincerity of purpose of the American Industrial Lenders Association and its constituent state bodies which are striving to police the business and maintain it upon its new and high plane.

These words of praise from the talented, irreproachable young man who had been opposed and mistrusted by many of his audience were probably heightened by the respect and appreciation they certainly held for him. Ham was not to let them off too easily:

I doubt whether you yet deserve a place in the roll of fame beside the Christian martyrs or those who have given their lives in the cause of humanity. You have simply had the good sense to recognize the right road when you saw it, the courage to stand up and be counted in favor of a proposition which to the lending fraternity generally was anathema, the will and determination to stick to your principles and by fair dealing and honest practice to gain the confidence of your clientele, the cooperation of the agencies of reform and respect of the general public.[12]

The address was more or less a summary and farewell by Ham as he was no longer actively engaged in the Department of Remedial Loans and was on the lookout for a successor who would finally appear in the person of Leon Henderson in 1925 to lead the Department in another burst of activity. Ham's imprint on the consumer finance business was tremendous, of course, and one might well speculate on what other direction it would have taken without his particular background and turn of mind. "For this accomplishment," wrote Frank B. Hubachek in 1941, "from the original studies to the enactment of the first twelve or fifteen laws, great credit is due to the vision, intelligence, courage and energy of Mr. Arthur H. Ham, then Director of the Department of Remedial Loans of the Russell Sage Foundation and now one of its Trustees." [13]

In 1937 Ham was elected to the Board of Overseers of Bowdoin College which bestowed upon him an honorary Master of Arts degree in 1947, the citation reading as follows:

. . . for some years vice president of the Provident Loan Society of New York; valiant, sensible and resourceful foe of loan sharks in whatever guise, showing that a good business head can be successfully combined with a heart set on social reform and progress; with his scholarly pen also a contributor to the literature on small loans and chattel loans; beloved and trusted by hundreds of friends and honored today by his alma mater for service well performed to her and his community.[14]

XII

WERE THERE ANY GOOD
LOAN SHARKS?

If Arthur Ham was an authentic hero of the consumer finance business, were the pre-regulation lenders authentic villains? Obviously, the Foundation did not expect a new crop of businessmen to appear overnight to operate under the new laws. It was fully aware that the only persons who would be lending money under the new statutes at the outset at least were those formerly labelled, without selectivity, as "loan sharks." For this reason, the Foundation felt justified in accepting the aid of the lenders who wished to assist in the passage of the Uniform Laws. Both the Foundation and the National Federation looked upon the first lenders' associations with apprehension and undoubtedly the relationship was regarded as one of necessity rather than choice. Still the only immediate source of capital, organization and lending techniques was the former high-rate lender, and in a very few years his sincerity and performance merited the trust of his benefactors. There are so many surprises revealed in the history of men and events, however, especially with the objectivity of time, that some speculation on the subject some fifty years later is in order.

Majorities of course can be tyrannical and the majorities are never more tyrannical than when they persecute minorities in the name of a false, or, as in the case of the loan sharks, an oversimplified morality. In 1930, Burr Blackburn, who had made a special study of the social effects of the small loan law in Wisconsin in 1929 before joining the staff of Household Finance Corporation's consumer education department, proposed the following on the subject:

> Previous to the adoption of the Small Loan Law lenders were serving a real need and no more guilty of violating the usury laws than the banks and discount companies today. Previous to the adoption of the Uniform Law lenders who advanced small amounts, charging the interest of 10% a month and providing a repayment of principal and interest on a six months schedule, were rendering a needed service at what, under existing conditions was probably not an exorbitant charge. I am convinced that any unemotional, unprejudiced discussion of the conditions existing before the Uniform Law would lay most of the onus and blame for conditions upon the usury law and the legislators and general public opinion toward lenders rather than upon the lenders themselves. Certainly a wide differentiation should be made between those who served the need without the type of exploitation which, of course, came out under the legally imposed conditions when the business was undertaken by persons of no character. The emotional approach to this subject parallels the general notion in the north that southern masters of slaves were brutal and vicious on the whole although the actual facts were that such brutality was the exception and not the rule.[1]

Most observers of the history of the loan business would regard this special pleading with a grain of salt, although there is no question that the system was as much to blame as the individuals. To balance Blackburn's appraisal, Walter S. Hilborn states flatly: "There were no good loan sharks. They were all bad until converted by the law." [2] Robinson and Nugent, in *Regulation of the Small Loan Business,* commented in 1935:

In any attempt to be fair to the lenders of the loan-shark era one must admit that they were working under a system, or rather a lack of system that tended to demoralize the business . . . It restricted the flow of capital into the small loan business and it drove the business underground and forced lenders to resort to all kinds of expedients to get around the law.

There is no desire here to excuse or condone the acts of the lenders. Had many been less prone to exact the last farthing from unfortunate debtors, the public would sooner have come to appreciate the necessary part they play in our social and economic life as it is presently organized. As it was, the men who undertook to deal fairly with their customers, and there were several such, received no recognition and the name "loan shark" was applied to all alike.[3]

These men included such outstanding examples of character and ability as L. C. Harbison and Byrd Henderson of Household Finance Corporation and Charles H. Watts of Beneficial Finance Co., who helped build their companies into major American corporations. Still, the pre-regulation days were rugged, even for the best. A down-to-earth description was given by Mr. Harry Gatter, a distinguished veteran and leader of the business, when he was honored on his fiftieth anniversary in consumer finance in 1956. Recalling his entry into the business in Philadelphia in 1906 for the Mackey chain, predecessor of Household Finance Corporation, he said:

Fifty years may seem like a long time but actually it is only a short time when you measure the growth and the importance of your business.

Few, if any, of you, recall what our business was like in its infancy. Few of you may want to. As an infant, it was a brat. Today's well operated offices bear little or no relation to those at the turn of the century. Those were the very dark days. Practices, too, were dark by today's high standards. There was little or no responsibility, financial or otherwise. Anyone with a few thousand dollars could hang out a shingle. No Uniform Small Loan Law. No licenses. No income tax.

Rates and terms were "what the traffic would bear"—often what it couldn't bear. A good size loan was $25. Large loans—the few that were made—could be as high as $50 or even $100.

Collections were tough. I know. I started with a bicycle, making them for a salary of less than $50 a month. After pedalling that thing 15 or 20 miles a day and making between 35 and 40 calls all over the city, that bike doubled and tripled in weight as the evening approached. We boys worked long hours, too, come rain, snow or high water and we fixed our own punctures in the bargain.

Losses were great. After repaying a loan—perhaps several times over —borrowers would become reluctant, even to the point of appealing to the D.A. for relief. In such case, the lender, like as not, would move his shingle to a new location and start all over again.

In retrospect, by way of comfort, our industry is not alone in origins that were, shall we say—"questionable." Many were the bucket shops dealing in "securities,"—many were the banks whose practices were far from proper by today's high standards. With a great mass of advertisers and merchandisers, morals were an unknown factor. Regulation as we know it today was all but nil. Hence, we need not blush now for our predecessors' practices, any more than legitimate and honorable members of the Stock Exchanges, the modern bankers and the great majority of sales units.

We welcomed and invited much needed regulation. The loan business itself initiated corrections and laws to rectify its activities.[4]

In summary, it appears that the loan business went through the stages of "get the business—get legal—and get respectable" which has been the sequence for so many other American businesses, particularly those connected with money. The borrower, especially the educated clerk, civil service worker or gentleman of the press, hardly deserved the sympathy he received from all quarters when he decided not to make his payments because of the exorbitant rates, except in the cases of the more flagrant overcharges. On the other hand, the harsh collection activities were inexcusable, but in no sense did they compare with today's version of the waterfront racketeering loan shark. One wonders, in retrospect, how these quick-witted, ingenious outlaws, with their virtual monopoly of their field, could have taken so long to recognize what Arthur Ham and the forces of reform were offering them.

II

One also wonders how such an ancient dragon as the "loan shark" should suddenly have come back to life once again. It is currently the subject of a House subcommittee inquiry under the leadership of Representative Charles L. Weltner and it is back on the agenda of the National Better Business Bureau, identified as a "$1 billion a year business that has mushroomed across the country."

This time the loan shark is a creature of the criminal underworld. No collateral is required of the borrower—"only his body." Although the new group indulges in occasional "six for five" street-corner lending, its basic activity is connected with the business world. A New York State Commission of Investigation study revealed loan-sharking as a method by which crime syndicates invaded legitimate manufacturing and merchandising firms, brokerage houses, restaurants and night clubs.

In most states, the criminal loan shark conducts his business within the usury laws, which generally are wide-open for business concerns, particularly corporations, on loans above the usual consumer finance law limits. An obvious remedy was achieved in New York and Illinois in 1965. Here new legislation has established usury as a crime if more than 25% annual interest, in New York, or 20% annual interest, in Illinois, is charged on such loans. The apparently high rate still permitted under this legislation is intended to allow continuance of legitimate business loans which might still serve a purpose at higher than banking rates. The criminal element, of course, was collecting 260% to 2,000% on its loans and at least no longer has the protection of the law in these states. Again it has been demonstrated that the lending of money calls for constant vigilance on behalf of both borrower and lender.

XIII

THE MASSACHUSETTS STORY—
A CASE HISTORY IN REGULATION

To me has been given the honor of placing in operation a system by which it can be demonstrated just what is beneficial, and thereby secure some dependable facts for general use. I shall endeavor by my work to justify the wisdom of the Legislature in creating this office and the judgement of the appointing power and the confirming power in making me the Supervisor of Loan Agencies.[1]

So wrote E. Gerry Brown shortly after his appointment as Supervisor of Small Loans on September 20, 1911. No man could have entered public service with more dedication than this high-minded Bostonian whose idealism crashed upon a reef of misunderstanding and ineptitude only three years later when he was ousted from office by Governor David I. Walsh on January 2, 1915. His story classically reveals the pitfalls and problems to be experienced in the regulation of the newly legislated loan business.

In the fullest tradition of progressive reform, E. Gerry Brown not only quoted his Wassam and Ham faithfully in his elaborately written Annual Reports but also noted the scope of his authority: "The office of the supervisor was established and power given to him to establish some reform." [2] Not laws alone, but the decrees of the powerful, impartial executive filled his visions of his new office, reflecting the high hopes for the executive branch which the La Follettes and Theodore Roosevelt had stimulated in the art of American government. This faithful public servant, however, made the mistake of trying to satisfy too many people at too many times, as revealed in his presumably excellent credo: "Honest capital, honestly employed, is entitled to honest treatment and an honest return." [3] He would find that relying upon businessmen to exercise self-control under such conditions was as naïve then as it would be now.

The Bay State has always had a distinguished record in social reform, no doubt reflecting its Puritan heritage and abolitionist militancy, so it is not surprising that it was a pioneer in small loan legislation and supervision. The Massachusetts law of 1911, though decidedly inferior in some respects, was a trail-blazer in the creation of a strong supervisor, one of the key requirements in any of the legislation to be proposed by the Russell Sage Foundation for either remedial or commercial lending organizations. The full-time employment of an expert administrator with the power to punish was certainly needed for a business which by its nature was one of the most ingenious of all times in finding alternate routes for raising its prices.

The history of modern legislation for the loan business, therefore, may well be said to date from the adoption of an order by the Massachusetts Legislature on April 11, 1911, appointing the House Committee on Banks and Banking to investigate the law "regulating the business of making loans by persons, firms or corporations engaged in the business of lending money upon mortgages or personal property, collateral securities or assignments of wages, or engaged in the business of making small loans without security." Public hearings were held in the State House and note was taken of the forthcoming Conference on the Loan Shark Evil in New York, as Arthur Ham, with his crusader's "hero and villain" terminology, had labelled the merchants' conference at which he would deliver his parade of the loan shark victims speech on May 18, 1911. A stenographer was delegated by the Massachusetts Committee to attend the New York conference, testifying to the national authority that Ham was already developing in matters relating to loans.

The existing law which the Committee was checking on was a crude one. It was administered through some archaic tradition by the Police Commissioner in Boston and by either the mayor, aldermen or selectmen in the smaller cities and towns. It applied to loans of $200 and less and allowed 2% per month on loans under $50 and 1½% per month on loans over $50, but there were so many charges, fees and fines allowed or taken that the rate was practically unregulated. The heart of the additional charges was the so-called "paper charge" which was a fee permitted by custom and indifference for what amounted to the shuffling of papers involved in making a new loan. In order to get as many paper charges as possible, borrowers would generally be made one-month loans, which encouraged additional renewals of the original loan. In addition, whenever possible, the amount requested would be "split" into two or more loans to get the extra set of charges. This created an intolerable situation with rates on smaller loans often averaging 240% or more a year and an investigation was inevitable.

Because of its historical implications, certain portions of the Committee's report, signed by its distinguished chairman, George Holden Tinkham, a goateed perennial in Massachusetts politics, are reprinted herewith:

Your Committee found the subject to be a highly technical one, with various statutes passed by several preceding Legislatures and that the complexity of the subject was such as to require careful but radical treatment and an entirely new method of effectively regulating the business.

After hearing much evidence and many suggestions your Committee came to the conclusion that there were two classes of borrowers the borrowers through necessity and the borrowers through im providence, and had impressed upon it that money hunger, either the hunger of necessity or the hunger of wilful extravagance, could not be satisfied by pure loan laws which amounted to prohibition any more than food hunger could be gratified by pure food law which amounted to prohibition; that pure loans laws will be bene ficial when they are practical; but that the operation of loan agencie under existing conditions approaching justice will do more to mini mize the evils incident to the loan business than a great many law based on suppression; that the class of borrowers through necessity must be provided for and that the class of borrowers through im providence must not be encouraged; that the entire business of small loans was fraught with dangers and with complications, but tha these dangers and complications made it the more necessary to have an adequate law and an adequate scheme for supervision.

The question of regulating the small loan business is one that ha occupied the attention of various philanthropic bodies and the Legis latures of almost every state, and many laws have been enacted in an attempt to confine and regulate the business within reasonable limits, but with ill success and in most cases failure. Your Committee believes that if the business is to be successfully regulated with equa justice to the borrower and the lender, legislation which is drastic must be placed upon the statute books. While the recommendation of the Committee are in their nature far-reaching, your Committee believes that the abuses and evils which today exist in this busines will be speedily eliminated, and that the business will be conducted upon a fair and honest basis if they are enacted into law.[4]

The "drastic recommendations," which of course became law established the position of Supervisor at a salary of \$2,500 a year, raised the limit on regulated loans from \$200 to \$300 increased the rate of interest to 3% a month and repealed the prior section of the law that authorized the so-called "paper charges."

RUSSELL SAGE AT THE TICKER TAPE. *CIRCA* 1900.

ARTHUR H. HAM
From Russell Sage Foundation
reprint of *The Trend and
Progress of the Movement to
Improve Small Loan Condi-
tions*, 1921.

It appears that the practice of loaning money at exorbitant rates of interest, has already
been opened as a field for discussion ; so I
suppose I may enter upon it without claiming
the honor, or risking the danger, which may
may await its first explorer. It seems as
though we are never to have an end to this
baneful and corroding system, acting almost
as prejudicial to the general interests of the
community as a direct tax of several thousand dollars annually laid on each county, for
the benefit of a few individuals only, unless
there be a law made setting a limit to the rates
of usury. A law for this purpose, I am of opinion, may be made, without materially injuring
any class of people.   In cases of extreme
necessity there could always be means found
to cheat the law, while in all other cases it
would have its intended effect.   I would not
favor the passage of a law upon this subject,
which might be very easily evaded.   Let it
be such that the labor and difficulty of evading it, could only be justified in cases of the
greatest necessity.

sate.   But if the good people in their wisdom shall see fit to keep me in the back
ground, I have been too familiar with disap-
pointments to be very much chagrined.
    Your friend and fellow-citizen,
                                 A. LINCOLN.
New Salem, March 9, 1832.

ABRAHAM LIN-
COLN proposes
usury limitations in
his first try for public
office. From the *San-
gamo Journal* of
March 9, 1832, cour-
tesy of the Illinois
State Historical So-
ciety.

PASS THE LOAN SHARK BILL!

HARRY MURPHY'S GREAT ANTI-LOAN
SHARK CARTOON

From the *Chicago Examiner* of March 26, 1917, in support of the
Russell Sage Foundation sponsored Uniform Small Loan Law.
The law was passed in 1917 against bitter opposition of the loan
sharks.

The Loan Shark's Office

THE USURER'S GRIP

A Motion-Picture Film on the

Evils of the Usurious Money-Lending Business

Produced by

THE EDISON COMPANY

In co-operation with the

Division of Remedial Loans

of the

RUSSELL SAGE FOUNDATION

31 Union Square, New York City

ARTHUR H. HAM, Director

The Clerk is Discharged

The Collector Threatens

FROM THE BROCHURE OF ARTHUR H. HAM'S FILM "THE USURER'S GRIP," PRODUCED IN 1912
Note the female "Bawlerout" in the lower left illustration.

UNREGULATED LENDERS'
ADVERTISING AT THE
TURN OF THE CENTURY

THE FIRST NATIONAL AUTO FINANCING ADVERTISEMENT

Saturday Evening Post of April 8, 1916

Guaranty Securities Corporation was later acquired by Commercial Credit Company.

LEON HENDERSON IN WAR-TIME ROLE

Members of the National Defense Advisory Commission hold their initial meeting on May 30, 1940. From left to right behind President Roosevelt are Edward R. Stettinius, Jr., Chairman of U. S. Steel; William S. Knudsen, President of General Motors; Miss Harriet Elliott, Dean of Women, North Carolina University; Leon Henderson; Chester C. Davis, Federal Reserve Board member. The agency was the forerunner of the War Production Board.

FRONT PAGE HEADLINE OF DETROIT NEWS OF JUNE 23, 1927

Leon Henderson arrives to aid Better Business Bureau campaign against salary-buyers.

WALTER S. HILBORN AND THE AUTHOR
Los Angeles, California, June 7, 1965
Mr. Hilborn represented the Russell Sage Foundation in the
drafting of the Uniform Small Loan Law of 1916.

Such was the experiment which E. Gerry Brown solemnly undertook to supervise. He first addressed himself to a few preliminary problems, such as dealing with D. H. Tolman, who thundered:

I do not come under the law at all. I buy the unsecured commercial paper of salaried people, or of women keeping house . . . Under the "law of the merchant," I have a right to buy notes by third parties at any price for value before maturity. I do not buy loans direct.[5]

By 1912, an amendment to the law brought note buyers under supervision and most of them went out of business rather than accept Brown's rates. Tolman stayed on in a few offices.

Next, Brown correctly utilized his powers by prohibiting absolutely all arbitrary fees, fines, and collection expenses, regardless of whether or not the borrower had voluntarily agreed to them. In addition, exercising a degree of old-time paternalism, he "denied to the borrowers, unless with the consent of the supervisor, the privilege of getting money from a lender if he or his family has engaged the services of some philanthropist to take him out of his debts to the moneylenders." [6]

So far so good, but inevitably he re-opened the box of paper charges which was to be his downfall. We have noted that the rate was increased from 2% to 3%, and that the old paper charges were revoked by the new law. Brown decided, however, that by "inference or implication" he was empowered to use his administrative regulations to permit a bonus or charge "as the expense of making and securing a loan, and such amount shall not be counted as part of the interest of such loan." He deemed this interpretation to be an injunction to the supervisor in his impartial wisdom to establish just enough paper charges to give the lender a fair return on his capital and to keep the borrower from paying the old unlimited charges. How much easier it would have been for Brown, had the concept of a "borrower's law" been paramount, as the Russell Sage Foundation would eventually propound! Brown wished to favor both borrower and lender and was caught between the two objectives.

Brown's paper charge procedures had both practical and theoretical foundations. He first consulted no less an authority than Boston Police Commissioner Stephen O'Meara, who was his predecessor in supervising the business, at least in Boston. Fortified with O'Meara's professional observation, as well as the pleas of the lenders, that about 5% a month was required for loans of $10 and under, Brown thereupon issued regulations permitting paper charges resulting in the equivalent rate for these loans. He then sighed a breath of relief:

An error of judgment could have destroyed the business of the moneylender. The supervisor reasoned that if the Legislature had intended to destroy the business it could have accomplished it without the aid of a supervisor, but in establishing supervision, it intended to initiate a system that would develop even and exact justice for both borrower and lender. This is the policy of the Commonwealth for all within its jurisdiction. Thus influenced, the conclusions were embodied in the rules and regulations and were given out as a system on which the business should be conducted.[7]

Before analyzing Brown's philosophical justification for these extra charges, we might consider his concern for loans of $10 and under in the first place. The Annual Reports reveal that such loans were indeed of the utmost importance in Massachusetts. For example, of the $1,078,000 in loans outstanding as of September 30, 1913 for 108 licensees, excluding the remedial loan associations, the average loan outstanding was only $20. To keep these figures in proportion, one should note also that the average manager's salary in the same report was listed as $27 per week and the average wage of the other employees was only $11 a week. Another major factor that created so many loans of $10 and under, of course, was the splitting of loans into two or more $10 loans in order to get the extra charges. In his sincere efforts to prevent this abuse, Brown allowed his new paper charges not as so many dollars per loan but instead as a percentage of the loan, which in effect made splitting no longer worthwhile, a considerable achievement. He also observed with disfavor the general practice of lenders to require the borrowers to pay in full at the end of the month in order to get additional paper charges. He therefore stipulated that the borrower must have the option to pay off these one-month loans on a weekly basis without any additional paper charges. This simple but basic desire to encourage borrowers to make weekly or monthly payments in order to liquidate their loans should have originated long before with the lenders themselves. Their reluctance to do so is one of the strongest indictments of the pre-regulation days.

Returning to Brown's theoretical defense of his paper charges, which also included a 10% fee for loans over $10, we find some rambling but well-meaning respects paid to Blackstone and others who had warned that interest would seek its own level between borrower and lender regardless of man-made laws. In Brown's case, he elevated his reasoning for 5% a month to a lofty plane:

It is another powerful, natural law which is often at work where human law is thought to be out of harmony with moral right.[8]

II

In New York City, Arthur Ham was not impressed with these platitudes. It is doubtful whether Ham at this point would have advocated anything above 2% plus some small fees had he been asked to testify before the Massachusetts Committee in the first place, although he was consulted by its investigator. If it were going to be 3% that was clearly enough in his opinion. In his report to the National Federation of Remedial Loan Associations on June 19, 1913, he stated:

The report of the Massachusetts Supervisor of Small Loans is an interesting document. After a careful analysis of about eighty money-lending offices in Massachusetts, the supervisor reached the conclusion that a flat rate of 3% per month is not sufficient to pay operating expenses, including cost of capital . . . His action opens the way to abuses in connection with the making of short term loans . . . I believe the supervisor's conclusions were erroneously reached. In averaging the percentages of operating costs to outstanding loans he included a large number of offices which employed a very meager capital, not through necessity but through the custom long in vogue among loan sharks not "to put all their eggs in one basket." That the disproportionate cost of operations among these offices greatly affected the result of his calculations is shown by the fact that the figures given for the percentage of operating costs, including cost of capital, to outstanding loans for the two remedial chattel societies in Massachusetts are 1⅓% and 1¾% per month, respectively. To argue that 3% per month is not a fair allowance because certain offices employing a small capital cannot make a satisfactory profit at that rate is not convincing. The argument might easily be carried to an absurdity and the Legislature asked to allow a charge under which offices employing a capital of $1,000 or $500 might pay expenses and a fair profit on the investment. The remedial loan societies have proved conclusively that with a fair amount of capital employed, 3% per month is a liberal allowance inclusive of all charges of whatever character; that at this rate honest capital can be attracted into the business and make a fair profit.[9]

Brown was not to let Ham's challenge go unanswered. Exceedingly proud of his approach, which he called "the Massachusetts system," he predicted that "Massachusetts at this moment has established a system that will become general wherever the business of small loans is regulated by law. The system in itself contains the possibilities of adapting itself step by step to changing conditions, until it has obtained the largest possible equity between borrower and lender." [10] In fairness to Brown, it must be admitted that he had indeed set up the most elaborate provisions for reporting income and expenses yet required from lenders anywhere and he apparently intended to reduce rates accordingly on these smaller loans when the lenders' earnings would permit it. For the year 1912 he had made a careful analysis of reported figures which proved that the Massachusetts companies lending on security, which he permitted for the time being to charge only 2% per month plus paper charges, would have lost money were it not for the paper charges. The unsecured lending companies were permitted the 3% per month rate plus paper charges but still only managed a slight profit. In fact, the gross income for eighty offices of all types throughout the state averaged only 2.8% per month against expenses of 2.72%, producing a negligible profit. One wonders where the widely advertised profits were in this business and it is apparent that for the Massachusetts offices, which averaged only $12,000 in outstandings in 1913, the new rates, even with the paper charges, were inadequate. Over half of the 151,037 loans made that year were for $10 or less. In summary, Mr. Brown was supervising a "nickels and dimes" business even in those days, a business incidentally which did not use borrowed money to increase the return on capital, since these companies did not yet have bank credit. It is quite probable that the Massachusetts companies were not typical because of their small size, as Ham indicated, as well as their penchant for $10 loans. The fact is, however, that in 1916, when the rate was cut to a flat 3% per month including all charges, 32 companies immediately closed their doors and within a year 16 more followed their example. Thus, we gain some new insight into the complex problems of rate-making for the business as it existed in those days.

Surveying his figures, Brown was convinced that the business of unsecured loans at least could not be operated at 3% a month and he published this opinion in his report for 1912. He thereupon drew upon himself the wrath of Arthur Ham, who easily recognized that a one-month loan at 3% a month plus a 15% paper charge for as long as six weeks was still at an annual rate of 156% a year. Ham furthermore was not at all impressed by the argument that short-term unsecured loans should get a higher rate. The remedial loan associations, which he was vigorously proposing as a model for the business, generally made loans secured by chattels and always with a weekly or monthly payment plan that would liquidate the loan in instalments. In fact, at its 1913 convention, the National Federation of Remedial Loan Associations had proposed that salary loans, which were the typical unsecured loans, be outlawed, a proposal which Brown condemned as an invasion of personal freedom of action. Thus, Brown, having been criticized by Ham for his 1912 report, addressed a lengthy rebuttal to Ham in his 1913 report and ordered 2,000 additional copies printed, as he regarded the Massachusetts reports to be messages of national importance for all concerned with lending problems. This stubborn New Englander confronted Ham in part with the following:

Mr. Ham is one who has given all of his time for some years to the study of the very important question: "What should be a fair allowance for capital engaged in the making of small loans?" His views are entitled to attention. The Supervisor of Loan Agencies of Massachusetts is giving, as he has given since his appointment, his best effort to the solution of this problem. Mr. Ham had the report of the supervisor before him.

If Mr. Ham is correct, then the supervisor is wrong; the system and conclusions derived from it are challenged. We propose to show conclusively, even to Mr. Ham, that he is wrong. The controversy is important because on the one hand is the system of the Federation of Remedial Loan Associations demanding legislation in line with this declaration that 3% a month is more than ample to command capital for the business of making small loans in general. We repeat that no law on this subject is wise unless its results are beneficial.[11]

With that opening gun, Brown proceeded to argue that the remedial loan associations were being inaccurately used for rate-making comparisons, taking an unkind pot-shot at Ham's brand new Chattel Loan Society in New York as a money-losing proposition. Other remedial associations throughout the country were carefully dissected to augment his point and Brown at least felt the issue was resolved.

By the time Brown was to write his next report, for the year 1914, he had already been levelled by Ham and Hilborn in the incident over the London Finance Company, whereby Hilborn and "persons interested in the small loans situation" had gone over his head to Governor Walsh. The ouster was front page news in Boston and was announced only "after the conclusion of the longest meeting of the Executive Council in the history of the Commonwealth." [12] Governor Walsh also released to the press his letter to Brown in which he charged Brown's office with being in conflict with the "spirit of the statutes." The letter took Brown to task for permitting Massachusetts lenders to make loans by mail against the objections of the New York District Attorney. It criticized the paper charges and questioned whether they were within the scope of Brown's authority. It also stated that Brown's "relations with certain money lenders had been so intimate you are not in a position to fearlessly and faithfully administer the duties of the office you now hold." This sting was made even more bitter by Walsh's claim that the Boston Typographers Union, those inveterate borrowers of the press, found the loan situation worse than before the 1911 law. In passing, Walsh also criticized Brown for appearing before a New York legislative committee in 1914 in opposition to a bill Ham was advocating.[13]

Brown fought back, asserting he was the "victim of a plot" and extended his sympathies to his successor, Frank H. Pope, on taking over an "office of misery personified." [14] He demanded a hearing before a special legislative committee that was held commencing January 26, 1915. At the hearing Brown was as articulate as ever, claiming he had told New York's District Attorney Whitman, now Governor Whitman, that inasmuch as

Brown had been able to keep New York lenders out of Massachusetts, Whitman ought to have been able to keep Massachusetts lenders out of New York. This moved the President of the Senate, a taciturn, sandy-haired man from Northampton named Calvin Coolidge, to ask the ambiguous question: "As I understand it, Mr. Brown, Mr. Whitman wanted you to treat New York borrowers better than you could those in Massachusetts?" "That is just it, Mr. President," answered Brown, who must have gained some satisfaction from the next day's headlines: "BROWN SATISFIED; EX-SUPERVISOR RESTS CASE." [15] The hearing continued for an additional session at which Brown's mental faculties were seriously questioned, leading to Brown's assertion that he was susceptible to hearing voices that gave him Divine guidance. Brown also stated: "If you will examine my reports, you will find that they show comparisons of the work done here with that of the Russell Sage Foundation, and you will find that the comparison is not to the advantage of the Russell Sage Foundation." [16]

Meanwhile, Deputy Chief of Police Neal had been pressed into duty as Loan Supervisor while Governor Walsh was appointing Pope to succeed Brown. In a kind of Keystone Comedy finish to this fiasco, Neal, in his three weeks in office, rendered the opinion that charges in excess of 3% a month were overcharges and should be rebated. This was duly reported in the papers and borrowers began to storm the State House to demand their rebates. Neal looked into the matter more carefully and said he meant only those paper charges that had been made more than once every three months, as Brown had provided for in his regulations. "Research revealed that the former supervisor had given verbal permission to certain lenders in Boston that they might make that paper charge each month with the understanding that if a borrower discovered it was not in accordance with the printed Rules and Regulations and expressed dissatisfaction with the proceedings, the overcharge would be refunded." [17]

This supervisor with the heart of gold for lenders had given the verbal permission because he felt without it the lenders could make no profit and might start forcing the borrower to go monthly from one lender to another on a reciprocal basis, according to Brown's successor's first report. Furthermore, Brown had actually printed and was about to send out a new set of regulations which would have raised the 15% paper charges permission from $10 loans to $15 loans.

In the long run, Brown was exonerated. First of all, the Attorney General ruled that Brown had the right under the law to allow paper charges, although they should have been in writing. Secondly, Frank Pope jettisoned the proposed regulations that would have allowed Brown's 15% paper charges on loans to $15, but substituted his own regulation of a 10% paper charge on loans up to $50, with the old Brown proviso that instalment payments could be started at the borrower's option within six weeks without further paper charges. Finally, Deputy Chief Neal, joining in the community's awareness of the utter probity of the misguided Brown, issued a press release: "NO WRONG IN BROWN'S DEALINGS, SAYS NEAL." [18]

Brown himself had some valedictory words to say in his final 1915 report which testify to the strong feelings, damaged reputations and fierce clashes which inevitably attend the growth of a new business:

At the opening there arose the question (of rates) which required perhaps even better judgment than the supervisor could bring forward for its solution. The supervisor had been entrusted with the duty; the state of Massachusetts had placed on his shoulders a superb cloak of authority over the whole situation. Unusual power was vested in him. The supervisor feels that no man could have a greater sense of responsibility resting upon him than the thoughts which have been with him night and day since he has assumed office. His work must necessarily be experimental . . . Unquestionably, his first duty was to find some ground upon which his feet could squarely rest while he proceeded to exercise this unusual power over the fortunes of men and corporations which were then engaged in the business. Millions of dollars were involved . . . He has conscientiously performed this service, but like all other men, his judgment is not infallible.[19]

E. Gerry Brown later became interested in the cause of labor and was serving as secretary of the Brockton Central Labor Union at the time of his death in 1928. The *Boston Evening Transcript* reported:

In 1911 he was appointed Supervisor of Small Loans, an office created that year, but later was ousted from office. His reputation, however, never suffered from this, as Mr. Brown, an idealist, was a man of the highest character, and had a personal record that was unblemished. He often attended meetings of the veteran newspapermen in the state and was also active in spiritualistic gatherings up to a few years ago in different parts of the state.[20]

Arthur Ham must have been puzzled by this doughty, moralizing Boston adversary. He also must have felt his own rigidity about rates weaken somewhat from the onslaught of figures produced by Brown, for it was about that time that he began to weaken on the old 2% per month stand and became more receptive to the higher rates that launched the regulated business under the Foundation's Uniform Small Loan Laws. Mr. Brown was effective after all.

III

Frank H. Pope served as supervisor for a period of ten years and had an easier time of it. As a newspaper correspondent and former State Auditor, he was more familiar with the State House atmosphere and met his problems with distinction. Still, his regime was not without excitement, and a review of some of his confrontations will complete this excursion into the trials of state supervision in the early days of the consumer finance business.

It was inevitable that Massachusetts would be faced with new legislation after the Brown publicity and this time the advice of Arthur Ham was requested. Ham advised in 1916 that on the basis of the evidence then at his disposal 3% a month including all charges was acceptable and such a law was passed and signed by Governor McCall on June 16, 1916. In the *Loan Gazette*, the new official publication of the American Association of Small Loan Brokers, the news was reported with grave concern:

Some lenders have already closed their offices, among them D. H. Tolman, while others who had several offices in the same city are consolidating them into one and have expressed themselves as "trying it out for a year to see if they can live under it."

Still there was hope expressed that if the record showed the rate was too low, the next legislature would raise it, as "none desire to deprive the public of small loan services." Pope was not too enthusiastic about the new law. He took great pride in the fact that his extension of the instalment privilege to loans up to $50 had been a great success: "Today thousands of loans are being paid on instalments as a result of the new opportunity given." He was further of the opinion that: "Had the instalment system applied to every loan there is a question whether the Legislature of 1916 would have enacted new legislation affecting the money-lending business, but as there were many who did not take advantage of the opportunity, and were unable to cancel their loans, they were subject to the then existing paper charges and were paying what was regarded by the Legislature as an exorbitant and unreasonable rate." [21]

The resourceful lenders were not long in testing Pope's mettle. After consulting eminent attorneys, thirty "unsecured lenders" decided to incorporate and require would-be borrowers to purchase stock in their corporations as a condition for obtaining loans. Under the Massachusetts corporation law, it was legal for corporations to sell stock payable in instalments. Pope apparently never understood completely the details of the plan, but it was clear enough that the device was for the purpose of evading the law and he put a stop to it after a few months by supervisory edict. A few lenders then decided to test the edict in the courts and Pope requested the help of the Boston Legal Aid Society to pursue the issue on behalf of his office. Representing the Legal Aid Society was young Reginald Heber Smith who was later to become a stalwart counsel for finance company interests and a great educating force concerning the business within the legal profession. Smith quickly killed the plan but some of the lenders had one more card to play, which caused Pope an embarrassing moment.

These lenders succeeded in arranging a conference with Smith and others in which they argued that they might exist under the 3% law if they had some security which psychologically would motivate the borrower to pay his loan. What better plan could there be than the discarded stock purchase plan revived with the borrower receiving a promise that if he completely paid for his stock in instalments, the stock would simply be converted into cash and used to repay his loan? Quite innocently, Pope enthusiastically describes in his report for 1916 the details of this plan as it applied to the still ever-present $10 loan. Instead of paying the paper charges, reasoned Pope, the borrower would pay his 3% interest each month on the $10 and would also buy $1.20 worth of "stock" each month for nine months. At the end of nine months, the $10.80 stock fund would be used to extinguish the $10 loan and 80¢ would be returned to the borrower. This was, of course, nothing but a variation of the Morris Plan, which was still new in Massachusetts and whose companies had reluctantly agreed to take out licenses under Pope's jurisdiction only the year before. It seems incredible that Pope, or for that matter, the approving Legal Aid Society, did not recognize that paying for the stock in instalments was no different than paying for the loan in instalments, and that the 3% a month should therefore be charged on a declining principal balance, rather than on the original $10 loan for each of the nine months. The actual rate permitted was therefore 72% a year instead of 36% and another scandal was in the making. Fortunately for Pope, he warned the lenders at the beginning of 1917 that all stock payments should be credited to the loan balance and that interest should be recalculated to apply to the unpaid balances when the final payment was made. In the early spring of 1917, Pope's auditors checked to see how the first batch of nine months' loans was gestating, and to their dismay they found such widespread overcharges by the lenders that Pope banned the practice altogether, whereupon sixteen additional companies surrendered their licenses declaring "it was an utter impossibility for them to do business at a rate of 3% a month."

Meanwhile, more progressive companies such as Beneficial Finance were interested in doing business in Massachusetts but they wanted the 3½% per month rate that had been established in other states such as Pennsylvania and Illinois with the Foundation's blessing. Pope duly reported in his report for 1917 that he had received information to the effect that in those states wherein the 3½% rate was adopted, it was known as the "scientific rate" and "it had been declared to be such by Professor E. E. Eubank of the Y.M.C.A. College in Chicago, who has given this subject very earnest and thoughtful consideration." The professors and their scientific testimony were to be held in abeyance during the war years (when Pope reported the loan business in Massachusetts was "looking up because there was no other direction in which it could look, it being flat on its back") but in 1920, the proponents of 3½% were ready to make their bid.

IV

In one of the lenders' first efforts to raise the rate of interest, Reginald Heber Smith, now representing the Legal Reform Bureau, advised the Massachusetts legislators that the 3½% rate "is the generally recognized scientific rate and the rate which has been fixed by the Uniform Small Loan Law drafted by the Russell Sage Foundation." He thereupon noted that every state which had passed an anti-loan shark law since 1917 had established such a rate. Mr. Smith added:

Massachusetts would have had the 3½% general rate if its law had been passed in 1917. In 1916, when the bill which became chapter 224 of the General Acts of 1916, was under consideration, the sponsors of the bill sought the advice of Arthur H. Ham, Director of Remedial Loans, Russell Sage Foundation. He is the greatest authority in the country, and on the basis of the evidence then at his disposal, he said that 3% was a good rate. Within six months, however, and on the basis of more complete data, he worked out 3½% as the general rate, and he put that rate in the first draft of the Uniform Small Loan Law. Had the bill been introduced in 1917, we should have followed Mr. Ham's advice and would have urged the 3½% general rate.[22]

Quite likely Mr. Smith's project would have had smooth sailing, but he also asked for an additional 1½%, or a total of 5% a month, for unsecured loans of $50 or less. "The data from which the 3½% rate was fixed," said Mr. Smith, "came primarily from the study of the records of the 34 organizations in the National Federation of Remedial Loan Agencies. The chart of their 1918-19 work shows, however, that their average loan (excluding the pawnbrokers' loans) was $68, and that these were *secured* loans."

The bill went through both the House and the Senate without opposition, and was returned to the House for the enactment stage, when Walter S. Hilborn suddenly appeared like an avenging angel, representing the Russell Sage Foundation, and flatly denounced the 5% provision. The Boston press wheeled into action urging the defeat of the loan bill and even the credit unions opposed "the measure that would give 'sharks' 60 per cent." [23] Smith beat a hasty retreat but instead of settling for 3½% across the board, offered an amendment making it 4% per month. The opposition which Hilborn had ignited, however, was unmistakably shown in the action of the House which not only rejected the 4% amendment but killed the entire bill and no change was made at all.

Pope reported in the same hectic year that in order to discourage repossessions of household furniture, he had devised the novel plan of writting a polite but firm collection letter to the borrower from his own office and he reprinted the letter, which warned the borrower: "Through such foreclosure you will be obliged to experience much discomfiture and humiliation from the taking away of the household goods which you have mortgaged which will result in the breaking up of your home." [24]

If this activity on the part of a state supervisor appears to be from a different world, we can at least be reassured that college students were as troublesome then as now. Pope closes his report for the year 1920 with the information that he noted in the papers that two Radcliffe College girls had opened a "bank" in Eliot Hall making 30 day loans at 10% to fellow students, and had sold 250 shares of stock for their enterprise. Pope thereupon wrote to them in order to ascertain whether their business came under the Small Loans Act. "The 'bank'," answered one of the girls, "was opened as the result of our interest in a course in economics which Miss Hastings and myself are taking in college. . . . Our 250 shares are sold at 5¢ per share; our loans are made at 10% for the month, but in view of the fact that they average possibly 50¢ per loan, and we want to declare dividends, we could hardly charge less." Pope pursued the matter of the 120% loans later and found the bank had ceased operations. He noted approvingly, however, that a 7% dividend had been declared.[25]

V

The Massachusetts law, like that of most states, went through a series of changes after 1916 marked by gradual reductions in rates and increases in "ceilings," which are the maximum amounts of loans allowed by the law. Presently the rate is 2½% per month on loans to $200, 2% on the portion from $201 to $600, 1¾% on the portion from $601 to $1,000, and ¾% on the portion from $1,001 to $3,000. Hundreds of millions of dollars are borrowed under this law each year.

The Massachusetts story is not yet finished, however, and even today its loan problems generate considerable publicity. In April 1965 a special Commission studying state government and administration released its recommendations for the regulation of small loans in Massachusetts. Among its recommendations are that the position of Supervisor of Small Loan Agencies be abolished and that the department report directly to the bank commissioner. It notes that presently rates are determined by a regulatory board consisting of the bank commissioner, the state treasurer, the commissioner of corporations and taxation and two public members appointed by the Governor, including one who represents organized labor. The report states:

As a result alternative methods of fixing interest rates have been considered. The Commission has concluded that rate-making authority should not be vested in the bank commissioner who also has enforcement responsibilities. Neither is the past practice of legislative determination of rates advisable. In the Commission's opinion the best solution would be the reorganization of the small loans regulatory board so that the members will be persons with the expert knowledge and detachment from politics necessary to enable it to regulate interest rates in a manner to protect the public interest without depriving the small loans industry of a fair and reasonable rate of return.[26]

To accomplish this, the commission recommends a board of three appointed by the Governor, consisting of a lawyer in private practice familiar with financial transactions, a certified public accountant and an executive experienced in small loan company or bank instalment work. Thus, the pioneer regulating state moves quite far away from the original Uniform Small Loan Law principles with their emphasis on strong, quasi-independent supervision and legislative rate-making. The establishment of rates by a commission was first proposed by one of the many professors who became interested in small loans, Professor John R. Commons of the University of Wisconsin, in a report for his home state in 1931. Indiana and Iowa were other states which early used such commissions.

A dependable witness to pass judgment on the proposals of the special Massachusetts Commission is Reginald Heber Smith. The Massachusetts case history in regulation may well end with his comments:

Ever since 1914 when I graduated from Law School and became counsel for the Boston Legal Aid Society, I have been deeply interested in the development of the small loan industry in Massachusetts, and the following comments are submitted in the light of fifty years of observation.

1. The position of Supervisor of Loan Agencies should be abolished.

When Massachusetts first began its effort to regulate small loans (then $300 or less) there was no one to do the regulating, and so the position of Supervisor was created by the Legislature.

Later, when Calvin Coolidge was Governor, there was a reorganization of the governmental structure, and the Bureau of Loan Agencies became a division of the State Banking Department.

177

Tradition enabled it to maintain a quasi-independent position, but which had no justification.

It is sound that the position of Supervisor should be abolished.

2. The Commission is sound in dealing with rates of charge on small loans—even if it miscalls them "rates of interest."

A legislative body exists to make broad policy decisions, not to fix any detailed tariff of charges. If Congress undertook to establish freight rates through the country, its work never could be finished and the results would be disapproved by all interested parties. The same would be true if a state legislature tried to fix telephone, gas, and electric rates.

A court is no better and can serve only as a final resort if a legislative body does interfere and fixes rates that are confiscating. That is a constitutional guaranty but it is not extended to small loan companies. It is constitutional—for historical reasons—to fix rates that are impossibly low, just as Congress has done for the District of Columbia. All that a law-abiding lender can do is liquidate his business and close his office.

Rate fixing is best done by an administrative tribunal or commission. Massachusetts has had such a commission but it has not worked too well, and that may be because some of the members had no particular qualifications for their responsibilities.

Indeed the essential point in any schedule of rates is whether it permits loans of $300 or less to be made lawfully by law-abiding loan agencies. These are the small loan companies. The banks greatly prefer larger loans.

If a truly fair rate is permitted on loans of $300 or less, it will follow that the lawful agencies will make the "little loans" of $100 or less which often are the most necessitous. It is on the most necessitous borrowers that the loan sharks prey. A prime objective of the Commission must be to keep them out of the state.

It is at this point that the morality underlying small loan regulation becomes apparent because, if the rate is made too low, the "little" loans cannot be made by law-abiding loan agencies.

Thus the loan shark is invited to return and take over again his dominion of the field of the little loans. It is an invitation for which he is ever on the alert.

It is to be hoped that these considerations may be brought to the attention of the Governor.

For many years licensed lenders have filed comprehensive annual reports with the Bank Commissioner. Thus the factual basis for rate determination already exists and has existed for a long time.

Intelligent men, activated solely by the desire to do an honest job, will find that their task is not too difficult and that, with the aid of public hearings, they can certainly arrive at the truth.[27]

XIV

COLONEL HODSON'S BUREAU
AND BONDS

When Reginald Heber Smith appeared before the Massachu-setts legislators in 1920 representing the Legal Reform Bureau, he represented an agency that was nothing but a creation of the fertile mind of Colonel Clarence Hodson, founder of Beneficial Loan Society, as it was known at that time. A born publicist, Hodson no doubt chose the name "Society" to obtain some carry-over from the semi-philanthropic image of the esteemed remedial loan societies. Colonel Hodson had participated in the framing of the Uniform Small Loan Law in 1916 and was also a key figure in the formation of the American Association of Small Loan Brokers. Disregarding the American Association's agreement with the Russell Sage Foundation to promote only the Uniform Small Loan Law, he soon began to promote a so-called "Ideal Law" under the sponsorship of his own Legal Reform Bureau. His draft was opposed by the Foundation wherever it was introduced and within a few years he dropped it and returned to his support of the Uniform Law.[1]

A man of great energy and imagination, the career of this colorful businessman affords fresh insight into the development of an industry, which, like history itself, reflects the impact of personalities as well as the march of time and events. He was born in Laurel, Maryland in 1868, descendant of an old and distinguished Maryland family whose founder settled in Dorchester County, Maryland in 1664. From this original colonist, a line of judges and men of affairs led to Colonel Hodson's father, a leader of the Republican party in Maryland and nominee for the U.S. Senate in 1886. Clarence Hodson was educated at Crisfield Academy in Maryland where his father was president of the board of trustees. He read law in his father's office and began to practice law with him in 1889. He quickly showed an aptitude for finance and organization, which eventually led him to abandon the law and devote his attention to launching banks, trust companies and other corporations. He established the Bank of Crisfield in 1893, becoming the youngest bank president in the United States at the age of twenty-five, a feat later equalled by Joseph P. Kennedy in Boston in 1914.

In the next ten years, Hodson is reported to have figured in the founding or organizing of over fifty banks and trust companies in New Jersey, Pennsylvania and New York with a capitalization in excess of $50,000,000. In 1896 in pursuit of this activity he had entered the securities business in Newark where he founded the New Jersey Fire Insurance Company in 1908 and the Eagle Fire Insurance Company in 1912. By 1913, he had discovered the possibilities of the small loan business and founded the Beneficial Loan Society, which became a New Jersey licensee under the new Egan Act in August, 1914. Other groups of offices in his system were the Industrial Bankers of America, incorporated in 1918, Collateral Bankers in 1921, known as Personal Finance Company, and the American Loan Company chain of 21 offices purchased in 1925. These were eventually consolidated into one major corporation in 1929, the year after

Hodson's death. At the time of his death, Beneficial had grown to over 200 offices.

In two particular areas, the raising of money and the writing of loan company literature, Hodson's contributions were noteworthy. As a securities specialist, Hodson undoubtedly did more than anyone else to bring capital and credit to the consumer finance business in its early days. It must be remembered that the pre-regulation history of the business made it an unlikely candidate for bank loans or for equity capital through the normal markets. A company like the Mackey chain, which had $3,000,000 outstanding in loans in 1908, was operating practically entirely on Mackey's personal fortune. John Mulholland, the Kansas City salary loan operator who had over one hundred offices scattered throughout the country in pre-regulation days, is said to have sold more than one million dollars' worth of stock through his New York office,[2] but the claim appears highly dubious. Beneficial, at any rate, sought public money from the very beginning under the leadership of Hodson who was primarily an investment banker. His firm, the "House of Hodson," specialized in the sale of bank and insurance securities and he was made to order to promote the difficult raising of capital for the new, misunderstood and untested industry. The magnitude of this task was compounded by the fact that within ten years after the founding of Beneficial, the country had undergone a war and a post-war depression but his results were spectacular. He was also astute enough to induce Charles H. Watts, Household's Eastern Supervisor and Hodson's successor as President of Beneficial, to join forces with him in 1925, allowing further concentration on financing. Hodson's instinct for hiring, incidentally, was also quite remarkable in his choice of personal secretaries. One of them, O. W. Caspersen, who was employed as such in 1920, rose to the top of Beneficial in a career spanning forty-two years and the other, Roy E. Tucker, who became Hodson's secretary in 1922, progressed to Vice-Chairman of the

Board in thirty-nine years at Beneficial. David H. Finck was hired by Hodson in 1924 directly from the faculty of the Harvard Business School. This brilliant executive was the first personnel expert in the industry. In the next forty years he supervised Beneficial's personnel development, making it possible for the firm to expand to over 1500 offices, and served in top management as well. Under his direction, Beneficial produced a correspondence school in the Twenties and Thirties known as the Industrial Lenders' Technical Institute for the purpose of training personnel. In a demonstration of unparalleled public relations within a highly competitive industry, Beneficial established this school as a non-profit institution available to anyone in the industry, the idea being that better personnel and better methods on the part of all competitors would raise the public acceptance and ethical standards of the business. This great service was matched in another direction by Household Finance Corporation's distribution of educational materials on money management to consumers throughout the country beginning in 1930. Since that date, Household has distributed over 23 million "Money Management" booklets.

Hodson was an unusual pamphleteer whose intense and often engaging rhetoric was placed in the service of advancing the cause of regulation in unregulated states and the cause of Beneficial's need for funds at the same time. In one booklet, published in 1919 when formal prospectuses were not yet required, he describes Beneficial's first public debentures:

The charter powers of the Society are broad and comprehensive. It is not a charity, but transacts a necessary and legal business upon fair and legal terms. It was not organized solely to make money, but to supply a popular loan service for which a public need exists in every State.

$2,000,000 of 6% debenture gold bonds, due 1939 dated as January 1, 1914 were authorized and about $1,250,000 have been sold, each with

183

bonus of a corresponding profit sharing certificate, which pays in addition at least one-third of net profits yearly. The Bonds are issued in denominations of $1,000, $500 and $100, with quarterly coupons attached. Among about 600 bond holders are many of the leading citizens of about thirty states and foreign countries.

These 6% debenture gold bonds, with profit sharing certificates, have proved satisfactory and popular with careful investors, who have given a preference to its securities. The total amount of bonds outstanding at the end of each year is as follows:

December 31, 1914—Bonds outstanding		$	100,200
December 31, 1915—	”	”	236,900
December 31, 1916—	”	”	750,000
December 31, 1917—	”	”	950,000
December 31, 1918—	”	”	1,150,000
February 28, 1919 —	”	”	1,250,000 [3]

If the amounts being raised seem small, one should remember that the loan offices were also very small. On December 31, 1922, when Beneficial had fifty-four offices, its outstanding loans were only $3,537,000. The raising of the money through these debentures with their profit-sharing bonus was therefore of the greatest importance. Perhaps this explains the ardent salesmanship with which Colonel Hodson wooed his bondholders who were also invited to an annual banquet which they attended in large numbers.

The title of this 1919 booklet, which was published by the Legal Reform Bureau to Eliminate the Loan Shark Evil, was *The Loan Shark Evil Is Now Superseded by Beneficial Licensed Money-Lenders of Small Loans in Many Cities—Public Spirited Men Have Enlisted*. Investors were urged not just to invest for profit but for good works:

More and more, good citizens recognize that they ought to do something in a practical and helpful way to assist their less fortunate though worthy fellow citizens. Every good citizen today should answer the question, "Am I my brother's keeper?" With a positive "Yes, I am." No gift of money is asked, only preference in making investment.

* * *

If every decent man declined to assist in forming or directing Beneficial Loan Societies, loans of that class and service would not be available to the public and the devil and his loan sharks would celebrate a happy holiday.

The honest thing for honest men to do is to invest their honest capital in an honestly conducted loan office, so that honest people will be able to obtain fair loans upon just terms.

Holding aloof accomplishes nothing. If this old world is ever to be made a better place for us all to live in, it will result from those who go in and make an earnest effort to accomplish something worth while, and it is worth while to save good people from the oppression of bad money-lenders. Beneficial Societies are doing it every day, and need more loan capital to extend the good work. For that reason they are offering more of their securities for sale.

* * *

Every loan society desires public recognition and encouragement and they are generally receiving it from those who happen to know what such service means to so many worthy men and women. No advantage is taken of their necessities, but all are treated alike, with respect and courtesy, without patronage, bullying, or charity sneer.

Under the heading "LET OTHERS PRAISE THEE—NOT THINE OWN LIPS," Hodson listed testimonials from satisfied bondholders. The list includes business executives and professional men, one of whom, a minister, stated: "My conviction grows that it is possible for high-souled men to place a good business on such a moral basis that the people will be protected from the unscrupulous sharks whose chief business seems to be to exploit the weak. I want to thank you personally for helping to make it possible for me to be made cognizant of the fine work your organization is conducting."[4] It was not too surprising that the clergy would invest in Beneficial as the officers of the Legal

185

Reform Bureau itself, in 1922 at least, drew heavily upon them Reverend King was President, Reverend Warren was Vice-President and Reverend Genthner was Field Director.

Among other booklets in the *Money-Lending Series* of the Bureau was one entitled *An Adequate Industrial Loans System Needed by the Masses,* published in 1922 when the industry had substituted "industrial loans" for brokered loans to describe itself. In this booklet, Hodson draws a strange conclusion about bank credit which reminds the modern reader how inconceivable it was at that time that banks would enter the consumer credit field:

It is generally accepted as a fact that only seven out of one hundred persons maintain a bank account, and from the coldly statistical standpoint of dollars and cents, eighty-six men out of one hundred fail in life. Of the fourteen who succeed, but two make a marked success. Therefore, as an outside figure, fourteen men out of one hundred are entitled to bank credit which calls for collateral that is accepted under the law.

To support his argument about what the masses needed, Hodson then detailed the occupations revealed in an analysis of one month's business by an industrial loan company in New York City. Why he chose New York, which did not have a commercial loan law at the time, is difficult to understand. No doubt the figures came through the courtesy of a remedial loan society, probably the Russell Sage Foundation's Chattel Loan Society. With that provision in mind, the occupations of the borrowers who had failed in life to gain bank status but were also active loan company borrowers is of interest:

Clerks 247, Post-office Employees 245, U.S. Employees 95, State Department and Court Employees 24, City Department and Court Employees 177, N.Y. County Employees 14, Fire Department 198, Police Department 114, Proprietors and Partners 344, Managers 67, Secretaries and Stenographers 44, Foremen 40, Agents 33, Salesmen

13, Factory Operators 81, Machinists 34, Inspectors 33, Tailors 39, Artisans 24, Pressmen, Compositors, etc., 108, Teachers 18, Doctors and Dentists 15, Writers 15, Telegraphers and Despatchers 18, Book-keepers and Accountants 64, Conductors 3, Miscellaneous 222.[5]

In another booklet published in 1922, *Financing the Working-man*, Hodson offers some observations concerning the changing structure of the business:

Professional money-lenders, on the other hand, seek borrowers and advertise in the classified columns of the daily newspapers in most cities and otherwise seek to attract the patronage of those who may have occasion to hire the use of small sums of money. Such money-lenders maintain loan offices, with staffs of employees whose duty it is to investigate the character and credit of loan applicants as well as the security or guaranty, if any is offered. This staff negotiate loans, collect instalment payments, keep the books and dun delin-quents. In many cases where borrowers "skip," the staff trace the absconding debtors and their goods as best they can. They must be credit and collection experts especially able to judge the moral hazard and avoid "dead beats."

Professional money-lenders, whether individuals, firms, associations or stock corporations or societies, have a permanent capital em-ployed in making small loans of not over $300 to any person. It is the usual practice to arrange for repayment of all loans in monthly instalments, usually from five to twenty months, although some loans are for a longer or shorter time to suit the convenience of the borrowers as to surplus they can spare from earnings. The ten monthly payment plan is most popular, though many loans are made on a weekly or semi-monthly payment plan to suit the borrowers' wages or income. The payment plan is always arranged to suit the convenience of borrowers both as to amounts and due dates, as it is recognized that living expenses must come first and the loan must be amortized out of surplus as available. As there are frequent disap-pointments, so many extensions must be allowed. If the delinquent doesn't call, he must be called upon and the matter arranged amicably, so he will not become discouraged. If he becomes involved an additional loan may be necessary. Such relations develop intimacy

187

and confidence, which frequently result in establishing patrons upon a sound financial basis and making better and happier homes.

* * *

Loans are usually closed in about two days, during which the necessary inquiry is made as to credit standing, and the home is visited so that both husband and wife are interviewed. Few loans are made to unmarried persons, as the reason for nearly all loans is to finance emergencies growing out of family life, as births, marriages, illness, deaths, vacations, etc. Reputable loan offices are to be accorded credit for making their investigations with tact whereby it will not become known that a loan is being negotiated.

* * *

It is surprising to note that when reform loan legislation has been enacted in various states, many of the loan sharks have remained in business under the new dispensation. Once their business was legalized and dignified, they have changed their methods to conform to lawful practices, preferring the open, dignified way of doing business. It is better that some should reform late, rather than never. Other lenders never reform and even if licensed, bear close watching for little abuses out of keeping with the spirit of anti-loan shark legislation. It is conceded by all that many loan sharks are efficient in credits collections and service in the small loan business, and that most of them would prefer to do business on a lawful and mutually fair basis. The extortionate rates of Loan Sharks and the dwindling of their borrowers are possible only and have been unduly prolonged by the absence of practical small loan legislation which will recognize actual conditions and will legalize a fair and necessary small loans service upon a practical and sound basis, mutually fair to borrowers, lenders and the public. To attain a fair rate the lender must have fair legal protection so that dead-beats cannot swindle him with impunity.

Another notable change observable as a result of proper legal regulation, has been the improved character of small loan business and of the borrower. Everything is then above-board and there is competition for the trade of borrowers. In the same office, run by the same men, the average loan, formerly of $15 to $30, has been found to increase from $60 to $125 per loan, and the old practice of requiring weekly payments has been abandoned in favor of the monthly instalment plan and the repayment period is increased from

hree to six months up to five to twenty months and extensions are
readily granted.

State after state is enacting uniform anti-loan shark legislation which
s effectively eliminating the loan shark evil and supplying a fair
and lawful small loan service, at an aggregate saving to necessitous
borrowers of many millions of dollars annually. The joy of it is that
the saving is to those who are least able to bear the burden of high
charges which an unlawful trade always requires. The saving of
self-respect and dignity to a multitude of American wage-earners is
also a consideration and inducement for legislation.[6]

Colonel Hodson, whose title was awarded to him by a Maryland Governor in 1896, was one of the first writers on the
subject of small loans and his pamphlets, distributed to libraries
and other sources of information, were pioneering efforts in that
direction. He was deeply interested in educational institutions
and served on the Board of Governors of Washington College
in Chesterton, Maryland, which awarded him an honorary degree of Doctor of Letters in 1922, which he proudly added to
his publications thereafter. He was also a benefactor of the
Princess Anne Academy, a trade school for Negroes in Maryland. Before his death he created a trust fund known as the
Hodson Trust, which still represents major holdings of Beneficial securities. The income has been a great assistance to
Washington College and other educational institutions. A dining
hall and dormitory at Washington College have been built from
the trust income and an endowment is being created for a Hodson professorship in economics at that college.

While considering the subject of early financing, note should
be taken of the first break-through in the sale of securities to the
public through an established, non-associated underwriting firm.
Household Finance Corporation, which had early established
credit lines with the First National Bank of Chicago, reputedly
the first bank to extend credit to a consumer finance company,
looked into the possibilities of selling stock to the public in 1928.

Lee Higginson & Co. made an analysis of Household's business
as well as the outlook for the industry in general, and made a
public offering of $7,000,000 of Participating Preference stock.
Considering that at the end of 1927 Household had only
$10,818,000 outstanding in loans, this amount of new capital
seems optimistic but the company opened or purchased close to
one hundred offices in the next five years and loans increased
to $39,367,000. The consumer finance business was well on its
way to phenomenal increases and its ability to weather the
depression of the Thirties made it one of the most favored
industries for the suppliers of money. The Russell Sage Foundation history notes that Leon Henderson, then Director of the
Department of Remedial Loans, assisted in the negotiations between Household and Lee Higginson & Co.[7] The investment
firm in turn emphasized the Foundation's sponsorship of loan
legislation in its promotional material for the sale of the stock.
The participation of Mr. Henderson was based on the reasoning
that access to greater financing would result in decreased rates
to the borrower. There was some voluntary rate reduction after
this security issue but Household and others soon found rising
costs generally made it advisable to operate at the maximum rates
permitted. Reductions in rates through legislative action were to
come soon enough as the industry gained in maturity and efficiency. The ability to borrow and raise money, following the
lead of Beneficial and Household, enabled lenders to adjust to
these reductions. Billions of dollars have been safely invested in
consumer finance companies by the public since the days of
Colonel Hodson's "gold bonds."

XV

DEVELOPMENT OF OTHER
CREDIT AGENCIES

While the loan industry was having its exciting and slightly illegitimate birth, other agencies of credit were also developing, some to become mighty components of our economic system. Credit unions, Morris Plan companies, sales finance companies and, finally, the commercial banks all began to carve their shares of the consumer credit pie. From virtually no outstandings at all in 1900, instalment credit alone, that is, monthly payment debt excluding home mortgage, credit card, charge account and other consumer debt, increased by billions, reaching the fantastic figure of sixty billions in the mid-sixties. Behind the bulk of this expansion were neither laws nor necessity, but instead the revolutionary consequences of the automobile age.

The credit unions, however, were an early response to a social need most closely paralleled by the loan companies. The growth of this cooperative type of enterprise is somewhat surprising in a country that professes to abhor the cooperative technique normally associated with socialist countries, but it is typical of

America's practicality that we easily accommodate institution
which threaten our myths and manage to use them to our ad
vantage. Not only credit unions fit into this category, but als
farm cooperatives in general, the tremendous educational subs
dies such as the G.I. Bill of Rights legislation and, of course, th
farmers' long and respectable affair with price supports.

It is highly doubtful if the original framers of the credit unio
legislation gave much thought to such doctrinaire consideration
as this relationship to capitalist enterprise. They were moved, a
was the Russell Sage Foundation, by a social problem that cried fo
a solution. Cooperative credit organizations had started in Ger
many as early as 1849 and had spread over many Europea
countries and even into India and Japan. A special type o
American millionaire such as E. A. Filene, the Boston departmer
store merchant, travelled broadly and cast an analytical eye o
such institutions. Just as James Speyer was inspired by the *mon*
de piété of France to help form the Provident Loan Society, s
did Filene see in the cooperative agencies of Europe a solutio
for small loans in America. Meanwhile, the movement had a
ready become strong in Canada. Alphonse Desjardins, a journa
ist of Levis, Quebec, had studied the European credit unions fo
years and started his own Caisse Populaire, or People's Bank, i
his home town at the turn of the century. Finding his missio
in life, Desjardins travelled through Quebec and Ontario estab
lishing credit unions. With his assistance the first credit union i
the United States was organized in a parish of French-Canadia
cotton mill workers in Manchester, New Hampshire in 190
Meanwhile, in Massachusetts, the aristocratic Pierre Jay, Con
missioner of Banks, actually drafted a law in collaboration wit
Desjardins and saw it enacted by the Massachusetts legislatur
in the same year. A movement such as this was eagerly studie
by Arthur Ham in his capacity as Director of the Departmer
of Remedial Loans at the Russell Sage Foundation. Familia
with the attitudes and habits of French-Canadians from his ow

background in neighboring Maine, Ham went to Quebec in the summer of 1912 to study the associations and confer with Desjardins himself. As a result, promotion of credit unions became a formal undertaking of the Russell Sage Foundation and actually took the place of the remedial loan associations in importance. Effective loan legislation would rapidly cause the remedial associations to lose their momentum. Also, in many ways, the credit unions had more appeal than the remedial loan associations, since they promoted thrift—the members supplied the capital through their own savings accounts—and were adaptable to rural areas as well as cities. In addition they were expected to discourage unnecessary borrowing, which was always close to the heart of the social worker. Ham's new allegiance to the credit union movement is shown in his solution to the dilemma of his victim in the film *The Usurer's Grip*, the script of which he sold to Edison in the fall of 1912. Ham has the young clerk fade out as a happy customer of a "cooperative savings and loan association" rather than of a remedial loan association, possibly reflecting his recent visit with Desjardins.

Following Ham's visit to Quebec, a conference was set up by the Foundation in New York in October 1912, at which Desjardins explained the Canadian movement. Pierre Jay had meanwhile come to New York as vice-president of the Bank of Manhattan Company. He responded warmly to the Foundation's program and had agreed to serve as treasurer of Ham's experimental Chattel Loan Society, founded earlier in that year. With the help of Jay, Desjardins and Leonard G. Robinson, general manager of the Jewish Agricultural and Industrial Aid Society, who had organized several credit unions among farmers in the eastern states, Ham drafted a bill providing for credit unions in New York State under the supervision of the Banking Department. The bill became law in 1913 and was used as a model for similar legislation throughout the country. In addition Ham wrote with Robinson the important *A Credit Union Primer*, which the

193

Foundation published in 1914 as a handbook describing in detail how to establish the new agencies.

In working with Robinson, Ham demonstrated the basic tolerance and contempt for racism that distinguishes the best of the Yankee tradition, conservative or liberal, on the American scene. This could not be said for Alphonse Desjardins, who revealed himself as a narrow-minded bigot in correspondence with Ham in 1918 in which he urged Ham to keep Jews out of the credit union movement, "for I fear the Jews and much more the merchant Jews above all." [1] Ham casually disregarded the advice. On the other hand, during the Thirties, the public relations program of the Foundation and the commercial lenders' association protested in a most unworthy and unnecessary manner that the regulated loan business was a "Gentile" business. [2]

Ham became a national speaker and writer on the credit union movement and in 1916 he engaged in a sharp debate with Myron T. Herrick on the subject. This prominent citizen, who was later to welcome Lindbergh in Paris as our Ambassador to France and had also been Governor of Ohio, denounced the credit unions and urged that they be "wiped off the statute books."

The reply of the young Director of the Department of Remedial Loans to Herrick gives fascinating insight into the attitudes towards loans and instalment credit at the time. Through this controversy, we are reminded that not only consumer finance but also credit unions had to struggle for recognition. In addition, Ham pointed out to Herrick: ". . . one cannot fail to remember that it required fifty years for the now well-known and widely appreciated building and loan associations to become a popular institution in this country and that in its early days it too had its critics as well as its defenders." Herrick's complaint could not be dismissed, as he was not only a national figure but also a leading expert on cooperative credit systems for farm areas and author of books on financing the farmers. His attacks were becoming so consistent that Ham felt it would destroy the movement and at that time Ham was a major spokesman for the movement. Herrick's criticisms were directed primarily against the indulgent hand of the government giving tax exemptions to organizations which he doubted should be relieving "distress and incompetence." This, of course, is still echoed by credit union opponents but Herrick went a step further and objected strenuously to credit unions for city dwellers, let alone farmers who were better off with his brand of credit agencies. He held in fact that loans should be made only for productive purposes and not for consumptive purposes. In this connection, Ham replied:

One instinctively rebels at the characterization of wage-earners and clerks as "thriftless incompetents" and inclines to the belief that it is an unfortunate choice of words rather than the reflection of any real feeling of distrust or pity for the army of men not engaged in enterprises of their own . . . The occasions upon which the wage-earner or clerk may have a legitimate reason for borrowing are so many that it would be hopeless to attempt to state them all . . . Has Mr. Herrick never heard of the evil of instalment purchasing which keeps so many clerks and wage-earners poor? Does he not know of the loan shark evil? Is a loan to a clerk to enable him to buy necessary supplies for cash instead of credit at ruinous prices, to escape from the continuous payment of extortionate interest charges, are these acts so inherently bad or unsafe as to be outside the pale of cooperative banking?

Ham's effective and analytical reply was published as a long article in the *New York Sunday Times* and served to silence Herrick. The redoubtable Ham could not resist one low punch:

It is doubly hard to reconcile this position (of Herrick) with the fact that he has taken the chairmanship of a committee in Cleveland organized to promote a company to operate under the so-called Morris Plan of Loans and Investments.[3]

The credit union movement had already found a strong enough champion, however, to launch it firmly in orbit. This was perhaps just as well for the fortunes of the consumer finance industry, which was to need Ham's support mightily. Edward A. Filene and later the Twentieth Century Fund which Filene established became the leading supporters of credit unions from the time the first law was passed in Massachusetts in 1909. In 1917 Filene established the Massachusetts Credit Union League and later he financed the Credit Union National Extension Bureau which still operates its massive program from headquarters in Madison, Wisconsin. Presently the credit union movement is extremely vigorous. After trailing the consumer finance companies in the previous decades, it has consistently kept over one billion dollars ahead of them in instalment credit outstandings, although this includes a great deal of credit union automobile finance paper. Still the credit unions are viewed with alarm as competitors inasmuch as they are the fastest growing segment in the instalment credit picture. The latent criticism that they are a threat to the existing social order has been disarmed by the conservatism of the movement itself as well as by the sponsorship of big business. The most logical complaint that can be levelled at credit unions is their tax-favored status as non-profit enterprises. Many are in fact multi-million dollar organizations whose operations are professionally managed and are essentially motivated by the prospects for profit. They have so broadened their basis for membership eligibility and the size and purposes of their loans that the competition validly questions why they shouldn't pay their taxes like everyone else. Meanwhile, the credit union movement flourishes, occasionally breaking forth with national advertising campaigns featuring testimonials from such stalwarts of free enterprise as Col. Eddie Rickenbacker on the subject of Eastern Airline's credit unions. Their loans are limited to members and the average rate is 12% a year, the same rate used by the old remedial loan associations. In addition to their tax exemptions, they also have the advantages of subsidized facilities and personnel from their sponsoring organizations.

The Russell Sage Foundation remained a strong supporter of

the credit union movement, concentrating on New York State, even after the Credit Union National Extension Bureau had opened its own office there. It was instrumental in changing an unfriendly attitude toward the credit unions, which were often badly managed, on the part of the Banking Department. In fact, during the depression, the Department of Remedial Loans, under Rolf Nugent, helped the Banking Department liquidate several defunct associations and remedy the laws in order to prevent future recurrences. After this endeavour, the Department ceased active propaganda on behalf of the credit unions but continued strongly its promotion of the Uniform Small Loan Law under the direction of Leon Henderson.

II

Arthur J. Morris enjoyed the unique privilege of having his name pass into the public domain as a generic term. Founded in 1910, the Morris Plan was as well known by the Twenties and Thirties in its field as the Babe and technocracy were known in their fields. The sheer originality of using one's own surname and endowing it with the prestige of a "plan"—long before the invention of the "five-year plans"—was remarkable in itself. At any rate, the Morris Plan achieved fame and publicity though its numbers were never large, so it must have been an inspired concept.

The inspiration came to Morris when the young Norfolk, Virginia attorney was struck by the growing perception that personal loans were as good as bank loans, provided of course they could be made at a sufficient rate of charge. As counsel for several banks he had the opportunity to guarantee several such loans when the customer's credit and security did not meet customary bank standards. These standards were generally so impossible no one could qualify and the plain fact of the matter was the banks did not want to make personal loans. They were

197

not equipped to check personal credit and handle small loans and they questioned the moral aspect of the whole transaction in the first place. Morris was aware that the banking system was distinctly weak in this respect and he decided to do something about it. He could have gone the way of the remedial loan societies or the credit unions but then there would have been no Morris Plan. What he wanted was a hybrid form of agency that would have the appearance and prestige of a banking firm and serve a higher type of clientele than would be expected to use the other agencies.

The first step was to avoid being licensed as a remedial type of agency in the few states that had remedial laws and to find a way to operate at the traditional 6% rate that prevailed in states such as Virginia at the time. He therefore figured out a plan as ingenious as any concocted by illegal lenders since the 1880's. The difference was that he kept his charges at a reasonable level and inaugurated his institutions under completely respectable auspices.

Funds for the business were to be raised by the sale of Class A certificates which in effect were the common stock of the corporation and were entitled to its profits. Class B certificates were savings certificates paying a fixed rate of interest to the saver and constituted an additional source of funds to lend to the public. Class C certificates were the "gimmick." They had to be purchased by the borrower on the instalment plan. When paid for, the proceeds were used to extinguish the loan. Fines were also charged for delinquency in making the instalment payments.

Since the Virginia legal rate was only 6%, that amount was deducted from the loan, along with a $2 per $100 investigation fee which the courts had generally allowed Virginia banks to charge without being accused of usury. Thus, the Morris Plan started out with $8 for $92, which is slightly in excess of 8%. It is 8.70% for a one-year loan. Not even the Morris Plan was

prepared to lend to consumers at that rate. The return of the
$100 by way of the instalment stock purchase made the differ-
ence. If you borrow $100 and have to pay it back in monthly
instalments, you don't have the use of the $100 all year. You
have the use—on the average—of only $50. Since interest is the
charge for the exact use of money, $8 for approximately $50 is
much closer to 17% than 8.7%. The simplest method for absorbing this fact of high finance is just to accept on faith that
any dollar charge per hundred per year for time payments is
double that amount in terms of true interest percentage. For
example: $6 is 12%; $7 is 14% and so on. If this seems to defy
logic, you are in good company. When William McC. Martin,
Jr., Chairman of the Federal Reserve Board, was being questioned
at a Committee hearing by Senator Paul F. Douglas, a former
economics professor, at one of Douglas' valiant attempts to pass
so-called "truth-in-lending" legislation, Martin obligingly remarked that he couldn't figure out true interest charges on instalment payments himself and was completely confused on the
subject.[2] As far as the general public is concerned, it is basically
interested in the dollar cost rather than the annual percentage,
but people concerned with the subject of credit should at least
grasp—or accept—this simple fact: double your annual dollar
charge to get the true rate of interest. If that appears to be too
easy, you must now accept an additional fact about loans, particularly consumer finance loans. If you are first quoted the
annual rate of interest as follows, "the average rate per year for
a medium-sized consumer finance loan is 24%," the dollar charge
is only one-half that figure, or $12. For example: 24% per year
costs the borrower $12, 20% per year $10 and so on.

With this in mind, it is easy to see why the Morris Plan was
well received and afforded incorporation privileges by willing
banking departments who either did not understand or care
about Mr. Morris' device for increasing his yield above the per-

mitted rate. Not only were the Morris Plan depositors to be protected by the cover of the banking charter but the community had given the institutions its moral support as well. The fears of usury charges thus never bothered the incorporators whom Morris enlisted from the best people in the community. The first Morris Plan company, the Fidelity Savings and Trust Company, opened its doors on March 23, 1910 in Norfolk.

The Morris Plan companies flourished and Morris chartered the system on a franchise basis in addition to his own controlled companies. Since they required two endorsers and aimed for the larger size loans, they did not displace the loan shark by any means. Their relationship with the Russell Sage Foundation was trying, however, as noted, particularly because of their self-styled 6% status. Their early literature leaves no doubt that they considered themselves and not the commercial lenders as the answer to small loan problems. In their 1912 and 1913 pamphlets, they claim to be "A Remedy for the Loan Shark Evil," and their recital of loan shark exploitation cases reads exactly like the literature of the Foundation and the Legal Reform Bureau in years to come. By 1913 Morris would claim:

> The Morris Plan has demonstrated by successful operation in Baltimore, Md., Atlanta, Ga., and Richmond, Va., Washington, D.C., St. Louis, Mo., and at other points that it is adaptable to local conditions everywhere, and by operating in each instance at a substantial profit to its stockholders, it has proven that it has the quality of permanence. It conforms to the borrowers' ability to supply security and make repayments, as is shown by the thousands of loans made to grateful borrowers. It has supplanted the Loan Shark wherever installed, and by its rapid adoption in various cities throughout the country apparently is destined to become the final Remedy for the Loan Shark Evil.[3]

In a 1912 pamphlet, the Morris Plan discussed the interest it charged its customers with the kind of reasoning that seems to have justified the Russell Sage Foundation's objections:

The question sometimes arises, if the Morris Plan bank can earn from 16 to 18 per cent on the money loaned, how much interest is charged the borrower?

The borrower is only charged, and he only pays, the legal rate of interest, which in most States is six per cent. On a $100.00 loan for a year he pays $6.00 interest.

From the fact that the borrower makes small weekly payments on his "C" Certificate, which he has to purchase in order to borrow money, it is patent that he does not have the use of all the money borrowed for a full year. These payments on the Certificates of Investment, however, are separate and distinct from his loan, and have no more to do with it than the deposits of a commercial bank have to do with the discounts or loans made by those institutions.[4]

The Morris Plan literature generally bore the mottoes "Providing Credit and Investments for the Masses" and "Character Is the Basis for Credit," the latter attributed to J. P. Morgan. Morris was fond of reminiscing that he saw the great man himself a few years after he started his plan and had received the wholehearted endorsement of the financier. Morgan, who had just suffered some indignities in the House's Pujo Investigating Committee hearings of 1912, was still the king of American finance and his chance testimonial to the effect that personal loans were as good as bank loans, both being based on character, was often quoted.

Indeed there was an aura of good breeding and respectability among the early Morris Plan activities which may have accounted for its ultimate inability to make a greater impression on the consumer loan field. From the October 5, 1912 *New York Times,* the following article speaks for itself:

TALES OF LIFE TOLD
AT BANKERS' SMOKER
————————

Consumer Finance: A Case History in American Business

Morris Plan Managers Swap
Stories of How Wage Earners
are Financed

$20,000,000 Lent in a Year

Young Doctor Enabled to Buy Auto;
Cash to Pay for Weddings
and Funerals Provided

The Morris Plan bankers, assembled at a smoker in the Hotel Astor last night, told many human interest stories about men and women who had escaped loan sharks and the humiliation of appealing to charitable institutions by borrowing money at a discount rate of 6%, with character as the basis of credit. Fifty-three Morris Plan banks now operating in the United States, it was said, are making loans amounting to $20,000,000 a year, and averaging between $100 and $125 each, to persons whose weekly income varies from $10 to $100 a week. . . . Arthur J. Morris, father of the Morris Plan, told how the New York bank in the Equitable building had lent the purchase price of an automobile to a young doctor who had promises of an extended practice, dependent upon his obtaining a car, but whose capital was not sufficient to cover the initial cost of even the cheapest automobile.

"And that's the kind of loan I like to make," said Mr. Morris, "for it furthers a constructive and productive purpose. If a man wanted an automobile for a luxury, we wouldn't lend him a cent, but we've lent money for the purchase of a piano in a case where someone in the family had musical talent and wanted to develop it."

* * *

There will be sessions of the convention today and tomorrow with a concluding dinner at the Hotel Astor tomorrow night, at which the speakers will be Eugene Lamb Richards, the State Superintendent of Banks, Thomas Mott Osborne, Warden of Sing Sing, George E. Canfield, Vice President of the State Charities Aid Association and Joseph F. Moran, President of the New York Patrolmen's Association. Brief remarks are expected from Mayor Mitchel, Theodore N. Vail, Percy Straus, Bishop Greer and others. Herbert L. Satterlee, the toastmaster, will be introduced by Clark Williams, President of the Industrial Finance Corporation.[5]

When the New York Morris Plan corporation was formed, its first directors included Columbia University's Nicholas Murray Butler, Vincent Astor, Oscar Straus and other luminaries. Differences of opinion on policy soon arose, however, and all of these men resigned from the Board. Meanwhile in 1915, David Stein of Newport News, Virginia, claimed he had originated this system of loans in 1901 and sued to enjoin his former friend, Arthur Morris, from its use.[6] This action died out, however, and the Morris Plan seemed to have an unlimited future at the time of the smoker in 1916.

How did it happen, then, that the consumer finance companies, charging a higher rate of interest, would eventually dominate the loan field, originating as they did under such poor circumstances? The answer lies in their greater understanding of the business of making loans, as well as their more human approach, which helped them stand off bank competition after the banks entered the field. The borrower simply felt more comfortable in the licensed lender's office and he preferred to pay the higher rate rather than get one or two endorsers to sign his note. The writer recalls the success of his own family's consumer finance business in Pittsfield, Massachusetts, founded in 1927. The local Morris Plan had been started some years earlier but was gradually outdistanced by the aggressive, friendly consumer finance company. To get a loan from the Morris Plan one had to reveal his secrets to a committee of local directors and to transact the loan one had to submit to the chill treatment of the local Morris Plan official who was hardly enthusiastic about a borrower's faulty financial condition. As a result, the Pittsfield Morris Plan was eventually absorbed by one of the local banks. The American public needed service as well as the servicing of its needs.

III

Service and not necessity was the key to the growth of the sales finance business. Once it was learned that more goods could be sold on time than for cash, an avalanche of credit buying swept over American life and became the feature, not the exception, of our economy. If there were any questions about its moral justification, they were cast aside with the introduction of the automobile and other "durable consumer goods," from washing machines to television, which could reach mass markets only through time payments.

As early as 1807, a furniture house named Cowperthwait & Sons is reported to have sold furniture on the instalment plan in New York City. Other New York firms such as Ludwig Bauman were also pioneers but the greatest breakthrough before the Civil War occurred when the Singer Sewing Machine Company began to sell on time not only in the United States but all over the world. The piano manufacturers joined the ranks soon afterwards. It was the automobile, however, which created and still maintains the great thrust in instalment credit.

The automobile was a luxury for the rich in the years before World War I and rarely would one be financed by a firm such as the Morris Plan and then only on a direct loan basis. In 1906, Woodrow Wilson, then President of Princeton University, commented: "Nothing has spread socialistic feeling in this country more than the automobile . . . a picture of the arrogance of wealth." [7] This type of moralizing made little impression, however, as the main reason for the automobile's slow reception was its unreliability. The early cars were uncomfortable, costly to operate and always breaking down, inspiring a popular song "Get Out and Get Under." Wall Street and the bankers made a collective bad guess about the future of the industry which would be the greatest in the country within thirty years and withheld financing of the manufacturers. This inability to raise money added to the mortality of manufacturers who rose and fell by the hundreds in the early years and further dampened customer interest. Progress was inevitable, however, and by 1909, the year in which Henry Ford decided to build only the Model T and reduce prices accordingly, total production of autos and trucks reached the impressive figure of 100,000. Equally responsible for the breaking down of sales resistance was Charles F. Kettering's invention of an effective self-starter in 1912, and above all, the introduction of the closed car. As late as 1916 only 2 per cent of cars were closed; by 1926, 72 per cent were closed. A storm-proof, reasonably quiet vehicle that could be locked and parked day and night in all kinds of weather was something quite different from the earlier "horseless carriage." Not only was the old American morality concerning buying on time about to crumble in the face of such a convenience but generations of young couples were handed a suitable locale for varying degrees of misconduct.

Though the instalment selling of cars was virtually unknown before World War I, by 1925 it had spread so rapidly that over three-quarters of all cars, new and old, were being sold this way and nearly 20 million cars were on the rapidly improving roads. The banks continued their monumental error concerning the undesirability of instalment credit and, as a result, a new type of specialized institution, the sales finance company, was created to fill the gap in the country's credit structure. The manufacturers themselves, starving for capital, were in no position to finance either their dealers or the auto purchasers, making the need for a specialized finance company all the more urgent. The dealers were mostly bicycle and machine shop operators and former wagon retailers with limited resources for their part, so the advent of the auto sales finance company, which would finance both the dealers and the purchasers, was a most desirable occasion.

Consumer Finance: A Case History in American Business

The first sales finance companies were originally accounts receivable financing companies which specialized in supplying working capital to manufacturers and wholesalers by lending against the borrowers' accounts receivables. Typical of these firms were CIT Financial Corporation, founded by Henry Ittleson in 1908 in St. Louis as the Commercial Credit and Investment Company, and the Manufacturers' Finance Company, founded in Baltimore in 1909 by Alexander E. Duncan who in turn established the Commercial Credit Company in 1912. These and similar companies quickly recognized the future in automobile financing and gradually developed into auto sales financing companies to fill an obvious need. Meanwhile, as early as 1913, a San Francisco auto dealer, L. F. Weaver, established an organization of his own to finance the instalment sales of his cars, making him the first person to operate a regular business of purchasing automobile time payment paper. In 1915, another sales finance company was organized in Toledo known as the Guaranty Securities Company. This firm intended to specialize in financing Willys Overland cars but was so flooded with business from other dealers it moved to New York and in 1916, as the Guaranty Securities Corporation, ran the famous two-page ad in the *Saturday Evening Post* which startled the nation. The ad announced that Guaranty would finance 21 different makes of automobiles which it listed. The headline: "You Can Now Get Your Favorite Car on Time" inspired the formation of numerous sales finance companies throughout the country and a new industry was born. Guaranty Securities, incidentally, was acquired by Commercial Credit Company, the official history of which comments as follows on the early days of this business:

It is doubtful if it was immediately realized what great changes would be brought about in automobile manufacturing and distribution through the undertaking of finance companies to meet the problems of carrying inventories during the intervals between manufacturing and sale. These companies proved to be the connecting link between mass production and mass consumption. They promoted all-year-round factory production and the elimination of the former periodic shutdowns made for stabilization of costs and labor conditions, and in consequence, a very marked lowering of prices which, together with prompt deliveries of cars, was bound to increase the number of buyers.[8]

In 1919 the last of the "Big Three," General Motors Acceptance Corporation, joined CIT and Commercial Credit to dominate the field in the same sense that Beneficial Finance Co. and Household Finance Corporation were to dominate the consumer finance field. The sales finance companies had no comparable legislative problems such as faced the loan companies. From the very beginning they avoided the usury laws under the shelter of the "time-price differential" concept, which treated their mark-up on the contracts they purchased from dealers as charges and not interest. This concept occasionally suffers judicial reversals, as it did in Nebraska in 1963, but the industry is too firmly entrenched as an agency of America's basic manufacturing product to be more than temporarily set back by such an occurrence. Like the consumer finance industry, it has also undergone a series of rate reductions since the early 1900's. Auto finance charges are roughly 25% less than they were at the outset, due to legislative and competitive influences. In the auto finance industry's case, not only the ability to raise tremendous amounts of borrowed money but also its entrance into the automobile insurance business made it possible for the present companies to survive.

The auto dealers were also vitally affected by the sales finance company. The sales finance company became their banker and also provided an important part of their net income, first through the "pack" or "kickback" to the dealer and later by the more legitimate return of bad debt reserves when the reserves more than covered the dealer's exposure as guarantor of the consumer's paper. Still another important change has been the competition of the "captive finance company," such as GMAC and the recently activated Ford Motor Credit Company, although Ford previously had withdrawn under a "consent decree" for restraint of competition by order of the Department of Justice in 1939. The frank dependence of many auto dealers on finance company and related insurance commission benefits for their margin of profit was revealed in the recent strong but unsuccessful opposition of dealers to the licensing of the Sears Roebuck auto loan program in California, which offered no participation to the dealers since the customers would apply for loans directly. The most significant structural change for the auto finance company, however, is the fact that the lion's share of its once exclusive automobile market has gone to the finally awakened banks, who now hold almost twice as much automobile consumer paper as the sales finance companies. The happiest small survivor in the picture is the occasional auto dealer who is prosperous enough to operate his own captive finance company. Otherwise, the number of smaller auto finance companies has greatly decreased in recent years. The larger companies, as always, have fared better than the smaller firms. Their major diversifications into non-auto finance fields, from industrial manufacturing and greeting cards to commercial banking, have placed them in the position where auto finance is no longer their dominant activity. At least they are no longer dependent on auto finance and can easily survive, as CIT did, the loss of the Ford Motor Company business.

The most drastic maneuver sales finance companies have made in recent years is their outright invasion of the consumer finance field. Possessing lists of prospects, ready-made security and credit records, they were able to capture almost overnight a significant share of direct loans, which are less volatile and more profitable than auto finance as a return on investment. Yet the consumer finance company, while viewing this development with dismay, must still acknowledge an overwhelming debt to the auto industry itself, for the reason that in a sense it made it what it is today. The basic consumer finance loan to consolidate many bills and instalment payments into one loan depends to a large extent on the existence of debt created by automobile purchasers. The automobile in turn has generated repair and maintenance bills, insurance needs and vacations, all of which are likely to end up as consumer finance loans directly or indirectly. In addition, an embarrassingly large number of consumer finance customers now become customers only by making a loan for all or part of the down payments on a new or used car or for the total purchase of a used car. The consumer finance company has long since lost its original function which made it more or less an arm of social work in meeting social problems. It has depended on America's emergence as a nation of time-buyers for its continued success. A final contribution of the sales finance company was to make the whole idea of instalments and loans so widespread it had to become respectable by the sheer force of numbers. One out of three American families could not be wrong, particularly when the White House itself, in an effort to head off the 1957-1958 recession, urged that "you auto buy now," knowing full well that this meant one-third down.

IV

The great depression of the Thirties failed to justify the fears of those banks whose doors still remained open about the new type of credit. Surprisingly, the record of the sales finance companies, and for that matter the consumer finance companies, was amazingly good, with only a negligible number of failures. There is indeed a question of whether banks lost more on finance companies or finance companies on banks which failed. These companies at any rate demonstrated extraordinary fluidity and flexibility in adjusting their operations to the severe downswing in the business cycle. Their fixed overhead was low and they were

209

able to reduce expenses accordingly. Having been able to go into the depression with the cream of credit risks as their accounts, neither type of credit agency found its share of unemployed customers fatal. The widely diversified borrowers made payments on their relatively small obligations to the best of their ability and again were the first to be re-employed when the nation began to climb from the depression. Naturally the finance company outstandings decreased, but the cost of their money, a most important expense factor, was also reduced as the government's easy money policy brought the banks' prime rate as low as 2%. The automobile finance companies witnessed the more drastic reduction in outstandings, reaching a point of only 43.1 per cent of their 1929 peak.[9] The consumer finance companies declined in number from 3,137 in December 1931 to 2,480 in March 1935, a reduction of 21 per cent. Household's outstandings dipped from $45 million in 1931 to $35 million in 1933. Beneficial experienced considerably less reduction in outstandings during this period but reported bad debt losses of $2,220,000 in 1933 compared with $605,000 in 1930. The finance industry nevertheless survived the depression with flying colors and this, more than anything else, guaranteed its access to the nation's money markets as a preferred customer. In the middle of the depression, Beneficial sold $7,000,000 of convertible debenture securities and it listed its common stock on the New York Stock Exchange in 1933, following the lead of Household, whose Participating Preference stock was listed in 1928.

With this lesson plain to see, the banks plunged into personal loans after the depression and ended up with the plum of the pie. The National City Bank in New York in 1928 was the first major bank to organize a personal loan department. The movement halted with the depression but today it would be difficult to find a bank that was not interested in making personal loans or in financing automobiles. Meanwhile the finance companies themselves have become the most sizeable and permanent cus-

tomers the banks have ever known and thus the banks are bene-
fitting both as a wholesaler and retailer of consumer credit. The
banks are so completely involved in consumer credit that it is
difficult to recall how strenuously they avoided it in the Twenties
and Thirties. A review of some of their literature for that period
reveals they were not only concerned with its operational problems and risks but also there was a strong prejudice against the
idea of consumers using credit. As late as 1938, many of them
joined wholeheartedly in the opinions of Roger Babson, an
economist and writer who was particularly esteemed by bankers
for having predicted the stock market collapse among other
things. In his *The Folly of Instalment Buying*, Babson wrote:

The crime of instalment selling is that it is causing manufacturers,
advertisers, merchants, and consumers to go more madly after material things to the neglect of the things of the spirit. One becomes
addicted to instalment buying as he would become addicted to liquor
or gambling or any other vice. The entire practice is dangerous
and vicious . . . The instalment business is making our citizens dis-
honest and unreliable. Those traits of thrift, industry, and reliability
which created America are fast becoming obsolete. The public thinks
it is "good business" to run up as much debt as possible with one
doctor, dentist, or merchant and then calmly change to another.
Entire communities are honey-combed with dishonesty. People fail
to realize that a very thin veil separates carelessness from crime. I
believe that the sale of automobiles on "easy terms" is in part responsible for the present serious state of the nation's morals.[10]

The banks recovered from Babson's folly soon enough and
have actually taken the lead in finding new ways to develop
consumer credit. Unrestrained by banking department regulations relating to charges, advertising or technique, they have
devised the ultimate in convenient credit with plans entitled
"Check Credit," "Instant Money" and so on which allow the
customer to draw checks against his credit rather than against an
actual deposit, with charges considerably in excess of those for

the usual personal loan. The credit card providing charge account or instalment privileges at subscribing stores has also become a bank specialty in recent years. The Bank of America, for example, has blanketed California with over 1,300,000 Bankamericard holders in a short time. The tremendous potential of consumer credit, however, has been so great that all of the major agencies of instalment credit, consumer finance companies, sales finance companies, credit unions and banks, have been reaching record levels year after year since the end of World War II.

XIV

THE MAN FROM
MILLVILLE, NEW JERSEY

In the roster of key men in the history of the consumer finance business, Leon Henderson stands just one notch below Arthur H. Ham. In addition, Henderson holds a secure place in history as a national figure on his own, which makes his association with the loan business all the more significant.

One of the most colorful men of the Roosevelt administration, this dynamic, vigorous personality brought the legislative program of the Department of Remedial Loans back to life in 1925 after the post-war hiatus during which it had no full-time leadership. In the nine years of his association with the Foundation, thirteen important states passed new or improved small loan laws and a fresh crop of loan sharks was ruthlessly mowed down by the fighting Director. In addition, the Department launched its study of the economic theory and implications of consumer credit. It was Henderson's lot not only to revive the passage of the Uniform Small Loan Law in key states but also to stem the tide of destructive rate reduction bills that suddenly appeared throughout the country, reflecting the unrest of the depression as well as the still imperfect understanding of the industry's claim for a special rate of interest. In 1931, for example, 215 bills affecting small loans were introduced in state legislatures, practically all for the purpose of rate reduction, and in 1933, 282 bills were introduced. It is realistic to state that without Henderson's tremendous drive and crusading spirit, the new industry might never have reached that second plateau of growth from which vantage point it would finally cut the umbilical cord to the Foundation after World War II. It would also appear that his departure from the Foundation directly to become the number two man in both the National Recovery Administration and the War Production Board gave the small loan business the distinction of having been endorsed by a person to whom the nation turned for leadership in times of grave national crises. The fact that in his public career he was known above all as the consumer's friend may not have endeared him to the general business community but it was obviously a bonus for the sensitive consumer finance business to have been championed by the consumer's champion, Leon Henderson. With this in mind, a full-scale review of Henderson's public career will be of interest before examining his 1925-1934 years with the Russell Sage Foundation.

II

Leon Henderson was born in 1895 in Millville, New Jersey, a town of about 16,000 population in Cumberland County. Like Arthur Ham, he was a small town boy who carried along the small town virtues while making good in the big city world. Their personalities were sharply in contrast. Ham, product of a genteel and comfortable Maine background, took Bowdoin College in his stride and easily adjusted to the patrician world of the trustees of the Russell Sage Foundation. Ham's point of view was anchored to the optimistic, secure era of T. R. Roosevelt and Woodrow Wilson. While choosing to become a social worker, in the sense that he limited his career to the Foundation and the non-profit Provident Loan Society, the urbane Ham also found time to relax in New York's Union League Club, to play excellent golf, to serve on the Board of Overseers of Bowdoin and to visit in the elegant surroundings of Pinehurst, North Carolina. Henderson was the son of a glass factory worker in Millville who had to scrape and fight to gain his education. His college career was interrupted by World War I and his middle years saw him engaged as a principal in the turbulent arena of the New Deal and World War II. Like Ham, his tough-mindedness was rooted in the moral rectitude of the best American small town tradition. Both men were products of devoutly religious families. Their fathers were Sunday School teachers, Deacon Ham serving as a Sunday School superintendent and Chester Henderson sometimes filling in for the regular minister as a "lay preacher."

The preacher's son, however, was the proverbial terror and his success might well be used as an inspiration for all bad boys. As a schoolboy, he developed a precocious standing in the local pool halls, where he argued about baseball averages and committed his meager resources to an occasional wager. No poolroom athlete, he soon became a high school hero playing on the football, basketball and baseball teams. He was best at baseball, where he early displayed the capacity for righteous anger and energy that marked his work both for the Foundation and in Washington. Grateful that his father did not make him work in the sand pits or glass factory at high school age, Henderson, who read Horatio Alger stories, displayed an early genius for self-help. He carried newspapers, became a reporter for the local paper, and played semi-pro baseball while helping out on the family farm. In high school he founded and edited the school paper but showed few signs of his future prodigious mastery of facts and theories. Instead, he gained distinction as the ruffian who arranged with a gateman to flood water over a dam on which the high school senior girls were posing for their class picture.

After a year at the University of Pennsylvania, Henderson dropped out and spent an indecisive year at Millville, but fortunately he received an athletic scholarship from Swarthmore where he started his education again in earnest. He switched his ambitions from journalism to economics which had immediately intrigued him. Meanwhile he played varsity baseball and basketball and set what was probably an all-time record at Swarthmore for self-help. At one point, he held fourteen jobs at the same time, including ditch-digging, book-selling, furnace-tending, baby-sitting and playing semi-pro football under an assumed name. Some of the baby-sitting was for a young professor named Louis N. Robinson who quickly spotted Henderson's potential. Robinson guided him into the classical Marshallian economics of the day, named after Alfred Marshall, the Cambridge professor whose respectable economics failed to recognize the excesses and disparities of the real world, which was so scrubbed up in his textbooks as to be almost unrecognizable. It was the school of economics which generally treated prices as the neatly predictable result of supply and demand, rather than an instrument which could be rigged or used for cutthroat competition. As far as depressions were concerned, they were periodic ills in the system which responded to a "wringing-out" process when the bottom of the business cycle was reached and wages had become so low that efficient producers could not resist the temptation to hire cheap labor once again. In his lifetime, Henderson was to observe most of the time-honored tenets of this "dismal science" rendered obsolete and, equally unexpected, men such as himself become palace advisers to Presidents.

Robinson, who was an inspiring and warm friend to Henderson, saw his prize student, who had also become his personal secretary, leave college and volunteer for the army three weeks after America declared war on Germany in 1917. Henderson entered the service as a private but characteristically ended up with the War Industries Board. At the end of the War, he was a twenty-three year old captain with an office in Washington and a job that made him accountable for a half-billion dollars worth of government property. His boss was Bernard Baruch, who was later to be his staunch defender when Henderson returned to Washington years later. When Henderson resumed his education at Swarthmore, things must have seemed pretty dull for the ex-captain but the academic world had its attractions and he decided to become an economics teacher. Although Robinson had resigned his professorship in 1918, Henderson's former teacher retained his connections with Swarthmore, became a Lecturer in Criminology and held an imposing number of memberships on outside commissions, parole boards and state authorities. In his capacity as a free-lancing expert, Robinson had begun a pioneering study, sponsored by some members of the American Industrial Lenders Association, of the new regulated small loan business. In November 1922, the Trustees of the Russell Sage Foundation engaged Robinson to transfer this project to the Foundation and turn it into a comprehensive survey. The plan was to include a history and description of the loan business in the United States, its legal setting, facts about borrowers and an account of the history of British money-lending. Robinson's first publication, co-authored with Maude E. Stearns, was *Ten Thousand Small Loans*, a statistical survey covering borrowers in 109 cities in 17 states. When the book was finally published under the imprimatur of the Russell Sage Foundation in 1930, the foreword was written by none other than Leon Henderson, who became Director of the Department of Remedial Loans in 1925, having been highly recommended by his former mentor at Swarthmore. Robinson's project had heretofore produced only a pamphlet on pawnbroking in 1924. One imagines that the former student may have delighted in igniting his former professor to get his book prepared for publication, although the survey had been completed some years earlier. Robinson later produced *Regulation of the Small Loan Business* in 1935 with Rolf Nugent, Henderson's successor. The former Swarthmore professor also became a member of the Board of Directors of Household Finance Corporation.

Before going to the Foundation, Henderson left his college teaching jobs to work for Gifford Pinchot, T. R. Roosevelt's fighting Chief of Forestry who had involved his President in the great advances in conservation and reclamation in the early 1900's. Pinchot was now the new reform governor of Pennsylvania and just the kind of man Henderson wanted to serve. He went to Harrisburg where he became Director of Accounts and also Deputy Secretary of the Commonwealth. In fact, he was a kind of major domo for Pinchot and held five different jobs at one time. Although his pay was only $5,000 a year, when he left the administration five different people had to pick up his jobs for salaries totalling $28,000. At Harrisburg, Henderson learned the art of public administration and discovered he enjoyed the experience of applying rather than discussing his theories so much that he decided not to return to teaching. In 1925, he accepted the offer of the Russell Sage Foundation, where he spent nine productive years until his destiny led him to Washington.

III

General Hugh Johnson, also a War Industries man, had been appointed administrator of the National Industrial Recovery Administration, the famous Blue Eagle agency, by President Roosevelt in June 1933. Square-jawed, profane, a table-pounder and shouter, he had performed miracles of organization and persuasion in getting the emergency experiment in industrial planning underway. The General had launched his agency with a tremendous campaign to get employers to pledge to uphold minimum wages and a forty-hour week—the idea being that this would increase purchasing power—until more formal industry codes could be arranged. The depression-struck country eagerly grasped at the symbol of the Blue Eagle with its Legend "We Do Our Part." Nearly everyone responded to the NRA's version of recovery amidst the high hopes stirred by the White House's surge of action during the First Hundred Days of the Roosevelt administration. Over two million employers quickly signed up in the preliminary campaign and the housewives of the nation signed a pledge of their own to patronize only NRA firms. The whole movement was endowed with a crusading, torchlight zeal unlike any other government peacetime program before or since. The climax came with the Blue Eagle parade in New York City in September. In the greatest march in the city's history, a quarter of a million men and women poured down Fifth Avenue cheered by close to two million spectators. The marchers included CCC boys in their olive drab, life insurance men, telephone linemen, stockbrokers and chorus girls. The bands played "Happy Days Are Here Again" and the ticker tape spilled from the windows. The happy days, however, were numbered for the valiant but unconstitutional agency which was to expire under the "sick chicken" case verdict of the Supreme Court less than two years later on May 27, 1935.

Hugh Johnson, in establishing the original NRA structure, had created three separate advisory boards representing labor, industry and the consumers in order to assure representation of these national interests in the code-making process. The Consumers' Advisory Board had no source of power, unlike the others, but it had a most unusual leader, Mary Harriman Rumsey. She was the daughter of E. H. Harriman, the railroad builder, and the older sister of W. Averell Harriman, whose great career in government included a year as administrative director of the NRA while Leon Henderson was serving as economist. Mary Rumsey led her board with great zest and spirit, enlisting such members as Dexter M. Keezer, now vice-president of McGraw Hill, Paul H. Douglas, still advancing the consumers' cause as Senator from Illinois and Leon Henderson, representing the Russell Sage Foundation. The Consumers' Advisory Board was primarily interested, of course, in keeping prices down. If employers and manufacturers were going to pass on the cost of increased wages and reduced hours to the consumer in the form of price increases, then all would be lost in a round of inflation. The problem was further compounded by the initial policy of the NRA to allow a certain amount of price-fixing, in an effort to discourage deflationary price-cutting, which was then a far greater problem than inflation. Prices fixed by business itself, however, inevitably led to monopoly and decreased production, as far as the consumer-oriented forces were concerned. In this dilemma, the harassed General Johnson's irritation over the constant criticism of the Consumers' Advisory Board is understandable. In one of his more stormy moods in December 1933, Johnson was confronted with a visitation from Mary Rumsey and her Board. They had just come from a consumers' conference, the very idea of which moved the General, who had personally selected the thunderbird as his inspiration for the NRA symbol, to shout at them and pound his desk fiercely. To the utter astonishment of everyone in the room, someone shouted back even louder than the General and pounded equally hard, shaking the General visibly. As often happens, however, one shouter respects another, and Johnson was entranced by the powerful Henderson and his articulate pugnacity. "If you're so god-damned smart," he bawled, "why don't you come down here and be my assistant on consumer problems?" Henderson accepted the challenge and the Russell Sage Foundation lost the services of Arthur Ham's one and only natural successor. "I got my job by hollering," Henderson later said, "and no day passes but what I holler about something."

IV

It took only a few weeks before Johnson promoted Henderson to head the Research and Planning Division of the NRA and become its chief economist. Meanwhile the Consumers' Advisory Board kept up pressure on Johnson to revise his policy on prices, charging the NRA was fostering monopoly. Henderson had a strong fear of monopoly and was later to become executive secretary and coordinator of the Temporary National Economic Committee (TNEC), the so-called "monopoly committee" of the United States Senate. As a supporter of his own agency, he had to go along for the time being with the General's position that cut-throat pricing produced a deflationary spiral of unemployment and reduced purchasing power. The corollary of this position was that price-fixing and the deliberate suspension of the antitrust laws in the NRA legislation in the first place were therefore justified. At the same time, the General recognized that his flanks were exposed by price increases and the charges of monopoly. In a speech to the National Retail Dry Goods Association shortly after Henderson joined NRA, the General said: "If I had only nine words with which to address you, I would rise here and say 'Keep prices down—for God's sake, keep prices down.' "

Yet prices steadily rose and Senator Nye gained headlines with charges that NRA was a breeder of monopoly. A National Recovery Review Board was thereupon established to investigate monopolistic tendencies in the codes. Old Clarence Darrow, whose memories stretched over fifty years of cases including the duel with William Jennings Bryan over evolution in Dayton, Tennessee, was the chairman. In four months, his committee considered over three thousand complaints and thirty-four industry codes. The Darrow report concluded that NRA was indeed an instrument of monopoly, which caused Johnson,

Donald Richberg, who was Johnson's number two man, and Darrow to engage in a battle of words that shook Washington. Johnson finally ordered a change in policy on price-fixing which so angered the business community, which felt it must have price controls as a concession for its increased labor costs, that he hastened to exempt existing codes from the new rules. One of Henderson's major tasks was to discourage price-fixing from this point on, or to allow it at levels so low that consumers need not be concerned. The era of large-scale price regulation was drawing to an end. Meanwhile, the NRA was involved in violent arguments over labor policy resulting from conflicting interpretations of the famous Section 7a of the NRA legislation which provided for collective bargaining for unions. Roosevelt, seeing that the NRA was out of its depth in labor matters, finally established the National Labor Relations Board in June 1934, but NRA had long since lost its initial glamor with most segments of the public.

General Johnson was not only becoming excessively irresponsible and irascible in his difficult job but he was also engaged in a power struggle with his sensitive, ambitious subordinate Donald Richberg. Roosevelt, indulging in his typical art of playing one administrator against another, kept an uneasy truce in the NRA. Meanwhile, Henderson emerged as the key public servant on the non-political level and concentrated on specific problems of control and recovery while his bosses made the headlines. Henderson correctly recognized that NRA had reached too far into areas of price and production and felt its energies should be focused on positive stimulants to greater productivity. Yet he could not escape from the problem of prices. When the Durable Goods Industries Committee recommended that prices should be controlled by that industry itself, Henderson stated:

This is contrary to the public interest. Price determination is not a proper function of industrial self-government. In this field, self-government would involve monopoly power, with an interest to securing maximum profits. Prices should be determined either by free competition or else by an independent agency which is concerned with the welfare of consumers and employees as well as equity holders.

Henderson gladly took the lead within the NRA in trying to create flexible prices, hoping that by gradual revisions of the codes in that direction increased buying would bring about increased production and employment. He was one of the few men in Washington at that time who recognized that immediate purchasing power itself would have to come from vastly increased public spending such as the Public Works Administration, which had been created at the same time as the NRA in 1933 and the Works Progress Administration (WPA), rushed into action under Harry Hopkins in April 1935.

One of the ironies of the history of the great depression is that so many business men wanted price protection instead of the traditional free prices. They welcomed government authority for their price-fixing and bitterly resisted the NRA's change in policy. *Time* magazine reported that of 2,000 businessmen attending an NRA conference as late as 1935, over 90% insisted on price protection. Meanwhile, NRA officials such as Averell Harriman and Henderson realized that the agency had become something of a bureaucratic monster in establishing codes and enforcing compliance for service industries and small businesses such as cleaners and dyers and beauty shops. In line with Henderson's common-sense plea for concentration on the major possibilities that would stimulate recovery, plans were established to withdraw from the service fields but labor resistance forced the suspension of this idea. Henderson also courageously stated that the basic code device itself may have been a mistake in relation to labor and that labor ought to solve its problems permanently through legislation, which of course it did through the eventual labor legislation of the Roosevelt era. This labor

223

legislation was to survive the feared Supreme Court tests of constitutionality. The same Supreme Court, however, rejected the NRA in the Schechter poultry case in 1935, causing NRA to vanish from the Washington scene. The imperturbable Roosevelt watched his experimental agency die and jauntily turned towards such measures as increased public works, new controls over money and banking and reciprocal trade agreements to revive world trade in the fight to end the depression.

Henderson had made a strong impression on Roosevelt and other influential people with his position that the NRA should not be allowed to become a restrictive rather than an expansive force in the economy because of price-fixing. At the same time, he did not want a return to a completely unregulated market for he recognized that the forces of government, labor and consumers should all be more closely coordinated with the marketplace in order to make capitalism work. In retrospect, his fear of controlled prices seems excessive in the light of the success of America's present system of administered prices, that is, prices that are determined by many other forces than supply and demand. Our present pricing system undoubtedly is much closer to the original concept of the NRA than anyone could possibly have anticipated in the 1930's.

Most observers would agree that although the NRA was an impossible agency, doomed to a short life, it still helped to revitalize the economy and contributed many lasting social gains. Its establishment of principles relating to maximum hours, child labor, minimum wages, collective bargaining, unfair trade practices and concern for the consumer soon became permanent features of the American system. It served as a great educational force in making business, labor and government do some hard thinking about the necessity of making our economy work so that a depression of such appalling magnitude might never be repeated. Furthermore, it produced an atmosphere of cooperation and leadership that would be sorely needed in the dark days of

World War II that were soon to arrive. The War Production Board was something of an NRA reunion, with men like Averell Harriman, Donald Nelson, Sidney Hillman, Edward Stettinius, Jr., Isador Lubin and Leon Henderson ready and trained to take over the great tasks of national mobilization of industrial resources.

IV

Henderson's subsequent career in the Roosevelt administration affords an opportunity to observe a basic change in the administration's prescription for curing the sick economy it inherited. The new approach was a particularly satisfactory one for Henderson, which helps explain his retention and influence in New Deal circles after the death of NRA. Basically the early New Deal, as expressed in the NRA, had made an emergency effort to centralize economic power. It accepted the necessity and rationale of a peacetime nationally planned economy. The key figures in this first approach, men like Raymond Moley, Rexford Tugwell, Adolf Berle, Donald Richberg and Hugh Johnson, saw their influence steadily decline after 1935, although some of these men, particularly Moley, changed their views as time went on. In their place, new figures like Ben Cohen, Thomas Corcoran, Harry Hopkins and Leon Henderson came into prominence as advisers and theorists for the President. These men favored a competitive rather than a planned society so long as it was based on ground rules that would create increasing prosperity, dignity and security for the broadest group of people. An important qualification, of course, was that the remedies must be consistent with political freedom, which they felt was always threatened by excessive central control, whether by business or by government. This explains the tremendous opposition which Justice Brandeis, for example, felt towards the NRA, in whose extinction he rejoiced. In general these men favored indirect methods, such as "pump-priming" through credit and other fiscal devices, to control the direction and pace of the economy. Although their opponents did not then and may not now distinguish between government intervention of the NRA type and the more subtle efforts of the "Second New Deal" to restore competition within a centrally defined social framework, the change was a decisive one for America. It is the economic style that has survived to this day as an essentially bi-partisan feature of our government. As early as 1934, Walter Lippmann in a remarkable analysis examined this change in direction. He called the new choice a "Compensated Economy" as against a "Directed Economy." The new version retained private initiative and decision so far as possible but committed the state to act when necessary to "redress the balance of private actions by compensating public actions." This would be accomplished by fiscal, taxation and monetary policies, by social insurance, by regulation of business and by the establishment of minimum economic levels below which no member of the community should be allowed to fall. Important institutional changes inevitably have arrived in the past thirty years which have refined this concept. There is, for example, J. K. Galbraith's identification of the modern pressure groups of big business, big labor and big consumers which also compensate or "countervail" against excesses. At any rate, if we are to pay our respects to the economists of the Thirties who made pioneering contributions towards our present reasonably happy solution, Leon Henderson is surely to be included in the august list. Roosevelt himself, incidentally, was primarily an experimenter who resisted abstract theories, economic or otherwise, that would require him to go all out in one direction or another. "This country is big enough to experiment with several diverse systems and follow several different lines," he once remarked to Adolf Berle in expressing his preference for a mixed system. "Why must we put our economic policy in a single systemic jacket?"

As Roosevelt turned away from detailed industrial planning, he found the ideas of John Maynard Keynes, the English economist, increasingly attractive. Keynes had been a steadfast critic of the NRA, disliking its potentially dangerous centralization and feeling absolutely confident in his own proposals for increasing purchasing power through public spending even if this meant massive budget deficits for the time being. The argument for public spending did not rest with Keynes alone for by 1935 the administration had already embraced it as a humane and political necessity regardless of theoretical considerations or budget deficits. America also had produced a few heretical economists of its own in that direction. William Trufant Foster, who was one of the earliest defenders of small loan legislation and consumer credit in general, had propounded deficit spending as a cure for cyclical downswings in the Twenties. Paul Douglas and other University of Chicago professors backed such a program. Roosevelt had already brought into his administration as a member of the Federal Reserve Board in 1934 Marriner S. Eccles, a distinguished Mormon banker. Eccles was an inspired advocate of public spending as a way out of the depression and of course was a rare and valuable representative of the business community in the government. Leon Henderson was an early Keynesian in this respect and did his part in educating the inner group of the administration in the theory of this new program for recovery. After the NRA, Henderson had been personally selected as economist for the Democratic National Committee by Roosevelt in preparation for the 1936 election campaign against Alf Landon. In a treatise entitled *Boom or Bust,* he emphasized the absolute necessity for increasing and sustaining purchasing power. In 1937-1938, the recession caused by Roosevelt's decision to put the brakes on the economy too soon proved Henderson to be quite right.

Henderson's tour in government progressed through consulting economist for the WPA and TNEC investigator to an appointment as a member of the Securities and Exchange Commission in 1939, succeeding William O. Douglas when the latter was appointed to the Supreme Court. Since Henderson's public relations with Congress were never in good repair, a product of his consummate independence and brashness, the appointment aroused a great deal of criticism via the business community. Wall Street was still smarting from his relentless exposure of the patterns of monopoly and price-fixing during the TNEC days. He served the SEC with distinction but by May 1940 had made up his mind to depart from government service and spend more time with his family. On the very day he was prepared to leave, President Roosevelt called and asked him to become a member of the National Defense Advisory Commission, a small group including among others William S. Knudsen, Sidney Hillman, Edward Stettinius, Jr., and Chester C. Davis. This governmental agency, which another erstwhile social worker, Harry Hopkins, had helped Roosevelt formulate, was the parent of all the war production, food production, priorities and price-control organizations that were to come. Its creation marked the beginning of the mobilization of manpower for the home front in those dark and unprepared days when German panzer divisions were already invading France. Henderson at once became the chief battler on this commission for the principle of unlimited production and was impatient with the caution of industrialists and Army and Navy officers who disagreed with his point of view. The situation reached the point where he resigned in a huff and went to Puerto Rico for a vacation. His strategy resulted in Roosevelt calling him back at once to receive increased authority as head of a newly created agency called OPACS, the Office of Price Administration and Civilian Supply, in April 1941.

The attack on Pearl Harbor galvanized the war effort and by January 1942, Roosevelt had transferred William Knudsen into the Army and installed Donald Nelson, the former Sears Roebuck executive, as head of the nine-member War Production Board which succeeded the NDAC. Nelson, as head of the WPB, was in charge of the production of war goods and the allocation of raw materials to producers. Henderson, as head of the WPB's Division of Civilian Supply, was to see to it that whatever raw materials were left were distributed in the best manner to the civilian economy. As head of the OPA, which succeeded OPACS in February 1942, he was directed to set prices for most goods and services for both industry and individuals and to ration scarce goods equitably to everyone, a job guaranteed to alienate every pressure group in the country. In the meantime, Congress had consistently refused to give the President's agency more rigid control of prices, particularly farm prices, many legislators keeping a weather eye on the 1942 elections which were in the offing. Henderson had repeatedly demanded such controls as well as larger appropriations for the enforcement of OPA. By the summer of 1942 he was bearing the brunt of considerable complaints directed towards the unprecedented agency and its 5,600 unpaid local volunteers who manned the price and rationing boards. In the fall of 1942 food prices were rising so rapidly that Roosevelt finally prepared to issue an Executive Order to stabilize prices and wages that would by-pass Congress. Hopkins and Henderson urged Roosevelt to hold up this action and give Congress an ultimatum to produce the legislation by October 1 or face the consequences. Congress passed the bill on the deadline date. The next day Roosevelt appointed Supreme Court Justice James F. Byrnes to assume the post of Director of Economic Stabilization which made him in effect Assistant President in charge of the home front. Under the new act, Roosevelt immediately froze agricultural prices, wages, salaries and rents throughout the country. Inequities inevitably arose and Henderson, as the target for complaints, resigned in December 1942, terminating a notable and durable career in the alphabetical agencies of his country. The OPA continued along the lines he had established and with its new authority managed to prevent runaway inflation on the high-living civilian front.

Administrators come and go with great frequency in Washington but only a few economists have left such a firm imprint as that of Leon Henderson. In 1942 a cover story article on Henderson in *Life* magazine stated: "It is arguable that Henderson has had as much real influence on the economic policies of the New Deal as any man except the President himself." Henderson, a semi-retired consultant, still recalls the government days with pride but also feels his work for the Russell Sage Foundation was in its own way of major importance as well as a source of deep satisfaction.

XVII

"THE TOUGHEST SOCIAL WORKER
I EVER MET"

Leon Henderson joined the Russell Sage Foundation in 1925 at age thirty, slightly older than Arthur Ham was when Ham preceded him in 1909. He was first employed as Associate Director but within nine months he had shown such capacity for work and eagerness for new conquests that he was made full director and authorized to bring in as his assistant Rolf Nugent. Rolf Nugent was an Amherst graduate who had been associated with Henderson in the Pennsylvania State offices. Nugent's primary assignment was to foster the credit union movement, particularly in New York State. Not only the fortunes of the credit union movement in New York but also those of the regulated loan business throughout the country had suffered considerably in the period following World War I when Ham had served only in an advisory capacity. The Foundation had hoped that the main responsibility for extending the business and protecting the public from loan sharks would be assumed by agencies such as the licensed lenders' own trade associations but it was apparent to the Foundation at least that they did not have sufficient power and authority to carry out this assignment. Thus the Foundation in another timely decision for the regulated loan industry decided to give it one more injection of strength in order to make sure the expectations of the earlier years would be realized.

Only six states had passed satisfactory loan laws since 1917 and although the total was now 18 and most of the important industrial states were covered, it was apparent that the rate of growth was unsatisfactory for a business which if good for one state should be good for all of the states in the country. In addition, another urgent responsibility awaited Henderson when he joined the Foundation. The loan sharks had come back to life under the guise of "purchasers" of wages or salaries.

II

This was a reincarnation of the loan sharkery typified by Mr. Tolman's former dealings with clerks and civil service employees. The lender did not necessarily look for states that had assignment of wages laws as the old salary-buyer did. He was perfectly content to have the borrower sign a statement that he had sold a certain amount of his wages to the salary-buyer and give him a power of attorney to collect that amount from the employer when the wages were due. Since the borrower did not want his employer to know about the transaction, he promised to collect the salary himself and turn over the amount he had "sold" to the lender. The nature of the transaction was such that most of the purchases were renewed without being paid off or were traded around to other salary-buyers. The discount, while not much in terms of dollars, amounted to an effective interest rate of 240% to 600% all over again and the procedure degenerated into borrowers paying a chronic tribute to the lender for the original loan as in the old days. The business started in the non-regulated states, as would be expected, but by 1923, the leading practitioners could not resist invading most of the 18 Uniform Law states. By 1925 the Foundation estimated that hundreds of thousands of borrowers had been trapped by these new loan sharks who were operating in two-thirds of the states of the country.[1] The Uniform Law had been amended in 1923 to include under Section 16 the "purchase of wages" as loans within the scope of the act. Progress in adding this amendment naturally took time. Maryland adopted it in 1924 and other states followed suit but the impudent salary-buyers began a series of attacks on the constitutionality of the provision in one state after another. The American Industrial Lenders Association and the firm of Hubachek and Hubachek immediately defended the section and it was sustained in the highest courts of Maryland, Virginia, Louisiana and Ohio and finally in the United States Supreme Court in 1930. Meanwhile, the profits were apparently so enormous that the salary-buyers moved in and out of states where Section 16 had not yet been added to the law or where the practice had never been tested in the courts in the first place, greatly embarrassing the whole concept of regulation in these states.

An incidental feature of this business revival was that the salary-buyer specialized whenever possible in dealing with railroad employees. Why these well-paid, hard-handed employees in the business that had made Russell Sage's fortune should have been so gullible as to fatten the purses of the salary-buyer, even in states where legitimate loans were available, is a mystery but so was the predilection of newspaper men for loan sharks at the turn of the century. At any rate, the practice is believed to have started with two railroad payroll clerks in Atlanta, Georgia about 1915 and from then on railroad employees were the prize prospects. The Department of Remedial Loans estimated in 1926 that one-third of all the railroad employees in the country were borrowing from at least two salary-buyers each.[2] There were far more railroad employees in the America of that day than there are now so it was a serious problem, compounded by the fact that the railroad men were subject to an employers' rule that withheld two weeks of their pay at any one time. Thus the salary-buyers could maintain that the employees did indeed have something to sell, wages already earned but unpaid. To add to the drama of the situation, the men who dominated the business were known mysteriously as the "Big Four." They were about to meet their match in the person of Leon Henderson.

Henderson's campaign against the salary-buyers was a classic demonstration of coordination and publicity. Its culmination was in Detroit where on June 30, 1927 the newspapers reported that the "Big Four Ring Agrees to Quit." [3] Behind this development, meticulous preparations had been made. All the elements of the ancient war on loan sharks were used—publicity in the newspapers, exposure of individuals, legal aid societies, social work organizations, lawsuits, enlistment of employer cooperation, additional legislation and one new ally, the Better Business Bureaus. In 1927 when the featured speaker, the President of the New York Stock Exchange, was delayed in his appearance at the annual convention of the National Better Business Bureau, Henderson extended his own remarks into a forty-minute speech on the loan shark peril and the Bureau's chance and responsibility to do something about it.[4] His remarks caught fire, particularly with Kenneth Barnard, manager, and S. B. Kempton, the attorney for the Detroit Better Business Bureau. A Sunday supplement full-page treatment in the *Detroit Free Press* shortly announced that "Detroit Grapples with the Loan Shark Peril—Shop Girls, Railroad Employees Being Preyed Upon Is Claim." Adding the shop girls was a neat touch by the Detroit Bureau since their perils were certainly more alarming than those of the railroad men. The article included the following message from Henderson:

In Atlanta, Ga., are the headquarters of the Big Four of the salary loan sharks, an unscrupulous clique, that has strung its chain of loan offices throughout the country, avoiding only stakes in New England and on the Pacific coast. These sharks purport to buy earned wages of workingmen, principally railroad employees, at a discount rate of 10 per cent per week, never more than two weeks distant, and under this flimsy pretense have enmeshed 100,000 railroad men in 200 cities. By giving their loans all the semblance of sales, these usurers have temporarily escaped the penalties accompanying violations of small loan laws, and have left a trail of bribery, corruption, intimidation and distress throughout the land. Some railroads, unfamiliar with the necessities of small loans, have given the salary buyers a club for enforcement of their usurious contracts by discharging employes who were garnisheed for selling wages.[5]

On June 23, 1927, the Detroit police made a series of lightning raids on the offices of five loan sharks and seven men were arraigned for trial on June 30 amidst reports that "their defense fund is said to be in millions." [6] On June 25, the *Detroit News* ran the biggest spread ever devoted to the fascinating subject of illegal lending. "LOAN SHARK WAR GETS NATIONAL AID" trumpeted from a front page banner headline of this newspaper. Below it was a picture of young Mr. Henderson entitled "RUSSELL SAGE DIRECTOR HERE" and bearing the news that he had arrived to offer the Foundation's help in driving the lenders out of business.[7] A few days later, Barnard met with the Big Four in the neutral city of Minneapolis at which summit meeting the Big Four apparently threw in the towel, enabling Kempton to announce: "We would like to see behind bars the men responsible for this national fraud, with its trail of corruption and misery, but if they have agreed to cease their operations for good in 25 or 30 states, we are satisfied." [8]

Henderson at least knew that these promises were worthless and continued his relentless attack throughout the country, including the home base in Atlanta. He obtained the support of railroad employers in refusing to honor the claims of salary-buyers and, above all, to stop firing the employees whose wages were attached, as this threat was the salary-buyers' basic security.

235

In cleaning house, the railroads found several of their own pay-masters were in league with the lenders and their departure hastened the end of the traffic. In some states where no decision by a court relating to buying salaries had been made, Henderson arranged for prosecutions to force a court decision that lending was involved. In others, he promoted amendments to the existing laws to include Section 16. Since the attack was basically a legal one, the Foundation's tremendous knowledge of laws and cases pertaining to loans was invaluable. By the end of 1927, the salary-buying menace was in full decline, having been beaten successfully in the courts of almost every state in which the Uniform Small Loan Law or its equivalent was in effect. What happened to the Big Four? The Russell Sage Foundation history soberly notes that the "Big Four had gone into the licensed loan business and were withdrawing from salary-purchasing." [9] Even then they apparently did not appreciate their safe haven. In Evans Clark's *Financing the Consumer*, the author, with an assist from Leon Henderson, named names and the number of offices of loan sharks extant in 1930.[10] At the head of the list were three of the Big Four, still operating 105 offices. As of today, their successors are probably all "legal" if for no other reason than the fact that practically every state in the union now has a reasonably good small loan law. Arkansas has the dubious distinction of being the only one of the fifty states which has neither a Uniform Small Loan Law nor a similar law under which the typical regulated commercial lender would provide a consumer finance service.

III

The campaign against the salary-buyers was not only a public service but it naturally helped set the stage for extending the Uniform Law into new states. A review of the experience in three of these states, Missouri, Louisiana and New York, will serve to recall the typical problems and accomplishments of the Henderson era.

As Rolf Nugent noted in a review of the loan shark situation in 1941, every time a statute was passed initiating the Uniform Law in a new state, the illegal lenders would generally move on to an adjacent unregulated state.[11] The lender who refused to embrace the new laws was a hard and tough opponent who foolishly felt that his present exorbitant profits were well worth the risk of an unregulated status. Perhaps he was also lulled into a false sense of security during the days before 1925 when Henderson had not yet taken over the temporarily restrained Department of Remedial Loans at the Foundation. At any rate, it is quite surprising to note that in 1930, Henderson and Evans Clark estimated that the volume of business of unlicensed lenders in that year would run at $750,000,000 involving 3,000,000 customers while the volume of the regulated companies would run at $500, 000,000 involving 2,000,000 customers.[12] Of course, the loan shark volume, made up of very small loans, would represent many times the yearly turnover of the regulated business, which means its loans outstanding were actually considerably less than those of the regulated lenders. Still, the fact that they dealt with approximately 1,000,000 more customers than did the regulated lenders, after 13 years of remedial legislation, is a sharp reminder that this was a major force to be reckoned with, a formidable adversary which would not give in easily, having managed to withstand all the pressures of the Foundation and the regulated lenders to date.

Missouri was always a stronghold for the loan shark interests, particularly since the nearby states of Iowa, Illinois, Indiana and Ohio were among the early regulated states, driving many of their loan sharks on to Missouri. Thus, when Leon Henderson and Rolf Nugent moved into Missouri in 1927 to try to obtain regulation, the odds were against them. As usual, there were not only the loan shark interests to contend with but also the well-meaning but unconvinced public which had little knowledge of the undercover loan sharks and a natural distrust for the high rate of interest recommended by the Foundation. It was not just a matter of lining up the usual respected forces of public opinion, such as social work organizations, the press and other friends of regulation. Care had to be taken to offset the well-financed and ruthless organization of loan sharks who very cleverly knew how to smear the reform forces with the big lie and similar tactics. In reminiscing about his fight to help obtain remedial legislation in Florida as late as 1939, John Kilgore, managing editor of the *Daily Democrat* in Tallahassee, Florida, offers an incredible experience of smear campaigns, intimidation and corruption directed against himself and the reform group. He states:

> It is necessary that a legislative committee, organized for such a purpose, understand fully that a fight against unlicensed lenders is difficult, exacting and fraught with peril. No one who shrinks from criticism or who is unwilling to swap verbal punches with ruthless and clever men should undertake the risk . . . They may expect to deliver hard work and to receive invective and abuse from cynical masters of venomous rhetoric—and very little else except the satisfaction of doing a job. It is no game for the faint-hearted.[13]

With this additional reminder from an impartial source about how much the consumer finance industry owes to the Foundation and its agents, we can observe the initial success and ensuing failure of Henderson and Nugent in Missouri in the Twenties. A Missouri chattel mortgage act of 1913 permitted charges in the range of 2% a month on certain loans, but few persons sought licenses under this act and the state was combed with loan sharks. Henderson first of all organized Citizens Committees in the major cities of Kansas City and St. Louis, drawing upon legal aid societies, better business bureaus, chambers of commerce, civic and charitable organizations and labor unions. This latter group became strong supporters of regulated lending, especially under the leadership of the liberal-minded Henderson, whose fight on behalf of their railroad brethren must have impressed them greatly. At that time, William L. Green, the American Federation of Labor President and A. F. Whitney, President of the Brotherhood of Railroad Trainmen, lent considerable prestige to the proposals for regulation throughout the country.

Public hearings were held in these cities and after several months of study, the Committees sponsored legislation in the 1927 session of the legislature for the Uniform Small Loan Law with the then recommended rate of $3\frac{1}{2}\%$ per month on loans up to $300. The bill was a model one except in one fatal respect. Section 16, the salary-buying section, was not included, as it was feared it would be declared invalid under the Missouri Constitution. Henderson had done his work well. Widescale newspaper support and well-organized, impressive delegations appearing at the legislative hearings on the bill succeeded in obtaining its enactment.

Meanwhile, the licensed lenders themselves assumed the responsibility of helping to drive out those salary-buyers who had stayed on in spite of the new regulation. The American Industrial Lenders Association had retained Charles N. Napier, a Chicago attorney with unusual experience in the field, to head its Vigilance Committee and to "police" violations of the small loan laws. Napier attended meetings held by Better Business Bureaus and similar agencies in Kansas City and St. Louis, at which employers were urged to refuse wage-assignments against their employees. Napier was able to refer to the progress made in beating the salary-buyer in Chicago and in Detroit and succeeded in enlisting considerable employer cooperation.[14]

The loan sharks rose to the occasion and decided the best tactic available was to turn the tables on the licensed lenders and get them and their vigilance committees out of Missouri. In 1929, both the House and Senate saw measures introduced to reduce

239

the rate to as low as 2% a month, no doubt sponsored by well-meaning legislators among others. The same Citizens Committees which had testified for the 1927 law opposed the rate reduction bills on the grounds that there had not been sufficient exposure under the Uniform Law in two years to demonstrate that it would be effective at the 2% rate, nor was there any record of effectiveness at such a rate in any other state. Both Leon Henderson and Rolf Nugent appeared before Senate Committees in support of continuing the 1927 act. The opposition had succeeded, however, in gaining support of a few labor unions, ostensibly because the cost to the consumer would be reduced. Capitalizing on this defection from the original ranks, the loan sharks launched a bitter attack on the Uniform Small Loan Law. The St. Louis *Post-Dispatch* printed a long interview with R. D. Ison of Atlanta, Georgia, admittedly a salary-buyer, who "reported" an alleged agreement between the Russell Sage Foundation and certain loan sharks. He admitted that no one from the Foundation was present at the alleged meeting but the impression was created that the Foundation had entered into an "unholy alliance" with commercial lenders.[15] R. D. Ison was one of the Big Four who supposedly had capitulated to the Better Business Bureaus in Minneapolis in 1927.

Next the Kansas City *Times* carried a statement by Clark G. Hardeman relating his intention to appear before a County Grand Jury to give "evidence" regarding a "slush fund" used by the small loan companies to gain their law in the 1927 session of the legislature. In spite of no substantiation to the charges and no action by a grand jury, some of the tar stuck and when the rate reduction bill was passed, the same paper stated: "Reports of a huge slush fund . . . are believed to have influenced the House in the passage of the Ballew bill." [16]

Incidentally, when the 1929 law was passed many of those who opposed the rate reduction were puzzled when the loan sharks did not oppose the inclusion of Section 16. They understood "why" a few months later when a salary buyer sued a borrower and was upheld by the Circuit Court on the grounds that Section 16 was unconstitutional because of a technical defect in the title of the 1929 act. The Supreme Court of Missouri eventually concurred, and in effect Section 16 had little more than five months of healthy existence. By 1935 salary-buyers were well-entrenched in Missouri. The regulated lenders had for the most part stayed on in Missouri at the new 2½% per month reduced rates but they did not seek the small loans at that rate, adding to the success of the salary-buyers. The Better Business Bureaus in Missouri kept up the fight, however, and in 1937 were hammering away at Clark G. Hardeman's salary-buying office in Kansas City and inviting borrowers to come to them for assistance.[17] Finally in 1939, an effective campaign spearheaded by the Governor, Attorney General and the former Governor who had signed the 1929 reduction bill resulted in a new law involving an increase in rate and an airtight Section 16. Within a month after the law was passed, all known salary-buyers in Missouri had closed their doors. To bring the Missouri story up to date, it must be noted that the state found itself without a law all over again on July 1, 1946. This resulted from the decision of the Missouri Supreme Court that the state's new Constitution had repealed the small loan law. The clause bringing about this decision required that statutes fixing maximum interest rates must apply to all lenders without regard to their type of business. The licensed companies left the state and almost immediately the old loan sharks, mostly with out-of-state headquarters, rushed in to fill the vacuum. In 1951, Missouri enacted a new consumer credit loan act, consistent with the Constitution, and the state was once again rid of its loan sharks.

IV

The doctrine that necessity makes strange bedfellows is illustrated in Leon Henderson's success in Louisiana with such an unlikely ally as Huey P. Long. When Henderson arrived there in 1928, Huey Long was the newly elected thirty-five year old Governor from the piny uplands of north central Louisiana who had just campaigned furiously throughout the state, winning an upset victory with the support of what he artfully called the "sapsucker, hillbilly and Cajun relations of mine." This was the first phase of that darkly sinister and sharply intelligent phenomenon in American politics, the reforming, anti-establishment young politician whose early period Robert Penn Warren was to describe with a certain compassion in the novel *All the King's Men.* In only a few more years, however, Huey Long was to become an authentic American menace and dictator, swaggering through the United States Senate, violating all the rules of decency and fair play as he rushed back and forth from Washington to Baton Rouge where he now exercised complete and corrupt control over the servile Governor and legislature. By March 1935, he had already become a third party threat and Henderson's ex-boss from the NRA days, General Hugh Johnson, was tapped by the administration to pay back the "Share the Wealth" prophet in kind. At a banquet at the Waldorf Astoria in Johnson's honor the eloquent general, who was in a class by himself for invective, attacked not only Long but that other "Pied Piper," Father Coughlin, whose admiration for Long was described by Johnson as an open alliance "between the great Louisiana demagogue and this political padre." Johnson continued:

You can laugh at Huey Long—but this country was never under a greater menace . . . Stripped to the facts—and whether consciously or not—these two men are raging up and down this land preaching not construction but destruction—not reform but revolution—not peace but a sword. I think we are dealing with a couple of Catilines, and that it is high time for somebody to say so.[18]

On September 8, 1935, President Roosevelt was lunching at Hyde Park with Father Coughlin and Joseph P. Kennedy, the latter having brought Coughlin to see the President in an attempt at reconciliation. The luncheon was interrupted by the news that Long had been shot in the rotunda of the statehouse at Baton Rouge by a young doctor whose strong antipathy for Long apparently made him willing to destroy himself at the same time. Long died on September 10, twelve days after his forty-second birthday.

When Henderson met Long in 1928, he was still the cunning clown, the rubbery-faced yokel about to turn the tables on the city slickers around him and little known beyond Louisiana. No doubt the Governor, who had not yet seized upon the immense press relations to be acquired by calling himself the "Kingfish," after the Amos 'n Andy radio character, took a liking to the bold young Foundation representative who was colorful and unpredictable in his own right. The preliminaries might well have touched on Mrs. Russell Sage's gift in 1912 of the 70,000 acre Marsh Island, off the coast of Louisiana, to the Bayou State as a bird refuge. Long knew all about the loan shark conditions in Louisiana. There had been an anti-loan shark crusade conducted by the newspapers in New Orleans in 1922 which had revealed rates being charged ranging from 600% to 1700% a year.[19] In addition, Long recognized that the loan shark interests were represented by the investments of his own legislators as well as by their high-powered lobbyists who were openly maintained in Baton Rouge to fight any Foundation bill. This lobby in fact was the best-financed and most bitter yet encountered by the Uniform Small Loan Law proponents in any state to date. Henderson and his group, however, had already obtained the support

243

of the newspapers of both political factions in the state. Long, whose rise to power was accompanied by attacks against the railroads and utilities and their prices to the public, decided to give the new law his public support. The degree to which he had been won over by Henderson is indicated by the fact that his special message to the legislature asking for favorable action on the bill was written by Henderson himself.[20]

The bill was passed as requested but the resourceful opposition had amended it to exempt several types of lending agencies before its passage. The next step was to test the constitutionality of the weakened bill in the courts, which obligingly declared it unconstitutional. Long could have walked away from the issue at this point, but under the pressure of Henderson and aware that his own power had been threatened, he called a special session of the legislature in December 1928 and rammed through another bill omitting the unconstitutional features. The bill was quickly passed and its constitutionality upheld by the Supreme Court of Louisiana in May 1929. Years later, when Henderson was in the NRA and Huey Long was a Senator, Long would occasionally meet Henderson and ask "What did you think of my message to the legislature on the Small Loan Bill?" and Henderson would give the straight-faced reply, "Senator, I am familiar with most everything written about this law and your message was one of the best." The Kingfish would then add a few choice words of his own, including a comment about "the toughest social worker I ever met!" [21]

V

Of all the states in the country, the failure of New York to pass a Uniform Loan Law was the most embarrassing. Here was the most populated state with the largest city, the scene and the home base of Arthur Ham's prodigious exploits against the loan sharks, still unrepresented by the commercial lenders who could

244

not operate at the 2% a month rates in effect. It was apparent that the remedial loan societies, including the Provident Loan Society, which was basically a pawnshop, could not supply the need for small loans. Their outstandings in 1930, excluding the Provident, were less than $3,000,000, a fraction of the amount owed to loan sharks.[22] In general the Foundation had enormous respect and excellent press relations in New York but over the years no readiness was found on the part of the legislature to increase the rates on the otherwise acceptable law which Arthur Ham himself had helped draft in 1914. As usual, it took a blatant abuse to produce the needed reform.

In the fall of 1927, the Foundation had been working with the New York Central Railroad on their troubles with salary-purchasers and together they brought the situation to the attention of New York's Attorney General, Albert Ottinger. Mr. Ottinger appointed Albert Raphael, a partner of Walter S. Hilborn, as his special deputy to conduct a campaign against the loan sharks. Raphael held a series of conferences to discuss proposals and remedies and meanwhile Henderson developed information and leads for the preparation of Raphael's report. In February 1928, at a hearing in Ottinger's office, it was announced that loan sharks were doing a $25,000,000 a year business in New York through salary purchases and other illegal methods of charging usurious interest. Also it was revealed that a nationwide ring was involved and that this ring had undertaken bribery, jury-buying and political influence.[23]

Ottinger asked the state legislature for help in his investigations. State Senator Baumes had a crime commission in operation at that time bearing his name and the legislature delegated the Baumes Crime Commission to take over the inquiry. In fact the life of the Baumes Commission was extended solely for that purpose. Next Ottinger obtained the help of the Postmaster General in taking action against out-of-state lenders who were making usurious loans by mail and by now the campaign was in high gear. Henderson was not satisfied with these moves alone and in March U.S. Attorney Tuttle announced he would conduct a Federal Grand Jury investigation with the aid of the Russell Sage Foundation, particularly in respect to blackmail methods allegedly being used against borrowers who didn't pay, notably taxi-drivers who had borrowed on their cabs. Soon Tuttle had directed Internal Revenue officials to examine the tax returns of 100 loan companies including auto loan companies and it would appear the lenders were being closed in from all sides. By May, the National City Bank had opened its personal loan department, taking advantage of all the publicity to extoll the value of its services and two branches of the Post Office announced establishment of credit unions. Arthur J. Morris welcomed the competition of the National City Bank but did not go so far as Chief Magistrate McAdoo who also held hearings and stated the National City Bank's action would "eliminate the loan sharks." [24] Henderson was not to lose sight of the objective of a remedial law, however, and soon Ottinger held a conference of bankers and others to draft plans for "chartering corporations under the present Small Loan Act." By September Ottinger's special committee, which included Leon Henderson, recommended that banks make short term small loans at 6% but also that "the Uniform Small Loan Law be enacted as a remedy for the existing evils." By the end of the year Ottinger had accepted the Republican nomination for Governor and in his acceptance speech called for the extermination of loan sharks. [25]

The Attorney General's committee report had specifically recommended that a higher rate law be enacted and that the peculiar New York State limitation on profits of loan companies be removed as discriminatory. The Baumes Crime Commission report also criticized these defects in the existing New York law. It would appear that with such backing the passage of the law would be guaranteed. It failed to pass, even with the additional approval of the State Banking Department, in 1929, 1930 and

246

1931. In the case of New York State, it is doubtful whether loan shark pressures significantly affected these reversals. The loan sharks had definitely taken cover, especially after Mr. Raphael's prosecutions resulted in several convictions and some prison sentences. It was more a matter of legislators just not being willing to accept the higher rates involved, which left a heavy burden of education on Henderson and the Foundation.

Franklin D. Roosevelt had become Governor of New York in 1928, stunningly defeating Albert Ottinger while Al Smith, the Democratic Presidential candidate, lost his own state to Herbert Hoover. Roosevelt did not oppose the loan legislation, even though it was part of the Republican program, and he was not pleased to see it sidetracked three successive times. Leon Henderson came to visit him before the fourth try and recalls difficulty in getting to the subject inasmuch as Roosevelt was extremely interested in hearing Henderson's opinions about his Presidential chances in the various states Henderson had been visiting. Roosevelt nevertheless assured Henderson that he would personally sponsor the bill, particularly in view of his high regard for John M. Glenn whom he had known well for some time.[26] Mrs. Roosevelt, a former social service worker and already a close political adviser to her husband, also held the Foundation in great esteem. The bill reached the final passage stage in the Assembly the day before adjournment of the session. At the last minute it was necessary to add several amendments to it in order to prevent conflict with certain collateral statutes. These circumstances nearly prevented its passage because of a provision in the New York Constitution which stipulates that a bill may not be passed or become law unless it has been printed and placed upon the desks of the members in its final form at least three calendar days prior to its final passage. An exception is possible if the Governor certifies to the necessity of its immediate passage.

Governor Roosevelt, keenly interested in the fate of the bill, sent a special message to the legislature certifying to the necessity of the immediate passage of the Uniform Small Loan Law. It thereupon received unanimous favorable votes from both the Assembly and the Senate and became law on June 1, 1932. Thus the most important state was added to the list shortly before both Roosevelt and Henderson moved on to more urgent business in Washington.

VI

When Henderson left New York for Washington in 1934, Congressman Fiorello H. La Guardia left Washington for New York, where he had finally achieved his ambition to become Mayor of America's greatest city. Since La Guardia was to spend a good portion of his twelve years as Mayor needling the licensed loan business as being in the same class as the underground loan sharks, one wonders if the New York law would have been passed at all had he won the mayoralty election on his previous try four years earlier.

Henderson had already experienced a clash with La Guardia on the subject of small loans, this time over a proposed bill for the District of Columbia. The District did not then and still does not have an acceptable small loan law, in spite of the fact that the borrowing propensity of employees in the nation's capital probably is greater than in any other city of the country. The District, which is administered by the Congress, had passed a loan law that became effective in 1913. It was legislated under the influence of the Russell Sage Foundation but in those trial and error days the rate had been established at 1% per month. In spite of anti-loan shark crusades before and after 1913, the District has since refused to increase the rate time and again.

It is interesting to note that the 1% bill of 1913 was not the one recommended by either the District Commissioners or the District Committee of legislators. These groups had come to the conclusion that a 2% a month law was needed, reflecting the current thinking of Arthur Ham and the Foundation at that time. Representative Dyer of Missouri introduced the 2% bill in the fall of 1912. Surprisingly enough, his chief supporters in the House gallery on the day of debate were the Women's Welfare Department of the National Civic Federation, in those days before the women even had the vote. Congressman George W. Norris of Nebraska who was later to co-sponsor the Norris-La Guardia labor bill in 1932 outlawing "yellow-dog" contracts, arose in the sparsely attended House and orated:

It seems to me a remarkable coincidence that those members whc favor the 24 per cent rate do it ostensibly in opposition to the so-called loan shark. The gentleman says that if the rate is fixed at 1 per cent a month it will not be effective; if they cannot afford to lend money at 1 per cent per month, there is no way to compel them to, and God knows nobody wants them to. We can get along without the loan sharks! [27]

This attack killed the bill and it was passed with a 1% a month amendment which has lasted to this day. As a result, cities bordering the District such as Alexandria, Virginia and Mt. Rainier, Maryland display the unusual spectacle of entire blocks of consumer finance companies established for the purpose of serving District borrowers who prefer not to use the loan sharks.

It was against this historical background that Leon Henderson was called as a witness in 1933 before a District of Columbia Committee which was considering the Uniform Small Loan Law. La Guardia appeared in order to express his violent objections against the proposed law as well as the Foundation. Henderson objected so sarcastically to what he called La Guardia's "half-truths" and "mis-statements of facts" that the Little Flower demanded unsuccessfully that Henderson be ejected from the Committee room. La Guardia then bombarded each Trustee of the Russell Sage Foundation with a telegram demanding that Henderson be fired. A meeting was called by John M. Glenn, at which Henderson told his version of the story. Glenn decided to ignore La Guardia and Henderson was urged to continue with his work.[28]

Still, members of the consumer finance industry should not be complacent about their business being blacklisted by La Guardia. Any unbiased observer of the American scene would have to admit that La Guardia was a great American and a great public servant. Indeed he was probably the only great American of consequence who was an implacable foe of the business. Demagogue and emotionally uncontrollable though he was, he certainly was always on the consumer's side and could be expected, with his reform background, to have approved of such well-sponsored legislation. An analysis of his background may supply the answer. La Guardia had first been elected to Congress as a Republican in 1916 but quickly went off to war where he became a Major and a much decorated combat aviator. His subsequent Congressional career found him a leader among the Progressive group in the House which traced its lineage back to the Populists of the 1890's and their exaggerated fears of bankers and big business. His boyhood idol had been Theodore Roosevelt, who had similar ideas, and now in Congress George W. Norris was his model. In the Twenties, La Guardia had been a lone voice attacking his own party's taxing, tariff, farm, labor and monopoly policies. He darkly predicted that because of them the boom would become a bust. By 1932, eighty-five thousand businesses had failed, five thousand banks had closed, nine million savings accounts were wiped out and nearly thirteen million Americans were unemployed. La Guardia had the distinction of being a prophet in his own time which increased the arrogance and intensity of his conviction that the banking and business interests were rightfully cast in the villain's role. In an article for *Liberty* magazine he wrote: "The bankers of this country are more to blame than are any other group for the present depression." [29]

Thus it was not only loan companies that he wished to squeeze but all kinds of financial institutions. In July 1932 the House was considering Hoover's Federal Home Loan Bank bill, which established twelve Federal Home Loan Banks to lend money to qualified home lending institutions. Its immediate objective was to enable home-owners to obtain easier terms and to help revive the economy through increased home construction. La Guardia attacked the bill with unreasoning fury: "The bastards broke the peoples' back with their usury and now they want to unload on the government. No . . . let them die." He quickly decided that it was a good bill, however, and he proposed an amendment, which became part of the law, to deny credit to any institution which charged more than the legal rate of interest in its state, or if there were no such rate, more than eight per cent.[30] Aside from the language, one would have hoped for an equal under- standing for consumer loans but apparently his ears were closed to any reasoning on this subject.

In 1944, members of the consumer finance industry had a per- plexing experience. They heard La Guardia attack the "six for five loan sharks" and the illegal "jewelry lenders" on one Sun- day's broadcast with the skill of a trained industry representative. On the following Sunday they heard him attack the licensed lenders with equal vigor.[31] In 1945 he carried his vendetta with the loan companies to the point of dictating orders to Governor Thomas E. Dewey to take action at his level.[32] Dewey had won distinction as a District Attorney ten years before by prosecuting and convicting 130 racketeering loan sharks. They had sprung up in New York County after the end of Prohibition, which brought many ex-bootleggers into this new field of endeavor. He had obtained his convictions under the penal provisions of the Uniform Small Loan Law, with the help of the Foundation, and he was not interested in La Guardia's pressures. It was at this juncture that La Guardia lost any chance for active Republican party backing and he was defeated in the forthcoming election by William O'Dwyer.

Leon Henderson recalls being told another reason for La Guardia's intransigence was because his family had been victimized by loan sharks in Italy. Henderson and La Guardia had the usual table-pounder's respect and friendship for each other on matters outside the Uniform Small Loan Law and La Guardia was particularly pleased with Rolf Nugent, Henderson's former assistant, who served in a senior capacity in UNRRA while La Guardia was Director-General. The history of consumer finance in the state of New York is an excellent example of the strong men and turbulent emotions that have accompanied the development of this unique industry.

Although the opposition stopped short of strong-arm tactics in Missouri and other states during Henderson's regime, they were not above attempts at bribery, intimidation and efforts to compromise Henderson and his family. During the days when Thomas E. Dewey was prosecuting the racketeering type of loan shark, Rolf Nugent was a similar target and was advised to go armed.[33] Even the mild Clarence Wassam, back in 1908, felt that he was in a dangerous activity, according to Mrs. Wassam.[34] The consumer finance industry does indeed owe a great deal to a very few.

VII

In 1927 Henderson's Department was confronted with eleven states that were considering reductions in the permitted interest rates to points below the current recommendations. Not one of these bills was enacted. By 1929, however, it was a different story. Hundreds of bills were being introduced and several reductions took place, especially with the advent of the depression. The New Jersey experience was a definitive case in this period and is worthy of review.

In New Jersey the rate was reduced in 1929 from 3% a month to 1½% a month. In 1928 a Joint Legislative Commission had been appointed to look into the matter of issuing charters to financial institutions and "any and all other matters" relating to the Department of Banking. It appears that the Commission had been encouraged to take a dim view of the loan business by the extravagant claims being made about its profitability in the radio advertising of certain loan companies. The loan companies sponsoring these ads were later found to be promotional enterprises seeking to make their profits from the sale of their securities rather than from their negligible loan operations. The Commission at any rate hired an accountant to study the reports of the licensees in New Jersey. The report charged that expenses were loaded and arbitrarily determined and that "the small loan business can be and has been profitably conducted at rates less than half the maximum now permitted." The rate was thereupon reduced to $1\frac{1}{2}\%$ a month, in spite of the protests of the New Jersey Industrial Lenders Association. The Association hired its own distinguished firm of accountants to prove that the Commission's analysis was inaccurate in every respect. It also hired Professor Willford I. King of New York University, who was later to become President of the American Statistical Association, to report on the necessity of the business in New Jersey from both an economic and a social point of view. Thus the tradition of student *vis à vis* legislature which originated with Ham and Wassam was invoked at still another critical point in the industry's growth. These two reports, while fully confirming the claims of their supporters, could not turn the wheels back and the New Jersey lending industry began to liquidate. By 1932, the original 437 loan offices had been reduced to 83. Of these 83, several were in receivership and all but 19 were liquidating. Meanwhile loans outstanding had dropped from $20,000,000 to $5,400,000. Of the latter amount, approximately 90% were receivables of Household Finance Corporation. which had agreed to undergo the unique experiment of continuing its eight offices in New Jersey and to submit the results of their operations to the Department of Banking in order to prove the necessity of a higher rate. This proposal of Household Finance in the home state of Beneficial Finance had an interesting antecedent. In January 1917, the *Loan Gazette*, publication of the infant American Association of Small Loan Brokers, carried the following news:

Being unable to continue business at a profit in New Jersey at the 3% per month legal rate, the Household Loan Company of Plainfield has been compelled to suspend business.

Of course, many changes had taken place since the days of 1917, not the least of which was the tremendous growth and acceptance of the industry. The ability to produce reasonable profits at lower rates as a result of this growth as well as the accompanying use of borrowed capital, did not extend to such a drastic rate cut as 1½%. In the spring of 1932, Household submitted its report and announced it too would have to leave the state unless a higher rate was made available. Meanwhile the inevitable loan sharks had reappeared. In 1932 the New Jersey legislature increased the rate to 2½%, which was hopefully accepted on the grounds that New Jersey's compact industrial cities would supply greater volume than could normally be obtained elsewhere. This painful experience was at least an object lesson to be used by an industry that would ever be on the defensive and its outcome was watched with keen interest throughout the country. In 1933 West Virginia, which also had a major rate reduction in 1929, followed New Jersey's lead and increased the rate to 3½% a month on the first $150 and 2½% a month on the balance of the loan.

The Foundation meanwhile was faced with the problem of deciding what rate it should now be recommending as the central authority on small loans in the country. To provide more reliable data on expenses and profits, a standard reporting form was produced, in cooperation with the lenders' association and the banking departments. In order to promote such uniform reporting and to improve regulatory proficiency, the Foundation also helped establish the National Conference of Small Loan Supervisors in 1935. By 1942 the Foundation had issued its final Seventh Draft of the Uniform Small Loan Law recommending 3% a month on the first $100 and 2% a month on the balance of the loan. By now the Foundation's Drafts were no longer released in conjunction with the lenders' association, which naturally was reluctant to recommend any further rate reductions. It was obvious that sooner or later active collaboration between the industry and the Foundation would have to end and the business would be required to defend itself. Henderson and the Foundation had already decided in 1928 to reduce legislative activity to the drafting of bills, correspondence, supplying of materials and appearances at hearings. The New York legislative activity was something of an exception due to the national importance of the state. The Department meanwhile not only continued its support of credit unions but also drafted bills for installment buying and assisted banks in entering the small loan business, on the theory that every legitimate consumer credit agency should be encouraged. In addition, both Henderson and Nugent felt it was now time to turn towards the study of the measurement and economic significance of consumer credit as a whole and important steps had been taken in that direction. The advent of World War II hastened the decision to cease active support in relation to the industry's legislative problems. Nugent had followed Henderson to Washington to become senior deputy administrator of the OPA. Although he had planned to return to full-time duty as Director of the Department of Consumer Credit Studies, as it was now called, Nugent tragically drowned in a swimming accident while on UNRRA duty off the coast of Yokohama in 1946. The Foundation, whose consumer credit interests were but one phase of its manifold activities, allowed the Department to terminate.

XVIII

GOVERNMENT CONTROL OF
CONSUMER CREDIT

"The ideas of economists and political philosophers," wrote
John Maynard Keynes, "both when they are right and when
they are wrong, are more powerful than is commonly understood. Indeed the world is ruled by little else." [1]

To support this claim that the academic ideas of economists
can be earth-shaking, Keynes himself must be included near the
top of the list. His ideas have actually revolutionized the way
the world thinks about its economic problems. They have dominated modern economic thought and government economic
action to a degree unmatched by any other man of his profession.
We are all now Keynesians in the sense that we were all Darwinists in the time of Arthur Ham's adolescence. The difference is
that Keynesian theories became the new orthodoxy in a much
shorter period of time. This was not accomplished without severe
cries of outrage and socialism on the part of Keynes' opponents,
but by the time President Eisenhower and his economic advisers
incurred a deficit of $9.4 billions in overcoming the recession of

1958, Keynesianism was firmly established as a bi-partisan government technique. Presidents Kennedy and Johnson have continued what is now a commonplace policy in this respect.

The relationship between Keynes' economics and consumer credit is not an important one. Keynes had little to say about consumer credit in the development of his theories which were originally conceived as a remedy for the great depression. In addition, they were formulated before the tremendous growth of consumer credit. Yet because the Keynesian approach emphasizes purchasing power, consumer credit glows in the reflected glory of such a congenial concept. Another by-product of Keynesianism is the reduced virtue attached to savings, in fact the actual danger inherent in what is termed "over-savings." Since consumer credit is on the surface an anti-thrift concept, again it finds the association advantageous. Meanwhile, consumer credit has developed a very attractive economic theory of its own, namely, that mass production (essential for defense as well as raising the standard of living) depends on mass distribution which depends on consumer credit. Why then should there be recurring demands for its regulation by the Federal Reserve Board? To understand more about the claims for and against consumer credit, a review of Keynes' theories is in order.

Keynes' fame, of course, rests on his remedies for bringing countries such as America and England out of a major depression. His future fame may rest, as is claimed for Franklin D. Roosevelt, on having brought Marxism to a halt in the advanced countries by reviving a very sick capitalism and launching it on the road to unparalleled prosperity. The fact that America's final emergence from the depression of the Thirties came from the tremendous spending and production related to preparations for World War II does not diminish the fact that the Keynesian deficit spending approach had already been clearly justified by results before the war. The control of consumer credit is related to the other side of the Keynes coin, that is, the matter of controlling inflation, which Keynes correctly predicted would be a major problem following a cured depression. It is as a "depression economist," however, that Keynes made his major contributions.

If you were one of the 13 million unemployed in the early 1930's, no economics textbook which taught that the capitalist system had a built-in mechanism that tended towards stable prices and full employment would be read with anything but bitter irony. Yet the typical college economics student was taught that production itself provided exactly enough purchasing power to buy whatever was produced. Unemployment could occur for various reasons, but the resulting reductions in wages would lead to increased production again and the economy would tend to stabilize at full employment. The economists naturally recognized that not all wages and income would be used for purchasing power. A substantial portion would be "saved" in one form or another rather than spent. Savings, however, were the stuff from which vital investments in plant and equipment were made. Savings therefore created additional jobs and took up the slack in purchasing power caused by the savers in the first place, so that full employment continued once again. This process depended not only on the imaginations of the economists but also on a special ingredient, the interest rate. The interest rate would be a regulator that encouraged both savers to save and investors to invest just enough to keep the economy in equilibrium. Too much savings, for example, would eventually result in interest rate reductions on a supply and demand basis. This would discourage further savings and at the same time encourage valuable investments in plant and equipment since the interest rate for borrowing would also be reduced. In fairness to the economists, most of them recognized that this time-honored view of the interest rate as an automatic balancing factor was something of a folk-tale. Practical experience had proved long before the great depression that people did not save and business did not invest as a reflection of the interest rate alone. Public confidence, the existence of markets for raising money, consumer income above the subsistence level, the distribution of income itself, the growth of institutions for savings and investments such as life insurance companies and pension funds, all these were equally if not more important. No one had pursued the process, however, with the logic and persuasion of Keynes, who began to lecture President Roosevelt on what to do as early as 1933 in letters to the *New York Times* and who would eventually convert the leading economics professors, particularly those at influential Harvard, to his point of view. Although his major book, *The General Theory of Employment, Interest and Money*, published in 1936, is so erudite and difficult to read that it is understood largely through the efforts of his disciples, the message seeped through that an undirected economy would not normally settle at full employment by way of the interaction of savings, investment and the interest rate. Indeed it was just as likely that savings would become "stagnant" or would actually dry up in a depression and would not result in investment. Production would therefore decrease and the economy could "normally" stabilize at a point of massive unemployment. In addition, although Keynes did not advance this argument, his followers such as J. K. Galbraith have discounted the likelihod of producers responding to lower wages. This also would be revealed as a myth since both wages and prices in the modern economy tend to be rigid rather than the true products of supply and demand. Moreover, investment comes in spurts, responding to inventions, family formations and other variables. All in all, the *laissez-faire* capitalist mechanism, in relation to major unemployment at least, was shown to be sadly in need of improvement.

The significance of Keynes' approach was that government had to step in to pull the country out of a depression reflecting a breakdown of investment. Since private investment had no incentive to risk what was left to create jobs, government spending of public funds was the only alternative. This could create enough purchasing power, or "aggregate demand," in the economy to revive production and private employment. It would create a budget deficit, but this would be offset by later budget surpluses and meanwhile the intolerable depression would be broken. Keynesians of course, advanced other remedies. Reduction of taxes in order to provide private individuals with more money to spend and measures to stimulate private investment such as insuring mortgages on behalf of lending institutions would have a similar effect. The $10 billion tax cut of 1964 was a classically Keynesian policy, with an estimated cumulative flow of three times that amount added to the national economy, according to the President's economic advisers. The boldness of this technique is brought into focus when one considers that President Hoover actually considered raising taxes during the depression and President Roosevelt at the outset of his administration spoke hopefully about a balanced budget. The problems of the Thirties were so completely unique, however, that Keynesianism has become basically associated with public spending financed by loans and resulting in budget deficits.

Thus we see that the relationship between Keynesianism and consumer credit in regard to their association with thrift is a completely tenuous one. If critics of consumer credit base their criticism on guilt by association with Keynesianism, they do an injustice both to Keynes and logic itself. Keynes did indeed bring thrift, a sacrosanct virtue, into disrepute in the sense that it was connected with redundant savings and depressions. In the context in which he criticized savings, however, he was concerned with the breakdown of the investment cycle and not with personal habits or attitudes. Nevertheless his dwindling band of critics have seen dark implications in the attack on savings as have others in the equally unorthodox idea of consumer credit. Interestingly enough, in Keynesian economics, as well as in the new, overall economic measurements it called into being, such as Gross National Product and National Income, repayments on consumer credit debt are treated as "savings," in the sense that anything not spent is saved. This pleasant about-face for consumer credit has been matched by the industry's own ingenious and convincing argument that buying durable consumer goods on credit is nothing but "savings-in-reverse," that is, satisfying today's needs by using tomorrow's savings. The association of consumer credit with purchasing power, on the other hand, is an extremely valid one. Consumer credit obviously increases purchasing power and is a major agent for helping us out of recessions, once the economy is strong enough to bring borrower and lender together again.

II

The upshot of Keynesianism was not merely that a way had been found to reverse the forces of depression but that government itself now became an indispensable partner of business. This was not an easy prescription for business to take in spite of the definite intentions of the Keynesians to make government activity an indirect rather than a direct matter. Thus the directly administered NRA was not a Keynesian program and Keynes himself viewed its centralized power with alarm. Business felt it could control the NRA, however, and had cooperated with it as an emergency situation. Vast public spending and deficits were a different type of meddling, and since the New Deal itself had fostered an anti-business sentiment, Keynesianism was not well received by the business world until it became standard procedure over the years. In a sense business was correct in its fears. The new managed type of capitalism did reduce the power and status of business in relation to government. Federal Reserve administrators and Secretaries of the Treasury could now make decisions that were likely to be more important than those of any banker or group of bankers. The obvious hindrance to purchasing power resting in the vastly unequal distribution of incomes such as existed in the Twenties would be redressed by income taxes designed to create a larger, better-paid middle class as well as a highly taxed upper class. Resistance to labor unions on the grounds that wage flexibility was essential for restoring equilibrium to the economy was also demolished by Keynesian theory. There was in addition the ever present threat of loss of liberty and efficiency inherent in the tremendous expansion of government services and bureaucracy connected with stabilizing the economy and encouraging its growth. By and large the American consensus has been to accept the risks involved and to recognize that individual liberties have not been seriously impaired by the present mixture of economics and politics.

The formal canonization of the new role of government was expressed in the Employment Act of 1946. This Act, which is always exhibited as background for any serious discussion of government regulation of consumer credit, makes it the duty of the federal government and its agencies to use all practicable means "to promote maximum employment, production and purchasing power." More a statement of intent than a detailed law, it means primarily that Congress voted to use government spending and taxing, or fiscal, powers and government monetary powers, such as central banking policy, for the purpose of avoiding major swings in the business cycle. This in turn has been elevated in practice as a mandate to use these tools to keep our economy in a state of constant growth from the point of view of both domestic and foreign policy considerations. Thus economics has become a keystone of government policy. The government's budget has become a dramatic determinant of what the economy will do, and federal spending now accounts for one-fifth of all economic activity.

III

Government control of consumer credit, known as Regulation W, was not a depression offspring. It was fostered by World War II and among its chief progenitors were Rolf Nugent and Leon Henderson. It was not established to prevent abuses of the consumer by the lender, as in the case of state regulation. It was created as part of the war effort, in this instance as a step to control prices and to promote guns rather than autos. Its method was to increase the down payment, shorten the number of monthly payments and limit the purposes of consumer credit, primarily consumer instalment credit.

Rolf Nugent, upon joining the Russell Sage Foundation in 1925, had been urged by Leon Henderson, its director of the Department of Remedial Loans, to pursue his scholarly interest in the economic significance of consumer credit. When Henderson left the Foundation to become General Johnson's assistant in the NRA in 1934, Nugent actively continued these studies. By 1938, he had completed his Ph.D. requirements at the New School in New York and his dissertation appeared as a Foundation book in 1939 entitled *Consumer Credit and Economic Stability*. Meanwhile Henderson had initiated federal interest in consumer credit by directing Nugent on behalf of the NRA Consumers' Advisory Board to study consumer credit in relation to its possible retarding effect upon industrial recovery. When the NRA bowed out prematurely in 1935 the study reverted to the Foundation where Nugent carried it to completion with the publication of his book.

Nugent accumulated some pioneering data at a time when the type of consumer credit statistics we now have were in their formative stage. In fact, he claimed that getting his figures was more a job for a detective than a statistician.[2] He pointed out that consumer credit directly expanded and contracted with good and bad times and produced significant aggravating effects on the business cycle. Following in part the Keynes theory, he deducted that consumer credit grossly accelerated booms by increasing purchasing power and deepened depressions because of the necessity to pay for past purchases during the downswings. His book was highly respected and drew attention to the possibility that control of consumer credit might help reduce business cycle changes. When the book appeared the war in Europe had already started. With considerable foresight, Nugent had included several last-minute observations on how to use consumer credit controls in times of national emergency, thus planting the seed for Regulation W. Meanwhile the National Bureau of Economic Research had started its research projects on the size, practice and significance of the various types of consumer credit agencies in 1937, so that by 1941 there was a literature, a statistical series and a corps of experts to draw upon for the first exercise in consumer credit control. Among the noted economists contributing to this series, Gottfried Haberler of Harvard reinforced Nugent's conclusions in his *Consumer Credit and Economic Fluctuations*, published in 1942.

By 1940 Leon Henderson had become one of the seven commissioners of the National Defense Advisory Commission, which had been established to speed up the country's defense program. Henderson's particular job was to prevent inflation through price control and by May 1941 he had brought Rolf Nugent into his department which eventually became the Office of Price Administration. Nugent vigorously pressed the case for control of consumer credit, which became more compelling as the inflationary forces rapidly mounted. Meanwhile Henderson had obtained the services of F. B. Hubachek, the Household Finance attorney, who also came to Washington and helped draft Regulation W. Since the Federal Reserve Board had the responsibility for the regulation of the country's flow of credit and was already administering selective controls for stock market credit, it was prepared to add another selective control to its duties. The combination of the Federal Reserve Board, the OPA and Nugent resulted in an Executive Order of the President establishing Regulation W on August 9, 1941. The Executive Order included among its reasons the necessity to transfer productive resources from consumer to defense industries. This aspect of Regulation W was a perfectly legitimate wartime endeavor which properly belonged in another sphere of control once the country was awakened by Pearl Harbor. In May 1942 the strategic materials argument for consumer credit control had ended, since the War Production Board called a halt to the unregulated production of major durable consumer goods. Regulation W remained in effect, however, as an anti-inflation device until the end of the war. The Federal Reserve Board requested permanent authority for the regulation as the war ended but Congress allowed it to expire in 1947. Eleven months later, when inflation seemed about to run rampant as pent-up purchasing power was released, Congress reinstituted Regulation W but allowed it to lapse again in 1949, despite the pleas of the money managers and of President Truman. Congress instituted it once again at the outset of the Korean War in 1950 and allowed it to expire on June 30, 1952.

The controversy over Regulation W is mainly whether or not a control that was installed in time of war should be continued in peacetime. Since our post-war economy has largely been a protracted brush with inflation, our Presidents, Economic Advisers and Federal Reserve Board managers have frequently recommended at the very least standby controls. Congress has been loath to accommodate these requests. Meanwhile the members of the consumer credit industry as well as numerous distinguished economists have assembled a formidable array of arguments against the bureaucracy, the discrimination and the ineffectiveness of Regulation W. The controversy has produced a torrent of words and articles among professors and economists beyond the dreams of the pioneering students of the industry. In

April of 1956, under the auspices of the Federal Reserve Board, the National Bureau of Economic Research called forth a veritable economical conference wherein 46 scholars from 28 universities and research institutions delivered papers devoted to "an analysis and discussion of the data and knowledge needed for effective decisions on, and application of, public policy in the field of consumer credit, especially instalment credit." When all was said and done the conference made no recommendations about standby authority to regulate consumer credit but their conclusions were printed in six volumes which are a monument in their own way to the importance of consumer credit in our times.

Since the negative arguments are in the ascendant and appear to be safely in the hands of Congress, some review of the positive arguments in favor of control will serve to keep our theory up to date. The late Professor Marcus Nadler proposed that since central banks in the governments of all the leading free countries have made such tremendous progress in influencing domestic business activity and employment, compared with their quite different function before the 1930's, they ought to be entitled to any of the tested indirect controls which can keep an economy healthful. Paraphrasing the modern interpreters of the Constitution, he states: "The scope and function of a central bank must reflect changed economic and social conditions. A nation's economy is a living organism, subject to constant changes, and the central bank must adjust itself to these developments and changes, irrespective of previous theory and practices." He finds that all the principal factors that have produced economic disturbances since World War II are responsive to control by the Federal Reserve Board or other government agencies with the exception of consumer credit, especially when it becomes "too large and harmful to the economy as a whole." [3]

There are still other arguments for control which reflect the thinking of Federal Reserve staff members from time to time.

266

There is, for example, the argument advanced in the Federal Reserve Bulletin of November 1965 that a major imbalance in a specific area, such as the purchasing of consumer durable goods, can lead to major fluctuations in the entire economy. Others feel that in boom periods the quality of credit falls and that this can later accelerate deflation by inhibiting the activities of both consumers and producers.

Other advocates of standby control such as Neil Jacoby, a former Eisenhower Economic Adviser, emphasize that monetary controls such as the Federal Reserve Board utilizes are now much more effective than they were in the post-war days. Until 1951 the Federal Reserve Board was obligated to support bond prices in order to aid the Treasury Department's financing of the war debt, which reduced its control ability in the general economy area. The Keynesian emphasis was also on fiscal rather than monetary policy, especially in downswings when it was claimed that low interest rates could no more induce investment than a string could be pushed uphill. Jacoby and other monetary advocates emphasize that Keynes missed the importance of the "availability" of money in influencing investment decisions, even if interest rates do tend to be disregarded by both lender and investor, especially when the downswing has not been too severe as to destroy confidence. Since they feel that our current long-run prosperity reflects an expanding money supply as well as an expansionary fiscal policy, they would advocate standby authority for selective control of consumer credit in order to help the general monetary controls work even more satisfactorily.[4]

The arguments against control seem to be overwhelming in their proof that the determination of "too much" consumer credit is arbitrary, that consumer credit does not significantly affect the stability of the economy and that it does not make that much difference in relation to effective monetary controls. In addition, the major sales finance companies have argued that over half of their short-term funds come from the sale of commercial paper to corporate and other investors rather than from bank borrowing, which involves considerably less inflationary pressure. There is also something ludicrous in the idea of one very personal section of the economy, instalment credit, being regulated via millions of transactions of a type that is most easily violated, especially in times not calling for patriotic compliance. Finally a host of refinements in consumer behavior have been introduced in evidence, such as the fact that people tend to acquire durable goods on time as part of their family formation and equipment purchasing life-cycles, which stabilizes the effect of credit buying,[5] or that consumers no longer decide to buy more goods on time simply because their income increases, as was the assumption and probably the fact in Rolf Nugent's day.[6] The most compelling argument is more sociological than economic. The consumer is so conditioned to buying his automobile on time that he is likely not to buy at all if terms are reduced to the point needed to make Regulation W worth invoking. This reticence would apply even if he has money in the bank. He will pass up new car purchases to the extent that a major recession could easily develop, a fact which the average Congressman, close to the fears of local businessmen, probably recognizes. Since auto buying comprises about one half of consumer instalment credit, this potential buyers' strike cannot be overlooked.

The consumer finance companies, of course, are only innocent by-standers in the great standby controversy. Since their loans are made to pay existing bills, they do not generally create accelerated purchasing power or drive up the price of durable consumer goods at the expense of other goods in the economy. Yet they could be used to frustrate Regulation W, considering the ingenuity of auto and other dealers as well as their own. As a result they have always been included in Regulation W, which hopefully will continue to remain a matter for the history books, as it has been since 1952.

IV

Regulation W did not attempt to go into the morality of buying on time, although some of its proponents claimed that shorter terms would be good medicine for consumers and could save them carrying charges. The Federal Reserve Board recognized it had no mandate to protect the consumer against himself in this respect and officially took the position that it was interested only in the health of the economy as a whole. Yet even this admirable agency is now tempted to examine the quality of consumer credit from the point of view that overloaded customers would be a greater drag on a declining economy than others. It recently started a pilot study of 10,000 bank personal loan department customers in order to see if guidelines could be established to find out why loans turn out to be losses for the lender. It already has decided that a borrower who commits himself to debt of more than 20% of his income after taxes is too heavily in debt and, with the help of its prime research contractor, the Survey Research Center of the University of Michigan, has issued a series of statistics based on admittedly fragmentary data in this respect. The figures, incidentally, show the "overloaded" consumers have been a constant 10% to 12% of total instalment credit users for the past five years.[7] It is doubtful if consumer credit agencies are enthusiastic about this new interest in their activities. They are quite capable of measuring and paying for their own mistakes in credit judgment and view any extension of federal control as a Pandora's box that were better not to be opened.

Government regulation of consumer credit is of course as old as the first small loan laws but these were enacted on the state and not the federal level. The consumer finance business was the creation of tightly restricted state regulatory laws and thrived upon the cloak of legitimacy they granted. The sales finance companies were not so happy about their state legislation but have managed to live with it as state after state finally passed sales finance legislation covering not only automobiles but the myriad of other items that are sold on credit. As difficult and unpredictable as state legislators have proved to be, at least they accounted for only their own state which could be dealt with on an individual basis. It is this same safety in numbers theory, as well as the desire to reserve for the states whatever Washington will leave them, that has encouraged other institutions such as insurance companies to resist federal legislation. The handwriting is always on the wall, however, and banks, savings and loan associations and securities dealers are already under the dual regulatory system.

It is interesting to note that Rolf Nugent and Leon Henderson were among the first to advocate regulation of instalment selling for the reason that, as in the case of loans, the customer was simply in too disadvantageous a bargaining position. "As in the small loan field," they wrote in 1934, "society will probably begin by restricting the use of certain collection instruments and end by finding complete supervision necessary." By society they meant the states but at this time the NRA was busy establishing a "Fair Practices and Competition Code for the Finance Company Industry" and they noted: "The Consumers' Advisory Board has wisely recommended the inclusion of a provision in the Finance Company Code requiring the statements of finance charges both as a money charge and as a rate per month on the unpaid balance of the contract." [8] The NRA was soon a buried agency, but one member of the Consumers' Advisory Board, Professor Paul A. Douglas of the University of Chicago, never gave up the quest for this potential federal regulation of consumer credit.

For the past five years, Senator Douglas has been proposing a so-called "truth-in-lending" law which, by its appropriated title, implies some present falsehood. Senator Douglas is one of America's most impressive Senators, a distinguished economist, war hero and legislator, a person whom one would rather have on his side of an issue. In fairness to the Senator, it must be noted that he refers to his Douglas Bill as a "truth-in-interest" bill and that he limits his objections to remedying the alleged misunderstanding of charges in consumer credit. He states that his bill does not seek to control credit but simply to require that credit grantors express their charges first, in dollar amounts and second, in terms of annual true interest rates. For example, if you are billed for a revolving charge account by your department store, your bill would note that the 1½% charge on your balance of $200 is $3.00 and the annual rate of interest you are paying is 18%. In its most recent revision, the Douglas Bill eliminates the annual interest rate requirements for revolving charge accounts because of difficulty in regard to an accurate statement, but this is considered an exception.

Banks, retailers, sales finance companies, manufacturers and consumer finance companies have closed ranks in opposition to the bill. They feel the states have adequate resources to protect their instalment-buying consumers. They also do not want to suffer the indignity of expressing their "retail mark-up" for credit as an annualized percentage which would create fear and distrust on the consumers' part. They point out that the dollar charge is what counts and that any consumer can get this by simple multiplication. An additional negative argument is that mathematicians come up with different answers for dollar charges expressed as an annual interest rate, although it is difficult to deny that some reasonable compromise could be reached in that respect, as Douglas apparently did for revolving charge accounts. The crux of the argument is over "add-on" charges, which we have already noted as being close to double the dollar charge in terms of annual interest when monthly payments are involved. For example, the Morris Plan's charge of $8.00 per $100 per year was shown to be in excess of 17% per year. Opponents of the Douglas Bill point out that insofar as misleading advertising is concerned, state regulations prevent deceptive financial advertising and the Federal Trade Commission is similarly effective, as in the case of its prohibition of GMAC's "6% plan" in 1935. To this date, the Congress has not yet seen fit to single out the consumer credit grantors for such discriminatory treatment in spite of the implied endorsements of Presidents Kennedy and Johnson.

The consumer finance companies have a strange position in this controversy. The very concept of the original Russell Sage Foundation program was to include a clear statement of the monthly rate of interest on the unpaid balance and to make a full disclosure of same on the customer's payment book as well as on the papers he signs. Any borrower from a consumer finance company can easily read his monthly interest rate and presumably multiply it by twelve to get his annual interest rate. It was this failure to show the monthly rate which engendered the original bitterness between the Foundation and the Morris Plan. For years the consumer finance companies venerated the spelling out of the monthly interest rate and the entering of separate monthly interest charges on the customer's payment book as payments were made. The established practice of banks, sales finance companies and even some credit unions, however, is to "add-on" the charges at the outset, in other words to refer to charges as six, seven or more dollars per hundred added to the principal borrowed. This system, known as "precomputation," has the advantage of eliminating monthly interest computations and of meeting less customer resistance. As a result, the consumer finance companies have swung over to the add-on method themselves although still complying with state regulations requiring the disclosure of the monthly interest rate, which is not the case with their competitors. At any rate, the consumer finance companies would have far less reason for objections than any other credit grantors under the Douglas Bill. Nevertheless, they resist it as unwarranted, unworkable and unnecessary as well as emanating from the all-embracing federal level.

Still another phase of government regulation has arrived on the scene and this appears to be the most controversial change of all. It is a new type of proposed state regulation bearing the same appellation of "uniform" which previously enlisted the support of consumer finance people all the way. The first major effort to draft a uniform consumer credit law, embracing all types of consumer credit, was launched in 1964. This undertaking was sponsored by the prestigious National Conference of Commissioners on Uniform State Laws. Its purpose is to produce model legislation to offer to the various states which would provide more protection for the consumer and permit business to operate more effectively. This National Conference of Commissioners has been in existence since 1892 and has a considerable record of accomplishment. Its most notable recent production is the monumental Uniform Commercial Code which includes a single system for covering all transactions in which debts are secured by personal property. This particular legislation, completed in 1952, has already been passed by a majority of states and the District of Columbia and will eventually be passed in all the states. The Conference is not a body of state officials. It was originally created by the American Bar Association and is a lawyers' group completely independent of officialdom. As a result its recommendations have the aura of complete detachment and its decision to promulgate a uniform consumer credit law is viewed with bated breath by all concerned. The Special Committee charged with drafting the law includes five practising lawyers, four professors of law and one judge. A twenty member Advisory Committee has been appointed which includes nine executives from the consumer credit industry and others representing the Better Business Bureau, state and federal government, American Bar Foundation, education and labor. It is the most eminent gathering since the Federal Reserve Board's conference on consumer credit regulations and in its potential much more loaded. The target date for the first draft is 1966 and it is predicted that the states will be passing the new law by 1968. The Russell Sage Foundation has contributed a substantial amount of money to the project.

Whereas Senator Douglas may be stymied in the Congress, he can take some satisfaction in that the Conference lists as one of the reasons for its activity the impetus created by his "truth-in-lending" bills. Alfred A. Buerger, Chairman of the Conference Commitee, has stated that the Douglas Bill, which has recently become a House measure as well, threatens federal invasion of state regulation of consumer credit. Federal legislation would inevitably expand and the question of where it would step in to nullify state legislation is also a worrisome problem. The presumption is that state laws are the lesser of the two evils. Although industry representatives have been invited to sit in on the National Conference proceedings, there is an uneasy feeling in many quarters that they may be presiding over their own liquidation. The reason for concern is that an omnibus consumer credit bill must inevitably take up the question of rate of charges. Professor Robert F. Shay of Columbia University, a consumer credit expert who has been directing consumer credit research for the National Bureau of Economic Research, points out that it is time a group such as the Conference sought to express uniform public policy based on the ample research on hand. He feels that the growth of consumer credit and the changing function of credit agencies, such as the consumer finance companies with their increased size of loans permitted, indicates that the present legal framework is antiquated. He advocates for the Conference's consideration a ceiling of relatively high rates under which competition and rate disclosure would tend to satisfy the consumer's need to make a proper choice of credit agency.[9] One can imagine the resistance of most consumer credit agencies to such a concept of competition which would invite every agency to invade the other's field of business overnight. It is more than likely that the various types of consumer credit agencies will want to preserve their own special rate structures and let the public continue to choose between competing agencies on the basis of service and specialization as well as cost. It may well be that consumer finance companies will view their present difficulties with state legislators as far less a problem than those arising from the umbrella-type legislation implicit in a uniform credit law. The heavy-handed uniformity of the states would be substituted for the threatened uniformity of the federal government. Semantically, the consumer finance business has always favored a "model law," with variations according to region and cumulative experience rather than the misnomer of a "uniform" law. The proposed uniform credit law will undoubtedly present the consumer finance industry with the most difficult decision in its unique history.

V

No review of government regulation would be complete without a glance at consumer credit in other parts of the world. When advocates of standby control of consumer credit remind us that countries such as Great Britain, France, the Netherlands, Denmark and others have used consumer credit control as an anti-inflationary technique, an awareness of the worldwide use of consumer credit is driven home. One of the strangest manifestations of its international significance was illustrated in a proposal made by the American Federation of Labor in 1955. This organization seriously proposed as a form of foreign aid that a $10 billion international consumer credit fund be established under the auspices of a free-world conference to enable participating countries to develop their economies with this mighty tool.[10] One country not included, of course, was the

Soviet Union. Russia, though it does not claim to have invented consumer credit, announced in 1958 that it was considering instalment buying for certain products. Since so many of our own economic decisions, such as the race to the moon and the race for annual rate of increase of Gross National Product, are related to the activities of our giant rival, the Russian experience with consumer credit is of interest. Visitors to the Soviet Union are surprised to hear their guides talk about purchases of pianos, fur coats and refrigerators on the instalment plan, but it seems to be firmly established, especially under the new look at the profit system. One of the few informed sources is Egon Neuberger, an economist with the RAND Corporation and former U.S. economic officer and trade delegate in Moscow, who is the authority for the following.

Until 1959 there was no consumer credit in the USSR, largely because of the relative scarcity of durable consumer goods as well as an emphasis on industrial expansion rather than a concern for consumer welfare. Credit is now available for both hard and soft goods, but not for automobiles. The required down payment is 20% and terms go up to one year. The credit is provided by the government owned retail stores rather than through the banking system and the customer may pay directly or through payroll deduction. Since individuals don't have checking accounts in the Soviet Union, direct payments are made in cash. Probably credit-checking is non-existent, since employer cooperation can be expected rather severely. Although credit charges are minimal, the late charges run at 1/10 of 1% per day, which is a healthy 36.5% per year. In 1961, according to government figures, $1.2 billion worth of goods were sold on credit. Assuming this is a volume figure, outstandings are probably close to that figure presently, assuming credit sales and consumer production have increased each year. This would compare with America's present instalment credit outstanding for goods other than automobiles of approximately $16 billion and is a very sizeable figure for a new service. According to data from the Ukrainian Republic, the proportion of manufactured goods sold on time has increased from 1.6% of retail sales in 1959 to 13.6% in 1964.[11] This appears to indicate that Soviet consumers are not much different from American consumers in preferring to buy now and pay later. In the wonderful world of consumer credit, which was practically unknown when the twentieth century dawned, there are many surprises. Perhaps the English, who call consumer credit "hire-purchase," have the best description for it. Among themselves, it is referred to as the "never-never."

XIX

THE MASS CONSUMPTION
SOCIETY

Keynes and his followers wanted to stabilize the capitalist system in order to avoid mass unemployment. Since the end of World War II, quite a different thrust has marked the goal of governments throughout the world. The race now is to secure perpetual economic growth, to use the techniques of the economists and the forces of government to increase the Gross National Product by at least three to five per cent a year and to bring a higher standard of living to more and more people, in spite of heavy defense commitments. Keynes himself cast a prophetic look in this direction. In the midst of the depression, he wrote a book in 1930 called *Economic Possibilities for Our Grandchildren* which forecast a millenium for the year 2030 simply because the cumulative productivity, or ability to produce per man hour, would have become so great that workers would be supermen compared with their grandfathers. There were few other writers at that time who would care to spin Utopias while distress was at every hand. One was Aldous Huxley, whose

Brave New World, a satirical novel unconcerned with economics, touched on an intriguing economic problem we face today. Huxley's nightmare world was a dictatorship that had solved the problems of production but not of consumption. As a result, the gorged consumers had to consume heroically, even though an accommodating policy of forced obsolescence destroyed whatever they could not consume.

Although it would be unwise to assume that today's capitalism, with its deliberate and successful option for indirect controls, is not susceptible to violent swings, the real concern centers on demand. Out of the most erudite conferences on the health and future of the economy, a deceptively simple statement always seems to be issued, usually running along these lines: "There cannot be too much productive capacity in a country that has mastered not only the problems of production but also *how to match the supply of production with effective demand for products.*" [1] The fact is the consumer, whom Adam Smith indulgently labelled as "king" when the consumer actually had little freedom of choice, now really is sovereign and is polled by marketing men and Presidents before decisions are made. A new science of psychological-economics has even been invented to chart and analyze his behavior and buying intentions. Consumerism, like consumer credit, is something new under the sun and its threads go back to the beginnings of the century.

II

The first pangs of identity among consumers occurred in the early 1900's in the same progressive era that ushered in the reform movement which created the consumer finance business. Indeed the elements in both cases were similar, the emergence of exploited groups in the mushrooming, oppressive cities of America. It was not a matter of the consumers themselves organizing, as traditionally consumers have never organized or cooperated as such in urban America, unlike their cousins on the farms. Their designation as victims, which was their first designation, was the work of reformers, as in the case of loan shark victims, or of politicians who recognized the value of appealing to them as consumers. It was in this era, for example, that the pioneering new laws regulating the sale of foods and drugs were passed on behalf of consumers as against the usual special interest groups. Meanwhile the muckraking magazines and the press, not willing to take up labor's cause, reached the same broad audience by appealing to the consuming public, caught as it was by the "high cost of living."

The legitimacy of this new class was not readily accepted. In 1897 when Louis D. Brandeis testified against a high tariff bill, not as a free-trader but "on behalf of America's 70,000,000 consumers," he was greeted with jeers by the House Ways and Means Committee.[2] By 1909, however, when Senator Payne defended the Payne-Aldrich high tariff bill against insurgents in his own Republican party with the sarcastic questions: "Who are the consumers? Is there any class except a very limited one that consumes and does not produce?" he hastened the eclipse of the Taft administration.[3] A subtle shift in American thought away from the primacy of the producing or manufacturing class was taking place, quite consistent with the reduction of business influence being so articulately advocated by Presidents Theodore Roosevelt and Woodrow Wilson. A modest new hero, who would soon take his place in the political cartoons as the man in the barrel and in the political speeches as the "common man," the "ultimate consumer," or the "man on the street," had permanently arrived. Although the newly regulated loan business was to use several names before latching on to "consumer finance," there is no doubt that increased consumer awareness in the state legislatures helped pass the first small loan laws.

One consumers' organization actually did arise in the progressive period which exerted influence far beyond its actual membership. This was the National Consumers' League, which had been established in 1899 to boycott the purchasing of articles manufactured in sweatshops. Florence Kelley became the vital leader of this organization and her influence persisted throughout the administrations of F. D. Roosevelt in the person of her protégé, Secretary of Labor Frances Perkins, the first woman cabinet member. Under Florence Kelley's direction, the Consumers' League fought early battles against sweatshop labor, child labor and excessive hours for women. Her League's investigators turned up facts which aroused the public conscience. Then the League would draft remedial bills and lobby for them in the state legislatures, gaining credit for the first minimum wage laws passed by the state legislatures. She was in fact a one-man Russell Sage Foundation of her own, and it is not surprising to note that in 1907, the first year of the Foundation's existence, she persuaded it to undertake an investigation of the working conditions in the canneries of the state of New York.[4]

The Consumers' League was more of a reform agency than an actual organization of consumers. Emphasis on the consumer as a class, or as a potential political group, never made much headway in America, although such proposals received considerable notice through the publications of F. J. Schlink, who wrote *Your Money's Worth* with Stuart Chase in 1927 and then in 1933 a best-seller entitled *100,000,000 Guinea Pigs* with Arthur Kallet. The heritage of these efforts is the current non-doctrinaire type of magazine such as *Consumer Reports*, which is published by Consumers Union, an independent non-profit testing organization founded in 1936. It claims a circulation in excess of 800,000 families. Occasionally, a writer such as Columbia University's Mario Pei will produce a book urging consumers to unite rather than be caught in the "wars between capital and labor" but consumerism on this level has practically no following.[5] On the other hand, ever since NRA's valiant but ineffectual Consumers' Advisory Board, both state and federal governments have tended to establish departments for consumer protection.

In keeping with this important role, today's consumer has become the ward of Presidents as well as legislators. John F. Kennedy summed up the matter as follows:

The consumer typically cannot know whether drug preparations meet minimum standards of safety, quality, and efficacy. He usually does not know how much he pays for consumer credit; whether one prepared food has more nutritional value than another; whether the performance of a product will in fact meet his needs; or whether the large "economy size" is really a bargain.[6]

President Kennedy established the first Consumer Advisory Council in 1962 and President Johnson extended the frontier by appointing his own Special Assistant for Consumer Affairs. President Johnson's consumer messages have been in the same vein as President Kennedy's, emphasizing "truth-in-packaging" as well as "truth-in-lending," and it is fair to say the consumer is not neglected in Washington. In fact, a recent House Committee report found that of 35 departments and agencies, only two were not active in the consumer field. Most of this activity, such as the work of the Food and Drug Administration, with its invaluable report on the drug thalidomide, for example, is of the greatest value to the nation. There is a strong school of opinion, however, which feels that many of the federal activities are unnecessary and purely for voter appeal. These objectors echo the opinion of ad man David Oglivy who states: "The consumer is no moron—she is your wife!"

III

The idea that the consumer could be a moron has a strong tradition in American thought and literature, perhaps tracing back to the western world's penchant for self-criticism from the prophets onward. In our own time, it has included H. L. Mencken's savage depiction of the "booboisie," Sinclair Lewis' dissection of middle-class American values and *Fortune* magazine's classic portrait of consumers drugged by credit. Keeping within the time scope of our subject, one would probably agree that to be an underprivileged consumer in the early 1900's was no laughing matter. It was an era characterized by a marginal standard of living for most people, excessive working hours and, from our point of view, outrageous conditions of "buyer beware" in advertising and marketing practices. Yet this was also the time when millions believed in the stories of Horatio Alger and optimistically held an unbounded faith in the future. Exposed evils, it was assumed, could be reformed by analysis and remedial laws, as in the case of the consumers' need for legitimate small loan facilities. Besides, there was the new world of consumer satisfactions beckoning in the prospects of mass production.

Before there could be a mass consumption society, America had to become the world's greatest mass producer. Like so much else in our history, this too has been a product of the fantastic twentieth century. Eli Whitney had long ago discovered the principle of interchangeable parts and Cyrus McCormick had produced reapers on the assembly line as far back as the 1850's but it was the application of the assembly line technique to automobile manufacture by such men as Henry Ford and Ransom Olds that ushered in the true meaning of the technical age for consumers. By 1930, Ford had produced 20,000,000 automobiles and it was obvious that the market for this vast production would have to include the laborers themselves who made the cars. The efficiency of mass production, along with Ford's inspired raising of wages in 1914 from a minimum of $2.40 to $5.00 per nine-hour day, brought the price of automobiles within their sight. The development of consumer credit from about 1916, as we have seen, guaranteed the mass distribution not only of automobiles but also of all the other so-called "durable consumer goods" which characterize our mass consumption society. The rest of the story is well-known. The great industrial machine broke down in the depression in a rash of speculation and inadequate, poorly distributed purchasing power. Bold repairs and experiments were demanded from the government and successfully provided as we emerged from the depression with an assist from World War II. The war, along with industry's own tremendous research expenditures, accelerated technological advances and created a huge pent-up store of demand and purchasing power. In spite of gradual inflation, a revolutionary change in real wages for the predominant laboring middle class, strengthened by the power of its unions, has sustained a prosperity of unparalleled duration and promise. It is a prosperity of mass consumption in which consumer credit has vitally stimulated purchasing power.

IV

There are two facets of the affluent consumer which attract the concern of American social critics and economists. One is a qualitative, spiritual problem. Is our age too involved with material possessions, with gadgets and tail-fins? Should not consumer expenditures be curtailed with a corresponding increased expenditure for hospitals, slum clearance and education, for example, which would enhance the quality of American life? These questions have been sharply posed by J. K. Galbraith, in *The Affluent Society*, and more recently by the British historian of civilizations, Arnold J. Toynbee. They are rhetorical in the sense that apparently the public expects both gadgets *and* good public works from our apparently limitless productive capacity, even in a period claiming a large percentage of our national spending on behalf of defense. In fact the worry has shifted towards another consideration: What would happen if people did not respond to the lures of advertising and keeping up with the Joneses, or did not regard yesterday's luxuries as today's necessities?

Most economists agree that much of what we consume is not only needless but immediately postponable. The hope is that we will continue to spend at least 94% of our income after taxes lest a recession ensue. We are highly dependent on what might be termed wasteful spending but we have a long way to go before our riches will be embarrassing. Millions of families still exist at an unacceptable standard of living and millions of others, particularly minorities, will expect new standards as a result of education and development of employment opportunities formerly denied to them. Ironically, we have to face up to the fact that in spite of our Puritan traditions of thrift and austerity, our founding fathers committed us to "the pursuit of happiness" among other goals. Besides, our expenditures no longer are concentrated so heavily on automobiles and other durable consumer goods which could conceivably exceed demand. We spend almost three times as much of our after-tax income on personal services, involving everything from haircuts to vacations, from education to amusements. These expenditures are expected to double in volume in the next fifteen years as the shorter work week becomes a reality. Finally, there is the dynamic of population increase which creates its own additional demand. In summary, there is no problem in the consumer's ability to consume in the manner expected of him, provided he has the prospect of steady employment. As for gadgets versus socially useful public spending, the Great Society and the elimination of poverty may finally depend on a highly material, tax-producing middle class. The next wave of economic theory may indeed call for both consumers and government to "spend and spend," thus creating a fantastic crop of income taxes, which the benign government will devote towards great improvements, resulting in even more prosperity. In this vein, Edwin L. Dale, Jr., the

Consumer Finance: A Case History in American Business

New York Times' financial specialist, speculates on a government embarrassed with a $50 billion budget surplus in 1970, based on present growth rates, no reductions in taxes and no war.[7] In effect, the Sears Roebuck catalog has long since replaced Horatio Alger as an index of our national character.

The other critical aspect of the consumer concerns his use of consumer credit. The consumer's enthusiastic employment of loans and time payments was bound to result in a body of satirical criticism, much as advertising, the function of which is quite similar to that of consumer credit, has been exposed as the province of the hidden persuaders. It would be foolish to deny that there is some truth in these charges, since very few of our contemporary institutions can stand the light of full examination.

Perhaps the most distinguished, or at least the most entertaining, exposé of consumer credit was William H. Whyte, Jr.'s *Budgetism: Opiate of the Middle Class*, in the *Fortune* magazine series on "Financing the New Economy" in 1956. Quite correctly, Whyte claims that people have a different attitude towards savings and going into debt than their fathers had. Examining the budgets of 83 young suburbanite couples in the $5,000 to $7,500 class, the *Fortune* researchers came to the conclusion that these young couples no longer associate cash savings with morality. On the other hand, they do not regard themselves as spendthrifts and gladly subscribe to what is called the Protestant ethic of hard work and thrift. It is simply a matter of their wanting to place all their major expenditures on monthly payment plans instead of using their best years glancing at the cash balances in their savings accounts. They are apparently unconcerned with the cost of the money they borrow. They want to enjoy an auto and a well-outfitted household before they are too old and they possess a great deal of optimism about continuing prosperity and increased incomes in the future. In addition, they accept without questioning most financial transactions as presented to them by any convenient source at hand because they

286

believe that the strict legislation about which they have heard and read guarantees the legitimacy of the transactions. In effect, *Fortune* comes to the conclusion that this particular group of consumers, most of them with two or more years of college education, is slightly bereft of intelligence when it comes to money matters.

Fortune does admit that to protest the illogic of "budgetism" would be futile, since it is a way of life. There is no compulsion for anyone to buy on the instalment plan. Since the merchants and financial institutions offer such an array of financing methods, understandably time payments seem as normal as checking accounts or paying one's income tax by monthly payroll deductions. Actually, *Fortune* did not survey a group which is even more time-payment conscious and certainly more important in numbers to the functioning of the mass consumption society. This would be the people in the same $5,000 to $7,500 bracket, which now accounts for about 27% of all families compared with 11% in 1930, who are not likely to be wearing white collars to work. This group, living in tract homes or in apartments, is barely concerned with status compared with the major task of outfitting and maintaining their generally larger families. They take great pride in their ability to obtain credit and would regard a survey team which treated the practice as news as bereft of common sense.

How is it, then, that record savings are reported year in and year out, accompanying the figures of record increases in consumer debt? First of all, there are tremendous savings generated from groups with more cash to spare than the young marrieds. Secondly, all groups of employed people have seen a good deal of their savings "institutionalized" for them, that is, their savings arise from automatic deductions or employer contributions for pension funds, profit sharing plans, group insurance plans and social security payments. This in turn encourages consumers to buy on credit rather than save first.

There are other factors which have encouraged consumers in all wage brackets to take the risks involved in instalment buying and loans. They do not have the "depression psychosis" of their elders who have lived through the depression, so they are not particularly worried about prolonged unemployment. If work does appear to be too uncertain, they generally hold back on new commitments or find the credit granters have already made the decision for them. The majority of families now have more than one breadwinner and most of them would be eligible for some unemployment insurance. They trust implicitly, on the basis of post World War II history, in an ever-expanding economy and they anticipate in time a guaranteed annual wage. The new family-forming groups, which account for the largest increases in credit each year, particularly believe in saving articles rather than cash. They often regard their equities in their homes and in their autos and household equipment as savings or family capital. It is the cash that is not committed to monthly payments that they frequently handle most poorly, a regrettable condition but a true one. In brief, today's hard-spending consumer looks to Washington to manage prosperity and keep the economy going at a level of full employment. While gazing towards the White House, he may also note with understanding that both President Truman and President Johnson announced they had to borrow money to pay their income taxes.

V

If you were a member of the Federal Reserve Board or of the President's Council of Economic Advisers, charged with avoiding both cyclical down-swings and runaway inflation, you might not accept so readily the tremendous recent growth of consumer credit on the grounds that it is a "way of life." The phrase is too general for professionals and has been used to justify too many special interest situations. Thus, though we have already noted the pros and cons of the regulation of consumer credit, an examination of the figures on debt in our mass consumption society is in order.

Altogether there is now over a trillion, or a thousand billion, dollars of debt in our economy. The total government debt portion is close to $270 billion and is no longer the "whipping boy" of debt critics since its rate of increase has actually been modest since World War II. In fact it is not unusual for administration officials to point out that government debt has been growing more slowly than other types of debt. State and local debt, for example, have tripled in the last decade to over $80 billion, whereas federal debt has increased only about 22%. The largest debt component is business and farm debt, in the half a trillion dollar class, and the remainder is in consumer long and short term debt, amounting to over a quarter trillion, or $265 billion at the end of 1964. Of this consumer debt, long term mortgages on home residences amounted to $187 billion. This leaves us with the remainder, consumer short-term debt, known as consumer credit, which amounted to $77 billion in 1964 and passed well beyond the $80 billion mark in 1965.

Once these breathtaking figures are absorbed, they must be placed in perspective. Most people now realize that the federal debt, including an increment of $200 billion from World War II, is easily handled by the borrower, the United States government. The debt burden, or the interest it has to pay on the debt, is quite manageable from its record tax collections and there is no intention on the part of the government to pay off this debt. In fact, it is quite necessary in providing a vehicle for the open market transactions of the Federal Reserve Banks, which are used in the regulation of the banking system's money supply.

Business debt of such proportions is a healthy sign and reflects the needs of our busy economy. Without it, our life insurance companies and other financial institutions would be sorely put to find investments for their funds. Without debt, corporations

289

would also be unable to show profits for their millions of stockholders including the new consumer-stockholder class. As it is, business is relying much less on debt as it creates its own huge investment sources in the form of depreciation allowances and retained profits.

The residential debt, or home mortgage debt, has increased over 300% in the last decade and this might be viewed with alarm. On examination, however, it represents primarily a change from a home rental to a home ownership economy and as far as most homeowners are concerned, they would prefer to be in debt paying their monthly home-owner's packaged payments rather than paying the same amounts to landlords. The beneficial effect on the economy of home ownership and, more important, of the more than one and one-half million new homes built each year, should be apparent.

Thus debt need not be looked upon as a mountainous villain but as an economic tool which has grown in proportion to an economy that has doubled in terms of Gross National Product in the past decade alone. Those who insist on treating this type of debt in terms of the family budget, or who dwell darkly upon the per capita total debt we are bequeathing to our grandchildren, are somewhat illiterate in terms of economic understanding.

Of the approximately $85 billion of consumer debt which is not related to home ownership, close to $70 billion is in instalment credit owed to banks, finance companies, credit unions and retail stores. The balance is in charge accounts, credit card accounts and other short term credit not payable in monthly instalments. It is this instalment credit component, now approaching $70 billion, or about 5% of the total debt picture, which periodically becomes a matter of major national discussion. Is it too much? Has it reached the point where the required monthly payments will seriously affect purchasing power and thus cut down next year's demand for goods and services? Should it be controlled, more or less like turning on a faucet, on the grounds that it is such a powerful stimulant?

To refine the problem, note that close to 50% of instalment credit represents automobile financing alone. (The consumer finance business, incidentally, comprises only about $5.5 billion of instalment credit, but its fortunes, as we have noted, are interdependent on what happens to the total.) Thus any action in relation to regulating instalment credit will affect most of all America's key business of making and selling autos. Now instalment credit has increased close to 50% since 1961, which is one of the causes for worry, although the growth rate has been a steady 10% each year. This rate of growth, however, is far more than the rate of growth for Gross National Product, personal income or retail sales. As a result, instalment debt is now at a record high of 16% of personal income after taxes compared with the previous norm of 12% to 13%. This causes the managers of our economy to take a hard look at it. The trouble is no one is certain as to what the ratios should be or how much is too much. For example, Arno H. Johnson, the J. Walter Thompson advertising agency economist, has been claiming for years that instalment credit, along with advertising agency budgets, must expand almost indefinitely if our consumers are going to supply the demand for the ever increasing Gross National Product required for prosperity and full employment. After several years of relating instalment credit to disposable income, or income after taxes, he has switched to relating it to "discretionary income," or income left to spend after taxes and necessities such as food, clothing and rent or home payments. Discretionary income, Mr. Johnson points out, has increased tenfold since 1940 and already exceeds consumer credit by more than a three to one ratio. Therefore, if discretionary income should follow Mr. Johnson's predictions and reach $495 billion in 1975, consumer credit may safely rise to $155 billion, or almost double today's $85 billion. The men in Washington may be pardoned if they don't accept these claims at face value, but neither may they disregard them. At any rate, the facts and figures have been presented and public policy will be determined on the basis of a variety of theories and pressures. Suffice it to say that consumer credit control is a convenient and quick expedient to prove that something is being done in the difficult new art of managing prosperity. It is much easier to get at than wage or price controls since it hurts only the lenders and consumers at the outset and can always be turned on again as easily as it was shut off. It is a tribute to the basic usefulness of consumer credit that control has been a lively but quite theoretical topic of conversation since 1952.

VI

Our society has been described as child-oriented, success-oriented and leisure-oriented. Quite understandably, the specialists on consumer behavior have described it as consumer-oriented. Since the success of our economy does depend on the appetites and pocketbooks of the consumer, this description is not overstated. As a result, the new science of psychological or behavioral economics has come of age. Its chief practitioner is George Katona, who has directed the Survey Research Center at the University of Michigan since 1939. The Center has been used by the Federal Reserve Board for its frequent surveys of consumer finances and buying intentions. Its findings always enjoy widespread publicity which is justified by its good track record.

Since its work is probably the most important recent development in consumer analysis, the technique of the Center is worth noting. It is an outgrowth of the sample interview survey, which only developed in the Thirties and almost died when the *Literary Digest* predicted that Alfred M. Landon would defeat Franklin D. Roosevelt by 209 electoral votes in 1936. It was the *Digest* that died, however, and polling received a boost from the correct forecasts of George Gallup and Elmo Roper, who had used statistical samplings for the election, whereas the *Digest* had used mail ballots. Katona's statistics do not compete with the invaluable national aggregates such as Gross National Product which came into use in the United States, the United Kingdom and Canada at the time of the commencement of World War II. The principal American inventor of these vitally important economic statistics was Professor Simon Kuznets, formerly of the University of Pennsylvania and now at Harvard. It was a contribution, according to J. K. Galbraith, which enabled the allies to mobilize their economic resources so much better than did the Germans that it became an essential factor in our victory.[8] Kuznets' type of national aggregates Katona calls "macroeconomic" measurement. His own type of survey, which measures consumer psychology in relation to economic decisions, is called, as might be expected, "microeconomic" measurement. For example, aggregate statistics, drawn from available total records rather than from sampling, tell us that the average American family owns common stock valued at $2,500, on the basis of dividing the amount of stock by the number of families. Survey sampling, however, would indicate that 80% of the families own no common stock at all and about three per cent own stock worth more than $25,000. Katona's sampling group comprises only about 1,000 to 3,000 families, which he feels is so carefully drawn from the income, age and residential groups of the country that they are representative of the more than 55 million families in the United States. It would be natural to question the micro-size of the surveys, but Katona has steadfastly limited the size of his samplings and offers good reasons for doing so. The surveys are intended to produce information on "the order of magnitude of values" rather than exact information and the resulting errors are not necessarily corrected by using a larger sampling. No organization except the Census Bureau uses a larger sampling, he claims, and that is only because it may want to show employment data, for example, for each state as well as for the nation, requiring more subgroups. In fact, says Katona, size of sampling is much less a problem for the survey researcher than the quality of the interviewer. By keeping down the size of his sampling, he can carefully select and train his interviewing staff, who are able to detect exaggerations and undue modesty on the part of respondents. Finally, the surveys are most interested in changes in consumer intentions and attitudes and these trends do not require a large group of respondents as much as they do frequent surveys of the same or different representative people.[9]

Granting the validity of the survey, what type of information is available? First of all, the basic justification for questioning the consumer in our mass consumption society is that he now has the discretion to buy or not to buy. This is because he possesses, along a broad middle class front, the discretionary income which was referred to by Arno Johnson. Given this discretionary power, the consumer must now have the willingness to buy as well as the cash on hand or the available credit. It is the willingness to buy that is subject to psychological influences, attitudes and motivations, which is what the researchers establish theoretically and then poll empirically by asking questions. Thus, the old notion that income alone is the key to demand is found to be inadequate. In fact, Katona points out that the consumer can even *create* income if he wants something badly enough, by putting his wife to work, for example, or by educating himself to command higher rewards. The Census Bureau, thoroughly converted, has gone on record recently with a label for one aspect of the economic effect of public thinking, namely, the "self-fulfilling prophecy." This is the theory that if most people think the economy is going to get better, it probably will get better and if they think it will get worse, it probably will get worse.

Applying Katona's approach to consumer credit, we can see that the survey might find, as it did, that because more families are beginning to accept credit as something more desirable and moral, an increase in credit may be expected. On the other hand, if they fear a recession or dislike the new car models, they may desire to hold back on new car purchases and again some reliable information is reported back to Washington and Detroit. In fact, based on his surveys, Katona has become an expert on consumer credit, and his findings have generally warmed the hearts of those who make their livings out of it.

Based on the findings, Senator Douglas' "truth-in-lending" legislation would not "assist in the promotion of economic stabilization" as claimed, because the cost is not a crucial consideration for consumers and a change upward or downward in competitive rates would hardly influence the rate of purchase of consumer durable goods. As to the preamble of the Douglas bill which once referred to "the excessive use of instalment credit," the survey finds a fairly conservative attitude on the part of most families towards instalment credit. When instalment credit did take a leap in the past few years, it was caused in good part, the survey showed, by an increase in the number of borrowers, not in debt load among old borrowers. As for those carrying the largest proportion of instalment debt to income, the survey indicates they are the young marrieds with the most legitimate needs for time-buying. Although Katona agrees with Rolf Nugent's original deduction in 1939 that instalment credit accelerates the swings in the business cycle, he sees it as so vital to the mass consumption society that its possible excesses are well worth the risks, particularly since he believes, speaking beyond his role as researcher, that the mass consumption society, both at home and abroad, is a key to peace.

On the subject of savings, Katona finds that the representative American family does not join the economists in regarding reduction of mortgage debt or payments on life insurance as savings. On the other hand, its desire to save and the esteem in which savings are held do not seem to have been blunted by the widespread use of instalment credit. Nor, for that matter, have savings been killed by the existence of social security and pension plans or the threat of inflation. The American family has decided to spend and save at the same time and tends to increase both actions as its income increases. A good many families, of course, report no conflict between saving and spending because they have nothing left to save after doing their spending, while others are able to save or to preserve their savings only because they are buying on the instalment plan.

VI

It would be pleasant to end this review of the mass consumer on the encouraging note of the survey, were not a growing statistic presented by the bankruptcy courts. If the consumer can take care of himself so well, how is it that he is going bankrupt at the rate of 160,000 cases a year? In 1950 there were only 19,033 consumer bankruptcy petitions filed, so the increase has been approximately 800% in fifteen years. The first line of defense would be to bring out the population growth statistics but population has increased only one-third since 1950. Using some microeconomic measurements, we find that over 80% of bankrupts are in the 25 to 44 age group. This is a group, however, which has only held its own as a segment of the total population, so no explanations are forthcoming from that quarter. It would be best to face the facts squarely. The consumer bankruptcies are largely among the younger marrieds who are the greatest users of instalment credit. They are "prosperity's orphans" and hold an embarrassingly large amount of consumer finance debt among the liabilities for which they seek relief. They do not jeopardize the institution of consumer credit, of course, as even at the current rate the annual number of bankrupts represents only one-third of one per cent of total American families. It is still a figure that does no credit to our affluent society. Moreover, there is reason to believe the trend can be reversed.

The idea of bankruptcy as a refuge for a hopeless debtor is a civilized and just social concept. Its modern development goes back to England's Henry VIII, the same Tudor monarch who defied the Church by permitting the charging of interest in 1545. The first English bankruptcy law was promulgated in his reign in 1542 and was essentially a law to make sure debtors would not outwit their creditors. The initiation of bankruptcy was reserved for the creditors only and the debtor could still find himself in prison if his seized assets did not satisfy his creditors. It was not until 1841 that American bankruptcy laws added the right of the debtor to seek bankruptcy voluntarily and to receive the protection of the court against creditors. In 1938, an important amendment known as Chapter XIII, or the "wage-earner plan," provided a legal framework for the debtor to pay his debts in full or in part under court administration over a period of time. Only the debtor can elect to use Chapter XIII. His creditors cannot force it upon him.

Bankruptcy incidence may have its own profile of the average bankrupt, usually a younger married man with a large family and debts about equal to his $4,000 to $5,000 average income, but its frequency varies surprisingly by states. Its frequency in Maine, Tennessee, Alabama, Georgia, Arizona, Colorado and Oregon, for example, exceeds 160 cases per 100,000 population per year, while 27 other states run at a rate half as much or far less. Such a dissimilar collection of high-incidence states suggests conditions in the states are far from uniform, even though the bankruptcy law is a federal law. Where severe state garnishment laws enable creditors to order a debtor's employer to pay a substantial portion of the debtor's wages to the creditor, there is a great inducement for the debtor to seek bankruptcy, even if only threatened with garnishment. States which have moderate and considerate garnishment laws, such as New York and New Jersey, on the other hand, have the lowest bankruptcy incidence. Another state factor is the prospect of deficiency judgments, meaning liability for the balance on a repossessed car, for example, after the car has been sold for less proceeds than the amount owed. Many bankrupts feel the deficiency claim is unjust and go into bankruptcy rather than attempt to pay their bills.

Whereas credit granters themselves have to bear part of the blame for the rising number of bankrupts, on the grounds that they "overload" debtors in their increasing competition for business, they would be the first to seek a reduction in bankruptcies because of the great financial losses involved. They grant the need for more careful credit checking and sharing of credit information in order to avoid their exposure but they also feel that in some areas debtors are being given the right to invoke bankruptcy needlessly. One of the few in-depth research surveys, conducted by Robert Dolphin, Jr., analyzed 482 bankruptcy cases in Genessee County, Michigan, in 1963. He came to the conclusion, affirmed by the referee in bankruptcy, that 50% of the bankrupts could have paid their bills in full under Chapter XIII.[10] His findings, incidentally, showed banks and sales finance companies each to have held a larger per cent of the bankrupts' debts than the consumer finance companies, contrary to general expectations. Moreover, 50 per cent of the consumer finance debt had been originated to consolidate existing bills, rather than create new debt. The survey further found a very definite change from previous attitudes on the consumers' part relating to the stigma of bankruptcy. Having accepted consumer credit so thoroughly, the bankrupts and their friends tend to accept bankruptcy as a normal casualty of the credit system.

As a result, creditors have initiated a movement to increase the use of Chapter XIII. They find that there are actually no Chapter XIII proceedings in some federal districts and virtually none in others, where the referees and lawyers happen to have little patience or interest in carrying out the expensive, time-consuming procedure. For years, the number of Chapter XIII cases filed has amounted to less than 20% of all cases, whereas it is felt as many as 50% could qualify. Legislation is therefore being sought in Congress, endorsed by the Consumer Bankruptcy Committee of the American Bar Association, to permit the referee to deny straight bankruptcy relief in wage-earner cases, if the debtor could pay his debts under Chapter XIII without undue hardship. Although an excellent case can be made for this proposal, including the rehabilitation of debtors under machinery ready and waiting, the bill will face a long struggle. It has been opposed by the Legal Aid and Defender Conference in 1964 on the grounds that the wage-earner ought not be compelled as a class to give up his voluntary rights to elect or not elect Chapter XIII. The Judicial Conference of the United States has also disapproved of the proposed amendment for similar reasons.[11]

Whether Chapter XIII is amended or not, the suppliers of consumer credit have recognized that financial counseling is a step that can be taken to remedy the situation. Community debt counseling services are being established throughout the country by committees of banks, consumer finance companies, retailers and others who recognize the problem. Free budget counseling and the distribution of income to creditors on a negotiated basis is provided by these relatively new non-profit agencies. This has resulted in a revival of a long-lost relationship with social work agencies on the part of the consumer finance companies, which provide much of the leadership for the movement.

A recent study of 28,000 bankruptcies in Ohio under the direction of Ohio State University indicates personal bankruptcy figures may be exaggerated as much as 10% because of duplications such as counting husband and wife as two cases.[12] Even allowing for such corrections, it is a sobering fact to contemplate that in a time of great prosperity, almost one million consumer bankruptcies could arise in a period of only seven years, assuming present growth rates continue.

XX

CONSUMER FINANCE TODAY

There are presently approximately 22,000 consumer finance offices in the United States, doing business in all the states except Arkansas. That the business still has its public relations problems is indicated by the District of Columbia which also has an inadequate law and thus no consumer finance companies. Government employees, however, are avid users of credit and the bordering consumer finance companies across the District lines include some of the country's largest individual consumer finance offices.

When the industry was still something of a novelty, it was analyzed structurally for the first time in 1935 by Professor Louis N. Robinson and Russell Sage Foundation executive Rolf Nugent. They noted that prior to 1929 only a few states published reports on the business but by the Thirties adequate data was available. What struck them as being particularly impressive was the increase in the size of the average loan office. Their benchmark, of course, was the old unregulated loan office, which now seems to us so unbelievably small, averaging about $10,000 in the preregulation days. In 1932, Robinson and Nugent reported that the average office had over $100,000 in loans. Today the figure would be close to $300,000, with the larger chains averaging considerably more. Today's consumer finance companies have total receivables of $5.5 billion compared with $258 million in 1932.

The figures have changed so thoroughly in this business, therefore, that the conditions in the Thirties are of interest only historically and perhaps to remind us of the inevitability of change. One remarkably consistent feature however, has been the predominance of Household Finance Corporation and Beneficial Finance Co. throughout the entire history of the business. Household was the first to exceed one billion dollars in receivables and Beneficial has also reached that figure, so that these two chains alone account for close to 35 per cent of the American consumer finance business. Interestingly enough, Beneficial has considerably more offices than Household, but less receivables, indicating a long-standing policy of being satisfied with smaller units, often in smaller towns. Although the business, because of its easily standardized nature, was from the beginning a "chain" type of business, there still exists a remarkable range of competition within the industry. Behind the half dozen giant chains, there are many smaller chains with thirty to two hundred offices and below these at least a thousand individual entrepreneurs with one to five offices. The consumer finance business is still one of the few businesses in which a principal can set up shop and charge the exact same price for the same commodity as the most powerful competitor in the industry. On the personnel front, this individual, often trained by the chains, can outperform his mentors, so that given adequate financing, the "independents" are still an important group in the consumer finance business. Although the trend is definitely towards concentration in consumer finance as well as in other businesses, its success at the bar of the all-powerful state legislatures is due in no small measure to its mix of both chains and independents. This fact, along with the anti-trust laws, has probably dulled any thoughts the larger chains may have had about achieving monopoly through rate reductions.

The most striking changes reflected in the profile of today's consumer finance business, besides the phenomenon of growth, are the following: increase in size of loan; reduction in rate of charge; dependence on credit life insurance; greater access to financing sources; diversification into other types of financing; and diversification into other types of business. All of these changes have insured the vitality and profitability of the industry. Yet in spite of these trends, consumer finance, as we shall see, though at the very height of its growth, is becoming an increasingly smaller segment of the personal loan market.

The increase in size of loans was an ingenious answer to a problem faced by the industry because of the decreased value of the dollar over the years. The old ceiling of $300, originally established to justify the special rate of charge for "small loans," had become outmoded and was actually preventing the consumer finance companies from serving an important segment of the population which qualified for larger loans. The privilege was not obtained easily, however, and the pattern has been for the state legislatures to grant the "ceiling increase" only on condition that the portion of the loan above $300 be made at a considerably lower rate. For example, in the state of Washington, the monthly rate is at 1½% for the balances between $300 and $500, and 1% for balances between $500 and $1000. The finance company still receives a larger rate on the portion below $300, and has gladly traded the lower over-all return on its loans for the chance to do a greater volume and retain its ability to serve its customers. In addition, its expenses did not increase accordingly as it made larger loans to the same number of people. Thus, the increase in ceilings in most states, along with the addition of 23 new state-enabling laws since 1932, had a great deal to do with the growth of the industry. The most important factor behind the growth, however, was the new inverted pyramid of wage-earners that followed the upheavals of the depression, creating more middle-income people towards the top and very few small-income people at the bottom of the pyramid. As a result, consumer finance companies now have loans with about one out of five American families. It must be remembered that even as the "risk lenders," consumer finance companies cannot make loans to the marginal families who are desperately in need of loans. The ability to pay, usually associated with larger, steady incomes, must be present. Another generally misunderstood fact about consumer finance companies is their acceptance ratio. Although their advertising blandly offers loans to one and all, it would be safe to assert that it is an extremely rare company which approves as many as 50% of new applications submitted. Considering that they are lenders of "last resort," compared with their lower-rate, more conservative bank and credit union competitors, consumer finance companies have to exercise this much care in order to keep their losses within reasonable limits. As it is, their delinquency and their losses exceed their competitors' by a proportionate ratio of at least two to one. One reason for the low acceptance ratio is the voluntary sharing of information with other lenders whereby the consumer finance companies arbitrarily limit the customers' loans, regardless of the customers' optimism about ability to carry additional debt. On the other hand, once a customer has demonstrated a good credit record, he is always welcome at the consumer finance company and the majority of the typical company's loans are made to present and former customers at a high acceptance ratio.

Who are the typical borrowers from the consumer finance companies and what are their reasons for borrowing in the midst of prosperity? They are no longer the predominantly white collar borrowers of the pre-World War I days nor are they the predominantly industrial borrowers of the pre-World War II days, when members of the industry briefly called themselves "industrial lenders." They are instead a true cross-section of the middle-income group in an economy which, for the first time, finds over fifty per cent of its work force employed in the service industries as against factory and farm employment. In 1960, an analysis by Dr. Katona's Survey Research Center also showed that sixty per cent of the consumer finance borrowers had incomes of over $4,800. Two-thirds of the borrowers were between 35 and 54 years of age and two-thirds owned their own homes. The survey revealed that these customers had liquid assets, in the form of savings accounts or government bonds, for example, of $100 or more. The data on consumer assets leads to some interesting observations on the "balance sheet" of consumers as a whole in the United States which are worthy of a digression. Whereas the consumer finance company borrowers understandably have meager cash assets on hand, consumers as a whole have a grand total of quick assets of $1,372 billion. Add to this their equity in their homes and in their durable consumer goods and the composite consumer owns total assets of $2,137 billion. Take away consumer debt on homes and for short-term consumer credit and the 1964 consumer ends up with a net worth of $1,874 billion. These figures, also produced by the Survey Research Center, would give small comfort to a consumer petitioning for bankruptcy. Yet they are factual and can be used to demonstrate that the consumer as a whole is not a hare-brained spender. Indeed his equity in his consumer durable goods is at least three times the consumer debt still owed on them. It is also worth noting that although instalment repayments now command a record 14% of income after taxes, much of these payments represent sociological change. Auto payments, for example, replace public transportation expenditures and television payments replace other amusement expenditures.

Still the consumer finance company borrower does not generally use his loans to finance equipment and the question of what he borrows for must be answered. The major reason, accounting for approximately fifty per cent of loans, is for the consolidation of existing bills. The very existence of the consumer credit economy has converted this former lender for emergencies into a consolidator of existing instalment credit on a grand scale. The rationale is simple: Combine many instalment payments into one monthly payment that is easier to meet out of income. The implication, of course, is that the consumer has committed himself too heavily in the first place, or finds the monthly payments too great when faced with an emergency or unexpected expense. The next largest reason for borrowing is associated with the purchase or repairs of automobiles, that consumer's luxury which has become a necessity. This is closely followed by a new item identified with the shift towards spending and working in the service industries, namely, loans for travel, vacation and education, accounting for about 10% of all loans. This item is probably the one that the original framers of the laws establishing the business would have least anticipated, but then who in 1914 would have predicted today's economy or the great acceptance of consumer credit which distinguishes it?

II

Volume and public acceptance alone, however, could not have saved the consumer finance companies from a possible precarious existence marked by the squeeze between rising costs and reducing rates of permitted charges. Into this breach in the post-World War II period came not only the increase in size and variety of loans but also credit life insurance. This commonsense device was originated by Arthur J. Morris, who organized the first credit life insurance company, known as the Morris Plan Insurance Society, in 1917. The sale of such insurance was formerly denied to the consumer finance companies in keeping with the original theory of the Russell Sage Foundation which looked upon any extra charge as a step toward evasion of interest limitations. Fortunately, the state legislatures have generally changed their opinion in regard to credit life insurance, which for a small premium and without physical examination requirements, pays off the balance of a deceased's debt. Recognizing the desirability of such coverage and the customer's willingness to pay for it, the insurance is widely permitted by state laws and the finance company is allowed a commission for its services in selling the insurance. The customer is protected from over-charge by model insurance legislation which tends to limit premiums to a level that actually requires at least half the premiums to be used for death claims. The remaining portion is deemed to be adequate for the expenses of the insurance company including commissions. The finance company commissions, or in some cases the underwriting profits of the finance company's own life insurance company, have become a most important part of the margin of profit in the consumer finance business, just as auto insurance has for the automobile finance companies. Thus, the by-product has unexpectedly come to the aid of the consumer finance industry at a most propitious time, a not uncommon experience in American business.

III

The structure of the consumer finance business would never have reached its present proportions had it not become, along with the sales finance business, a favorite customer of the American banking system. We have seen how these finance industries first had to prove themselves during the depression of the 1930's and at the same time overcome the banking fraternity's initial suspicions about consumer credit before the banks themselves became its greatest exponent. The financing of the consumer finance business is no longer confined to its original source, the banks. In fact, bank borrowings have actually declined as a percentage of the total funds used by the consumer finance business. In recent years, the sale of commercial paper to corporate investors and the use of long-term loans from non-banking sources have become increasingly important. The banks, however, are the key figure in the financing picture and the other sources would not be available without the banks' participation and traditional sensitivity to current developments. A recent Federal Reserve Board Bulletin reports that commercial banks through their loans to credit agencies supply 10% of all the funds used in instalment credit. A decade ago it was almost 20%, signifying a major change.

Although the larger consumer finance companies have long qualified for the lowest borrowing rates, an interesting major source of credit for the independent company has developed at the high interest end of the scale. Many of the large commercial finance companies such as Commercial Credit Company have developed a business of becoming exclusive banker to the small company, offering in exchange for a comparatively high interest rate specialized auditing services and a more liberal line of credit than banks would supply. It is often worth the extra cost for the borrower to employ the additional funds thus obtained without adding to his ownership capital.

This desire to borrow as much as possible for working capital is a distinguishing feature of the consumer finance company's financial program and has been cultivated to a fine art of borrowing based on the "leverage" principle. Just as Archimedes could tip the world given a long enough pole, consumer finance companies could manage a reasonable return of profit on a relatively small capital investment if they could borrow enough money for their increased volume. As a result, first the medium-size and later the smaller-size companies have become large borrowers of subordinated term loans from institutions such as life insurance companies. The subordinated loans are in a junior position to the senior debt supplied by the banks and the banks accordingly increase their loans as though new capital had been invested. Since the banks lend two to three times the capital which is below them in priority, the principle of pyramiding a company's borrowing power is apparent. This is especially true when it is considered that these subordinated loans have been supplemented by a hierarchy of "junior subordinated" and "capital subordinated" term loans to go below the "senior subordinated" loans. Although the leading five or six chains conservatively avoid subordinated term loans, other less well-entrenched competitors have employed them enthusiastically. It may be said that this device, only developed since World War II, ranks as an invention of the first magnitude in the consumer finance business, creating many strong challengers in the competitive picture. Meanwhile, practically all finance companies which qualify for institutional long-term loans, subordinated or unsubordinated, have increasingly shifted towards such loans, since they guarantee a steady flow of funds. At the same time, the increasing cost of bank funds with compensating balance requirements, uncertainty resulting from the heavy invasion of banks into the small loan field and occasional reductions or cancellations of bank lines have all encouraged this swing. In turn, the institutional investors have become more sophisticated in their approach to such loans and have gradually modified their restrictive covenants to allow the finance companies more liberal borrowing ratios and greater diversification into allied fields of finance and insurance. The insurance companies and pension funds, repositories of the consumers' savings, thus form a large reservoir for his borrowings.

IV

If there is one word that is in style in today's consumer finance business, it is "diversification." By its very nature, the consumer finance business starts out as a lesson in diversification, for it was the spreading of risks among thousands of small borrowers that originally made the business more or less depression proof and a permanent part of our financial system. Yet the original small loan laws were almost monolithic in their rejection of any services for the beleaguered consumer other than the making of pure and simple small loans. This state of affairs seemed generally satisfactory to all concerned through the Thirties. Meanwhile, the automobile finance companies and the loan companies seemed to have an unwritten understanding not to invade each other's fields.

The early Uniform Small Loan Laws actually prohibited the conduct of any other business in the same premises and it was not until those interested managed to amend these laws that instalment financing could be carried on as an allied business. Today's typical consumer finance company aggressively seeks non-automobile financing from merchants up and down its main street. The techniques of credit checking are similar, the size of the units are small and the new customers become a major source of loan business once their credit has been established through the financing of their retail purchases. The main reason for not seeking automobile finance business is that it is too specialized a business for the typical loan manager to handle. In addition, the financial structure of the consumer finance company, whose short term borrowings from banks are kept to a much more conservative basis than that of the highly secured auto finance company, makes auto finance an undesirable investment.

This is hardly the case with the auto finance company and the worst competitive blow suffered by the consumer finance industry has been the wide-spread entry into its field by the auto finance industry. The auto finance companies, gravely wounded by bank competition as well as by manufacturers' captive finance companies, had a ready-made customer list to which they could offer loans. In a sense, the auto finance companies might claim they have not invaded the field since they operate at the same rates as the consumer finance companies and have generally opened separate offices which in most cases are indistinguishable from consumer finance companies. They have simply become a part of the field and find the diversification very much to their liking. Almost overnight, Commercial Credit Company and CIT Financial Corporation have become major factors in consumer finance, joining Associates Investment Company, Pacific Finance, General Finance and General Acceptance, which had previously made themselves very much at home in this field. Diversification was an old story for the major auto finance companies, some of whom had been involved in commercial financing of various kinds before auto finance appeared. This was not the case with the much more limited consumer finance company, which had no desire to retaliate by going into the declining auto finance business.

As corporate enterprises, however, many consumer finance companies have strong financial positions and are committed towards diversifying into other fields of finance and insurance. Commercial finance, factoring, leasing, automobile insurance and life insurance are the typical first steps taken in the road to diversification. The road is not an easy one and several mishaps have occurred, such as some spectacular losses in recent years in the credit card and commercial finance fields. The most satisfactory loan diversification has been to make large consumer loans, up to $5,000, in the branch offices whenever possible, often on the security of second mortgages on real estate. These loans are generally made under so-called industrial loan laws in many states but there is a recent trend to establish new and separate real estate lending laws for consumers. At least 15% of consumer finance company receivables are now in "large loans" which are very profitable, considering the shared overhead, and help offset the declining rate of earnings on smaller loans.

Diversification within the consumer finance office or even within the world of finance itself fades in significance upon comparison with the decision of the twin giants, Household and Beneficial, to diversify into retailing. For Beneficial, a driving curiosity to look into new fields has been traditional, involving mild forays into bus lines, banking, real estate, commercial finance and life insurance over the years as well as non-auto instalment financing whenever possible. When it acquired the Western Auto Supply chain in 1960, a distinct change in emphasis was impressed upon the consumer finance industry because of the great size and dissimilarity of the acquisition. Although practically every retailer issues consumer credit, it could hardly be said that the industries have much in common, although the balance of strength from the investor's point of view was obvious. By the time Beneficial acquired Spiegel in 1965, it was apparent that the old days of the finance business were gone forever, at least in respect to the old leaders in the field. Hard upon Beneficial's diversification, Household acquired chains of auto supply and paint and hardware stores prior to the great leap of absorbing City Products, whose 1965 sales exceeded $400 million. At the time of its acquisition by Beneficial, Spiegel had $373,043,000 of instalment accounts on its books, owed by over 2,000,000 customers. This was, of course, far more than the entire receivables of the consumer finance business in its 26 states as reported by Robinson and Nugent for the year 1932.

The final change in the pattern of the consumer finance business has been a reverse diversification into consumer finance on the part of other industries. Recently Avco Corporation absorbed Delta Finance and International Telephone and Telegraph took over Aetna Finance, two medium-size consumer finance chains. The reasoning in both cases was the same. These already highly diversified companies thought it was time to get into the service industries, which might be less vulnerable to technological swings and which might be considered to have a good future in the growing service area economy. Although both finance companies were predominantly loan companies, their new owners confidently assume they can easily convert to sales financing for the parent company's consumer products divisions. Other industrial giants have already established their own captive finance companies in an effort to make a profit at more levels of the manufacturing and distributing process. In turn, sales finance companies like CIT and Commercial Credit have become industrial manufacturers on a large scale. The trend is further complicated by mergers such as Pacific Finance into the family of Transamerica Corporation, a massive holding company. Since Pacific was already a successful half-billion dollar company, publicly-owned and highly diversified, its match with Transamerica provided no particular purpose so much as making Transamerica more attractive for its stockholders. Meanwhile, Commercial Credit's recent proposed merger with General Finance Company was cancelled because of objections from the government's anti-trust officials. This will give further impetus to mergers of finance companies with non-financial enterprises. History may find that such mergers will also serve eventually to stimulate a reappraisal of our anti-trust theory, which could be found in need of restatement relative to restraint of competition among unlike as well as like industries.

XXI
THE FUTURE

This is the era of optimistic predictions for the future of the American economy. Economists and government advisers vie with each other in predicting continued growth and good things for all. A favorite reference is to the "golden harvest" which will follow the "fabulous Sixties." All predictions are contingent, of course, on some reservations. These would include no major war, no wage increases in excess of productivity and no let-up in the unprecedented scale of business investment in research and job-producing plant and equipment. With these and a few other hedges, such as sustained consumer demand and the exercise of judicious skill in government spending and taxing programs, the economists predict a trillion dollar Gross National Product in terms of 1964 dollars by 1980 or earlier. The average family income will increase from $7,500 to $10,000 by 1975 and the average family will have more leisure time for enjoying its prosperity.

This millenium is not a century away. It is predicted for ten or fifteen years hence, subject to reservations, by responsible economists. The National Industrial Conference Board, for example, has assembled forecasts from seven of the leading study groups, such as the Committee for Economic Development, *Fortune* magazine and the Twentieth Century Fund, which concur on a target of $800 billion Gross National Product for 1970 on the way to the incredible trillion dollar figure. Personal income would follow the Gross National Product, as it always does, to produce the above family income figures. The exciting prospect has been placed on an elevated scale by Barbara Ward, the British economist, who has stated: "The mass consumption economies of the Atlantic world represent a wholly new phenomenon in human history. In them, not simply individuals, or groups, or classes but society as a whole is rich and expects to get richer."

If consumer credit follows the Gross National Product and personal income in the familiar pattern it has established since World War II, then consumer credit could reach the $100 billion mark, probably by 1970. In this area it would be well to check with the consumer credit experts. Dr. Ernst M. Dauer, Household Finance economist, has been predicting consumer credit growth, with emphasis on instalment credit in particular, for many years and has found it to be so dynamic that he is often shown to be on the conservative side. At the National Industrial Conference Board Annual Meeting in 1960, Dr. Dauer predicted a 60% "reasonable" increase in instalment credit which would bring it to $64 billion by 1970. The figure was reached in 1965. In the fall of 1964, Dr. Dauer again erred on the conservative side, predicting the short run gain in instalment credit for 1965 at a few billion dollars less than actually occurred. No doubt Dr. Dauer's associates in the consumer finance industry were especially happy with the results but the difficulties in forecasting are apparent since so much in the instalment credit picture depends on automobile purchases as well as the psychological reflexes Dr. Katona has described.

Let us suppose consumer credit does reach the $100 billion

figure in 1970. In proportion to present distribution, the instalment credit portion will reach $80 billion and the personal loan portion will increase from $18 billion to $22 billion. How much will the consumer finance companies share in the $22 billion? First of all, the figures below will show that the consumer finance companies have not been doing very well in the total instalment credit picture.

CONSUMER INSTALMENT CREDIT BY HOLDER 1958-1965
(*In billions of dollars*)

	1958	1959	1960	1961	1962	1963	1964	1965
Outstanding at year end	33.6	39.2	42.8	43.5	48.0	53.7	59.4	67.4
Commercial banks	12.8	15.2	16.7	17.0	19.0	21.6	23.9	28.0
Sales finance companies	8.8	10.3	11.5	11.3	12.2	13.5	14.8	16.1
Consumer finance companies	3.1	3.3	3.7	3.8	4.1	4.6	5.1	5.6
Credit unions	2.7	3.3	3.9	4.3	4.9	5.6	6.5	7.5
Other financial institutions	1.3	1.4	1.5	1.5	1.6	1.6	1.7	1.8
Retail outlets	5.0	5.7	5.6	5.6	6.3	6.8	7.4	8.3

Source: Federal Reserve Board

In terms of proportionate increase, banks, sales finance companies and credit unions have each been growing more dynamically than the consumer finance companies since 1958. The credit unions passed the consumer finance companies in 1960 and now exceed them by one-third. The sales finance companies, in spite of losing the bulk of their auto finance business to the banks, have still registered large gains, partially by invading the personal loan field, in which they now hold over $2 billion of

315

receivables, practically all acquired in the past six years. Among the retail outlets, incidentally, Sears Roebuck alone now has 14 million customer accounts, with credit receivables of $2.5 billion. The overwhelming use of retail store credit has, of course, absorbed a great deal of the market which formerly went into personal loans.

There are still some good signs, reflecting the consumer finance company's specialized skill in direct loans. The banks, for example, have maintained only the same amount of personal loans as the consumer finance companies each year since 1960. Their 1964 total was $5.3 billions compared with $5.1 for consumer finance and their major instalment credit increases have come from financing automobiles and other large items. Very few banks are reported to have been able to develop profitably the "over-draft" check plan for personal lending and many have backed away from the merchants' charge programs which were widely publicized about five years ago. The credit unions, which have shown the most rapid growth since World War II, seem to have succeeded most significantly in convincing their members to finance autos and other consumer durable goods with them. Their personal cash loans have been the least rapidly increasing portion of their receivables. Nevertheless, their dynamic growth in the past fifteen years was hardly expected and their rivals have been all the more stimulated to encourage Congress to put them on an equal tax basis. Meanwhile, the fastest growing financial institutions of all, the savings and loan associations, have cast an eye on the consumer instalment credit field and want to get established in it. They are already making consumer loans indirectly through their refinancing of mortgages for non-housing purposes. Precise figures on the extent of this activity aren't available but the volume of such loans is surging and will continue to increase as funds remain available. In California, it is estimated that 35% of their mortgage loans in 1964 were for non-housing purposes. The savings and loan associations are seeking Congressional approval to make a variety of direct consumer loans in addition to the permission already received to make loans up to 5% of their assets for college education. It seems unlikely they would want to make consumer loans at unprofitable mortgage rates. Yet the whole package of a homeowners' indebtedness could be attractive for both association and borrower.

II

Thus the outlook for consumer finance companies is slightly less than optimistic in spite of its record growth in receivables. Although the larger companies are reporting increasing profits for shareholders, the profit margins from their loan divisions alone are continually declining. Across the ranks of the industry there is a temptation to meet the excessive competition from both within and outside the business by lowering credit standards, although it has been demonstrated that prosperity does not prevent a high level of credit losses. One remedy lies in upgrading the consumer finance services in order to concentrate on families that are earning more than $6,000 instead of less than that amount. This is the fastest growing segment of the population and by 1970 will obviously be the majority segment. A business which does not succeed in changing its office appearance, quality of personnel and lending techniques, many of which are hobbled by archaic state legislation, will find it difficult to get its share of the 1970 market. Constant pressure must be applied upon the regulatory authorities for equal treatment in relation to size and type of loans in the fight for survival.

Consumer finance companies will also have to consider the changing purposes for the loans which will be made in the 1970's. When the average family earns $10,000 in terms of present dollars, it stands to reason that its discretionary income will be considerably greater as a portion of its total income. A good deal of this additional income will be translated into better autos and home equipment which will require consumer credit but not necessarily loan credit. Some of the surplus income may actually be used to reduce existing loans or to cut down their use as the consumer falls back on additional reserves to meet emergencies. Although loans to consolidate bills will still be impressive, a substantial amount of all loans under such conditions will very likely be related to service economy needs, such as hobbies, travel and education. The new type of consumer, more educated and with more leisure time, will not choose a lending agency that does not understand his new needs or, for that matter, does not suit his new status. As an example of a change already here, one-third of all American families with heads under 45 now own encyclopedeas selling in the $300 to $400 price range.

The ideal consumer finance office within ten years may well be a carpeted, banking type of office with the traditional private consultation rooms replaced by open area desk clusters. The manager would be a highly educated financial consultant who might issue quarterly financial statements to his customers showing them their net worth position and commenting on their financial programs for saving, investing, goods acquisition and special leisure time projects. His loans would be made on an open-end basis, without the red tape of additional signatures and closing papers for additional advances. His office would offer a variety of services including charge account privileges at subscribing stores, travel information and highly-researched consumer buying information. There will be fewer offices than exist presently and each unit will be much larger. For a reminder of what it was like in the pioneering days, his library may include a history such as this.

III

In summary, consumer credit will reach the $100 billion goal but of all the consumer credit agencies, the consumer finance company faces the greatest challenge. If it can adjust its styling and services to the new consumer, it will retain its share of the market, as no other finance group has such a great store of knowledge and experience in relation to making and collecting loans. As for financing this expansion, if the volume requires it, banks will eventually raise their lending ratios for consumer finance companies to those now permitted for the sales finance companies. Meanwhile, the efficiencies of automation hold out the possibilities of expense reduction which may also be needed to maintain a competitive rate of charge.

The problems the consumer finance industry faces are no greater than other businesses have faced as they reached maturity and found the price of success included an onslaught of competition and a wave of consolidation. With a product that will never become obsolescent and with a strong foothold in the mass consumption society, the prospects for this business which originated so uniquely at the start of this aging century are excellent.

FOOTNOTES

The basic histories for the early days of the consumer finance business and its relationship with the Russell Sage Foundation are John M. Glenn, Lilian Brandt, and F. Emerson Andrews, *Russell Sage Foundation 1907-1946* (Russell Sage Foundation, New York, 1947) and Louis N. Robinson and Rolf Nugent, *Regulation of the Small Loan Business* (Russell Sage Foundation, New York, 1935). M. R. Neifeld's *Manual on Consumer Credit* (Mack Publishing, Easton, 1961) surveys the function of various types of consumer credit agencies. The National Consumer Finance Association's *The Consumer Finance Industry* (Prentice-Hall, Inc., 1962) is the most noteworthy modern contribution to the consumer finance industry itself. Published as a monograph for the Commission on Money and Credit of the Committee for Economic Development, it analyzes the structure and performance of the business in depth, coordinating the mass of statistics now available.

For background on the intellectual, social and cultural climate of the early 1900's, I am particularly indebted to Richard Hofstadter, *The Age of Reform* (New York, 1955), Eric F. Goldman, *Rendezvous with Destiny* (New York, 1952), Roger Burlingame, *The American Conscience* (New York, 1957), and Frederick Lewis Allen, *The Big Change* (New York, 1931).

Chapter I—The Meanest Skinflint (Pages 17-27)

1. La Guardia on Station WNYC, April 29, 1945.
2. *New York Times*, June 3, 1904, p. 10.
3. *Wheeler v. Sage*, Wallace's Reports, pp. 518-531, 1863.
4. Paul Sarnoff, *Russell Sage: The Money King* (New York, 1965), p. 67.
5. William Rainey, *Wisconsin* (New York, 1940), p. 183.
6. Leon Henderson to the author.
7. *New York Times*, August 11, 1869, p. 2.
8. *Ibid.*, August 18, 1869, p. 2.
9. Thurman W. Arnold, *The Symbols of Government* (New Haven, 1935), p. 125.

Chapter II—Mrs. Sage's Foundation (Pages 28-44)

1. Robert W. de Forest, "Margaret Olivia Sage, Philanthropist," *Survey* (November 9, 1918), p. 151.
2. *New York Times*, June 20, 1895, p. 4.
3. de Forest, *loc. cit.*
4. *Ibid.*
5. John M. Glenn, Lilian Brandt and F. Emerson Andrews, *Russell Sage Foundation 1907-1946* (New York, 1947), p. 66.
6. *Ibid.*, pp. 4-5.
7. *Ibid.*, p. 7.
8. Leon Henderson to the author.
9. Glenn, *et al.*, *op. cit.*, p. 17.
10. *Ibid.*, p. 7.
11. *New York Times*, April 17, 1965, p. 72.
12. *Ibid.*, May 17, 1913, p. 11.
13. Glenn, *et al.*, *op. cit.*, p. 169.

Chapter III—The Man from Livermore Falls (Pages 45-52)

For background on the Ham family in Livermore Falls, the author is indebted to Florence E. Mixer, Librarian, Treat Memorial Library, Livermore Falls, Maine.

Chapter IV—*The Impulse to Reform* (Pages *53-67*)

1. Alfred D. Chandler, Jr., "The Origins of Progressive Leadership," in Elting Morison, ed., *The Letters of Theodore Roosevelt* (Cambridge, 1954), VIII, pp. 1462-1465.
2. Baxter Ware, "The Lures of the Loan Shark," *Harper's Weekly* (July 11, 1908), p. 32; "Parasites of the Poor" (August 8, 1908), p. 32.
3. Louis N. Robinson and Rolf Nugent, *Regulation of the Small Loan Business* (New York, 1935), p. 120.

Chapter V—*New York, New York* (Pages *68-85*)

1. *New York Times Magazine*, March 25, 1917, p. 4. A feature article by Frank Marshall White, entitled "Loan Sharks Have at Last Been Put Out of Business by United Effort Against Them, Headed by the Russell Sage Foundation," in which Ham's speech of six years earlier is quoted.
2. Clarence W. Wassam, *Salary Loan Business in New York City* (New York, 1908), pp. 11-13.
3. *Ibid.*, p. 13.
4. Walter S. Hilborn in a letter to the author dated May 21, 1965. See also *New York Times*, January 3, 1913, p. 5.
5. Wassam, *op. cit.*, pp. 74-75.
6. *Ibid.*, pp. 62-63.
7. Clarence Hodson, *Financing the Workingman* (New York, 1922), p. 2.
8. Wassam, *op. cit.*, p. 21.
9. *Ibid.*, p. 78 (*Wassam* v. *H. A. Courtright*).
10. Arthur H. Ham, *The Chattel Loan Business* (New York, 1909), pp. 32-33.
11. *Ibid.*, p. 36.
12. *Ibid.*, p. 39.

Chapter VI—*An Old Profession* (Pages *86-96*)

1. Glenn, *et al.*, *op. cit.*, p. 136.
2. Cyrus H. Gordon, *Hammurabi's Code* (New York, 1963), p. 8.
3. *Ibid.*

4. Robert L. Heilbroner, *The Quest for Wealth* (New York, 1956), p. 72.
5. R. H. Tawney, *Religion and the Rise of Capitalism* (New York, 1926), p. 131.
6. C. G. Coulton, *Medieval Panorama* (New York, 1955), p. 338.
7. James Penderel-Brodhurst, "Pawnbroking," *Encyclopaedia Brittanica*, 1953, 17, p. 404.
8. Tawney, *op. cit.*, p. 153.

Chapter VII—Early Lending in America (Pages 97-105)

1. *The Works of Thomas Jefferson* (Federal Edition), V, p. 28.
2. *Ibid.*, p. 308.
3. Wilbur C. Plummer, "Consumer Credit in Colonial Philadelphia," *The Pennsylvania Magazine of History and Biography* (October, 1942), p. 396.
4. *Ibid.*, p. 402.
5. *A Sketch of the Original Object and Character of the Franklin Fund*, published by the Board of Aldermen of the City of Boston in 1866.
6. Samuel F. McCleary, "Sketch of the Franklin Fund," *Proceedings of the Massachusetts Historical Society* (October, 1897).
7. Arthur H. Ham, *The Campaign Against the Loan Shark* (New York, 1914), p. 3.
8. Robinson, *et al.*, *op. cit.*, p. 30.
9. Abraham Lincoln, "Communication to the Voters of Sangamo County," *Sangamo Journal* (March 15, 1832).
10. Paul H. Johnstone, "Old Ideals versus New Ideas in Farm Life," in *Farmers in a Changing World*, U. S. Department of Agriculture Yearbook (Washington, 1940), pp. 118-119.

Chapter VIII—Growth of Unregulated Lending (Pages 106-111)

1. Robinson, *et al.*, *op. cit.*, p. 38.
2. *Ibid.*, pp. 41-42.
3. *A History of Household Finance Corporation* (Company Booklet, 1965), p. 7.
4. Robinson, *et al.*, *op. cit.*, p. 47.

5. Wassam, *op. cit.*, p. 42.
6. Robinson, *et al.*, *op. cit.*, p. 72.
7. *Ibid.*
8. *A History of Household Finance Corporation*, *op. cit.*, p. 9.
9. *Ibid.*

Chapter IX—Fighting the Loan Sharks (Pages 112-129)

1. "South Sea Bubble," *Encyclopaedia Brittanica*, 1953, 21, p. 94.
2. *Ibid.*, pp. 41-42.
3. *Report of the Supervisor of Loan Agencies*, Massachusetts (January, 1912), p. 14.
4. Richard J. Whalen, *The Founding Father: The Story of Joseph P. Kennedy* (New York, 1964), pp. 43-44.
5. *Report of the Supervisor*, *loc. cit.*
6. Glenn, *et al.*, *op. cit.*, p. 340.
7. *Ibid.*, p. 139.
8. Robinson, *et al.*, *op. cit.*, p. 96.
9. *Ibid.*, p. 99.
10. *Ibid.*, p. 100.
11. Glenn, *et al.*, *op. cit.*, p. 140.
12. Herbert Corey, "Franklin Brooks," *System* (February, 1913), 23, pp. 164-168.
13. *Report of the Supervisor of Loan Agencies*, Massachusetts (January, 1913), p. 29.
14. Corey, *op. cit.*, p. 166.
15. *Bulletin of the National Federation of Remedial Loan Associations* (1913), p. 12.
16. Glenn, *et al.*, *op. cit.*, p. 141.
17. Walter S. Heilborn (now Hilborn), "Report on the Prosecution of the Loan Shark, 1914" (Typed Document). Copy provided to the author by Mr. Hilborn, p. 2.
18. Walter S. Hilborn to the author.
19. *Report of the Supervisor of Loan Agencies*, Massachusetts (January, 1914), p. 15.
20. Arthur H. Ham, "N. Y. Loan Sharks under Brooks Law," *Survey* (October 7, 1911), p. 920.
21. *Ibid.*, p. 921.

22. *Ibid.*, p. 920.
23. Glenn, *et al.*, *op. cit.*, p. 141.
24. "Progress of Campaign Against Loan Sharks," *Survey* (June 10, 1911), p. 405.
25. Correspondence of Arthur H. Ham in files of Russell Sage Foundation in stacks of Library of Congress.
26. Louis R. Harrison, "The Usurer's Grip," reviewed in *The Moving Picture World* (October 5, 1912), pp. 22-25.
27. Correspondence of Arthur H. Ham, *op. cit.*
28. Arthur H. Ham, "Hard Times for the Loan Sharks," *Survey* (November 20, 1912), p. 256.

Chapter X—Mr. Tolman Goes to Jail (Pages 130-135)

1. Hilborn, "Report," *op. cit.*, p. 1.
2. "Millionaire Loan Shark Behind Bars," *Survey* (February 10, 1912), pp. 1728-1729.
3. *New York Times*, October 10, 1913, p. 9.
4. *Ibid.*, October 11, 1913, p. 14.
5. *Ibid.*, December 24, 1913, p. 5.
6. *Ibid.*, December 26, 1913, p. 1.
7. *Ibid.*, December 27, 1913, p. 1.
8. Hilborn, "Report," *op. cit.*, pp. 8-9.
9. Leon Henderson to the author.
10. *New York Times*, December 26, 1913, p. 1.

Chapter XI—The Beginnings of Effective Legislation (Pages 136-150)

1. Glenn, *et al.*, *op. cit.*, p. 145.
2. Robinson, *et al.*, *op. cit.*, pp. 98–99.
3. Glenn, *et al.*, *op. cit.*, p. 143.
4. Robinson, *et al.*, *op. cit.*, p. 103. For details of legislation in this chapter, see Robinson, chapters 5 and 6.
5. Robinson, *et al.*, *op. cit.*, p. 133.
6. *Ibid.*, pp. 115-116.
7. Clarence Hodson, *Money-Lenders, License Laws and the Business of Making Small Loans* (New York, 1919), p. 95.
8. *Ibid.*, p. 99.
9. *Ibid.*, pp. 102-103.

10. Walter S. Hilborn, *Philosophy of the Uniform Small Loan Law* (New York, 1922), p. 5.
11. *New York Times*, September 23, 1922, p. 14.
12. Arthur H. Ham, *The Trend and Progress of the Movement to Improve Small Loan Conditions* (New York, 1921), pp. 4 ff.
13. F. B. Hubachek, "The Development of Regulatory Small Loan Laws," *Law and Contemporary Problems*, Duke University School of Law (Winter, 1941), p. 113.
14. Alumni Office of Bowdoin College.

Chapter XII—Were There Any Good Loan Sharks? (Pages 151-156)

1. Evans Clark, *Financing the Consumer* (New York, 1930), pp. 33-34.
2. Walter S. Hilborn to the author.
3. Robinson, *et al.*, *op. cit.*, p. 138.
4. Harry P. Gatter, quoted in *Pennsylvania Consumer Finance News* (December, 1956), p. 41.

Chapter XIII—The Massachusetts Story—A Case History in Regulation (Pages 157-179)

1. *Report of the Supervisor* (January, 1912), p. 13.
2. *Ibid.*, p. 3.
3. *Ibid.*, January, 1913, p. 30.
4. *Ibid.*, January, 1914, pp. 6-8.
5. *Ibid.*, January, 1912, p. 9.
6. *Ibid.*, p. 4.
7. *Ibid.*, January, 1913, p. 8.
8. *Ibid.*, January, 1914, p. 16.
9. *Ibid.*, pp. 20-21.
10. *Ibid.*, p. 19.
11. *Ibid.*, p. 21.
12. *Boston Daily Globe*, January 2, 1915, p. 1.
13. *Ibid.*, p. 4.
14. *Ibid.*, January 9, 1915, p. 14.
15. *Ibid.*, January 27, 1915, p. 5.
16. *Ibid.*, January 28, 1915, pp. 1, 4.

17. *Report of the Supervisor* (January, 1916), p. 8.
18. *Boston Daily Globe*, January 29, 1915, p. 1.
19. *Report of the Supervisor* (January, 1915), pp. 17-18.
20. *Boston Evening Transcript*, August 30, 1928, p. 1.
21. *Report of the Supervisor* (January, 1917), p. 5.
22. *Ibid.*, January, 1921, p. 7.
23. *Boston Daily Advertiser*, April 27, 1920, p. 2.
24. *Report of the Supervisor* (January, 1921), p. 18.
25. *Ibid.*, pp. 19-20.
26. Reginald Heber Smith, "Massachusetts Commission Report on Bureau of Loan Agencies," *Quarterly Report on Personal Finance Law* (Summer, 1965), pp. 92-93.
27. *Ibid.*

Chapter XIV—Colonel Hodson's Bureau and Bonds (Pages 180-190)

1. Glenn, *et al.*, *op. cit.*, p. 337.
2. Robinson, *et al.*, *op. cit.*, p. 47.
3. Clarence Hodson, *The Loan Shark Evil is Now Superseded by Beneficial Licensed Money-Lenders of Small Loans in Many Cities* (New York, 1919), p. 10.
4. *Ibid.*, pp. 6 ff.
5. Clarence Hodson, *An Adequate Industrial Loans System Needed by the Masses* (New York, 1923), pp. 4-5.
6. Clarence Hodson, *Financing the Workingman* (New York, 1922), pp. 4 ff.
7. Glenn, *et al.*, *op. cit.*, p. 345.
8. Lee Higginson & Co., *Lending Money to Small Borrowers* (1928), p. 8.

Chapter XV—Development of Other Credit Agencies (Pages 191-212)

1. Letter from Alphonse Desjardins to Arthur H. Ham, May 20, 1918, (in files of Bergengren Memorial Library, Madison, Wisconsin).
2. Robinson, *et al.*, *op. cit.*, p. 144. See also *Time* magazine, March 23, 1931, article on Charles H. Watts, p. 51.

3. Arthur H. Ham, *An Answer to Myron T. Herrick,* February 19, 1916, (in files of Bergengren Memorial Library).
4. Hillel Black, *Buy Now, Pay Later* (New York, 1961), p. 79.
5. Robert McBlair, *The Morris Plan of Industrial Banking* (New York, 1913), p. 16.
6. Robert McBlair, *The Morris Plan of Industrial Banking Providing Credit and Investments for the Masses* (New York, 1912), p. 12.
7. *New York Times,* October 5, 1916, p. 17.
8. *Ibid.,* November 20, 1915, p. 1.
9. Frederick Lewis Allen, *The Big Change* (New York, 1952), p. 107.
10. William H. Grimes, *The Story of Commercial Credit Company* (Baltimore, 1946), p. 30.
11. Clyde William Phelps, *The Role of the Sales Finance Companies in the American Economy* (Baltimore, 1962), p. 66.
12. Roger W. Babson, *The Folly of Instalment Buying* (New York, 1938), pp. 108, 220-222, 238, 244.

Chapter XVI—The Man from Millville, New Jersey (Pages 213-230)

This chapter has drawn on references from *Business Week,* February 16, 1935, p. 7 and December 3, 1938, p. 13; also *New Republic,* May 10, 1939, p. 3; *Saturday Evening Post,* March 30, 1940, p. 11; *Time,* May 1, 1939, p. 20 and *Life,* September 14, 1942, p. 104. The NRA is fully and philosophically treated in Arthur M. Schlesinger, Jr.'s *The Crisis of The Old Order* (Boston, 1957). Some acute observations on Henderson's role in the WPB are found in Robert E. Sherwood's *Roosevelt and Hopkins* (New York, 1948).

Chapter XVII—"The Toughest Social Worker I Ever Met" (Pages 231-255)

1. Robinson, *et al., op. cit.,* p. 158.
2. Glenn, *et al., op. cit.,* p. 341.
3. *Detroit Free Press,* June 30, 1927, p. 1.
4. Leon Henderson to the author.
5. *Detroit Free Press,* February 20, 1927, p. 9.

6. *Ibid.*, June 23, 1927, p. 1.
7. *Detroit News*, June 25, 1927, p. 1.
8. *Detroit Free Press*, June 30, 1927, p. 1.
9. Glenn, *et al.*, *op. cit.*, p. 342.
10. Clark, *op. cit.*, p. 39.
11. Rolf Nugent, "The Loan Shark Problem," *Law and Contemporary Problems*, Duke University School of Law (Winter, 1941), p. 7.
12. Clark, *op. cit.*, p. 30.
13. John Kilgore, "Legislative Tactics of Unregulated Lenders," Duke University, *op. cit.*, p. 182.
14. *Better Business Bureau Bulletin*, Kansas City, Missouri, June 6, 1928, p. 1.
15. George L. Gisler, "Organization of Public Opinion for Effective Measures Against Loan Sharks," Duke University, *op. cit.*, p. 188.
16. *Ibid.*
17. *St. Louis Better Business Bureau Bulletin*, St. Louis, Missouri, May 3, 1937, p. 3.
18. Arthur Schlesinger, Jr., *The Politics of Upheaval* (Boston, 1960), p. 245.
19. Robinson, *et al.*, *op. cit.*, p. 58.
20. Glenn, *et al.*, *op. cit.*, p. 343.
21. Leon Henderson to the author.
22. "Credit for the Consumer," published by the New York State Consumer Finance Association, 1956, p. 11.
23. *New York Times*, February 17, 1928, p. 23.
24. *Ibid.*, May 9, 1928, p. 30.
25. *Ibid.*, October 16, 1928, p. 30.
26. Leon Henderson to the author.
27. Constance D. Leupp, "Showing the Man from Missouri," *Survey* (September 7, 1912), pp. 699-700.
28. Leon Henderson to the author.
29. Arthur Mann, *La Guardia, A Fighter Against His Times* (Philadelphia, 1959), p. 286.
30. *Ibid.*, p. 306.
31. Paul B. Weston, *A Hammer in the City* (Evanston, 1962), pp. 127-128.

32. *Ibid.*, p. 138.
33. Glenn, *et al.*, *op. cit.*, p. 538.
34. Letter from Mrs. Clarence W. Wassam to author, August 8, 1965.

Chapter XVIII—Government Regulation of Consumer Credit (Pages 256-277)

1. J. M. Keynes, *The General Theory of Employment, Interest and Money* (New York, 1936), p. 383.
2. Rolf Nugent, "Tendencies in Consumer Financing," *Journal of the American Statistical Association* (March, 1938), p. 50.
3. Marcus Nadler, "For Standby Consumer Credit Control," *Consumer Instalment Credit Conference on Regulation,* National Bureau of Economic Research, 1957, Part II, Volume 2, p. 22.
4. Neil H. Jacoby, *Can Prosperity Be Sustained?* (New York, 1956), p. 53 and pp. 87-96.
5. Paul W. McCracken, *et al.*, *Consumer Instalment Credit and Public Policy* (University of Michigan, 1965), pp. 42-44.
6. George Katona, *The Mass Consumption Society* (New York, 1964), pp. 230-231.
7. *Federal Reserve Bulletin*, July, 1965.
8. Rolf Nugent and Leon Henderson, "Instalment Selling and the Consumer: A Brief for Regulation," *Annals of the American Academy of Political Science* (May, 1934), pp. 99 and 102.
9. Robert P. Shay, "The Proposed Uniform Credit Law," *Quarterly Report of the Conference on Personal Finance Law* (Winter, 1964), pp. 9 ff.
10. *New York Times*, February 6, 1955, p. 4.
11. Egon Neuberger, "Banking in the Soviet Union: An American View," *The Bankers Magazine* (Winter, 1965), pp. 28 ff.

Chapter XIX—The Mass Consumption Society (Pages 278-299)

1. Colin Clark, quoted in Jules Backman and Martin R. Gainsbrugh, *The Forces Influencing the American Economy* (New York, 1965), p. 99.

2. Alpheus T. Mason, *Brandeis* (New York, 1946), p. 92.
3. Richard T. Hofstadter, *The Age of Reform* (New York, 1955), p. 172.
4. Glenn, *et al., op. cit.,* pp. 30-31.
5. Mario Pei, *The Consumer's Manifesto* (New York, 1960), p. 55.
6. John F. Kennedy, "Message to the Congress on Consumers' Protection and Interest Program," March 15, 1962, House Document No. 364 of the 87th Congress, 2nd Session.
7. Edwin L. Dale, Jr., "Uncle Sam's $50,000,000,000 Surplus," *New York Times Magazine* (November 7, 1965), pp. 32 ff.
8. J. K. Galbraith, *American Capitalism* (Boston, 1952), pp. 79-80.
9. Katona, *op. cit.,* pp. 404-443.
10. Robert Dolphin, Jr., *Analysis of Economic and Personal Factors Leading to Consumer Bankruptcy* (Michigan, 1965), Occasional Paper No. 15, Michigan State University Graduate School of Business Administration, p. 99.
11. *The Legal Aid Society Brief Case,* June, 1965, pp. 259-263.
12. George A. Brunner, *Personal Bankruptcies: Trends and Characteristics* (Columbus, Ohio, 1965), pp. 101-102.

INDEX

Advertising, and first lenders' newspapers ads, 87, 107-108; of unregulated lenders refused by newspapers, 124, 140; and first national
auto financing ads, 206; and prohibition of GMAC's "6% plan,"
272; in relation to acceptance ratio
of loans, 303
Aetna Finance Company, 311
Affluent Society, The (Galbraith),
284
American Association of Small Loan
Brokers, The, 78, 136, 140, 171,
180, 254
American Industrial Licensed Lenders Association, 141, 149, 217, 233,
239
Associates Investment Company, 310
Aufderheide, J. H., 141-142

Bank of America, 212
Bankruptcy, personal, 296-299
Banks, personal loan departments of,
186, 197-198, 208-212, 255, 269,
306, 316
Barnard, Kenneth, 234-235
Bawlerout, 80, 109, 126
Bawlerout, The (Halsey), 80
Beneficial Finance Co., 117, 137, 140,
173, 181-185, 207, 210, 301, 311
Bentham, Jeremy, 101
Better Business Bureau, 234, 239
"Big Four," The, 234, 236
Blackburn, Burr, 152
Blackstone, 101, 163
Brandeis, Louis D., 36, 42, 135, 225,
280
Brave New World (Huxley), 279
Brooks, Franklin, 119-123

Brown, E. Gerry, 122, 157-170
Buerger, Alfred A., 274

Caisse Populaire, 192
Caspersen, O. W., 182
Charitable Corporation, The, 114
Charity Organization Society, 29,
31-35, 41, 113, 118
Chattel Loan Association of Balti-
more, The, 84, 112
Chattel Loan Business, The (Ham),
70, 82-85
Chattel Loan Society, The, 117, 119,
167, 186, 193
CIT Financial Corporation, 206-207,
310, 312
Clark, Evans, 87, 236-237
Collateral Loan Company, 115
Commercial Credit Company, 206-
207, 307, 310, 312
Commons, John R., 177
Consumer, development as special
interest group, 64, 279-282; and
Consumers' Advisory Board, 220,
270, 282; and National Consumers' League, 41, 64, 281; NRA
concern for, 224; behavior in relation to credit use, 268, 292-296;
and the mass consumption society,
278-299; and *Consumer Reports*
magazine, 281; Presidents Kennedy
and Johnson on, 282; criticism by
J. K. Galbraith and Arnold Toynbee of, 284; bankruptcy, 296-299;
debt counseling service, 299; balance sheet, 304
Consumer credit, effect of automobile on, 58, 204-209; and purchasing power, 261, 284; outside U. S.,

275-277; *Fortune* magazine on, 286-287; Arno Johnson on amount of, 291-292; Survey Research Center on, 292-296; predictions of amount of, 291, 314
Consumer Credit and Economic Fluctuations (Haberler), 264
Consumer Credit and Economic Stability (Nugent), 263-264
"Consumer Credit in Philadelphia" (Plummer), 98
Consumer finance companies, and theory of strong supervision, 61; financing of, 146, 182-184, 189-190, 209, 306-308; early clientele of, 186-187; and competition with Morris Plan, 203; and dependence on auto economy, 209, 305; derivation of name of, 280; number and type of, 300-301; loan acceptance ratio of, 303; trend towards diversification of, 308-312; future of, 313-319
Consumers' League, 41, 64, 281
Consumer Reports, 281
Coolidge, Calvin, 168, 177
Courtright, H. A., 78, 82
Credit life insurance, 305-306
Credit unions, 175; history of, 191-197; sponsor *Financing the Consumer*, 87; and Sage Foundation, 125, 147, 191-197, 231, 255; growth since World War II of, 315-316

Dale, Edwin L., Jr., 285-286
Dauer, Dr. Ernst, 314
Debt, total in U.S., 289-290; counseling service, 299
De Forest, Robert W., organizer of Provident Loan Society, 29, 70, 113; as adviser to Margaret Olivia Sage, 29, 32-33; as president of the Chattel Loan Society, 116
Delta Finance Company, 311
Desjardins, Alphonse, 192-194
Dewey, Thomas E., 119, 252
Dolphin, Robert, Jr., 298
Douglas, Senator Paul F., member of Consumers' Advisory Board of NRA, 220; and "truth-in-lending" bills, 199, 270-272, 274, 295
Duncan, Alexander E., 206

East, E. P., 141-142
Economic Possibilities for Our Grandchildren (Keynes), 278
Egan, Charles M., 137

Employment Act of 1946, 262
Eubank, E. E., 144, 173
Federal Reserve Board, 199, 227, 257, 263-268, 288, 292, 307, 315
Filene, Edward A., 192, 196
Financing the Consumer (Clark), 87, 236
Finck, David H., 183
First National Bank of Chicago, 189
Folly of Installment Buying, The (Babson), 211
Fortune magazine, 283, 286, 314
Foster, William Trufant, 227
Franklin, Benjamin, attitude towards credit, 98-99; loan funds of, 99-100

Galbraith, J. K., 226, 259, 284, 293
Gallert, David J., 123, 145
Gatter, Harry P., 153-154
General Acceptance Corporation, 310
General Finance Company, 310
General Motors Acceptance Corp., 207-208, 272
General Theory of Employment, Interest and Money (Keynes), 259
Gimbel Brothers, 122
Glenn, John M., 32, 34, 43, 247, 249-250
Gordon, Cyrus, 89
Gould, Jay, 23, 27, 29, 124

Ham, Arthur H., early years, 45; at Bowdoin College, 57; at Columbia University, 69; speech to Merchants' Association, 1911, 68, 159; writes *The Chattel Loan Business*, 70, 82-85; and files in Library of Congress, 87, 110, 125; appointed first Director of Sage Foundation Department of Remedial Loans, 112; as secretary of the Chattel Loan Society, 117; fighting the loan sharks in New York City, 119-129; and the film *The Usurer's Grip*, 125-127; and motivation in opinion of Leon Henderson, 134; lobbies for New Jersey 1914 law, 137; and drafting of first Uniform Small Loan Law, 141-142; and War Savings activity, 145; and Provident Loan Society, 112, 114, 145; and speech "The Trend and Progress of the Movement to Improve Small

Index

Loan Conditions," 147-150; and honorary degree from Bowdoin, 150; and conflict with E. Gerry Brown, 163-170; quoted as authority by R. H. Smith, 174; and Alphonse Desjardins, 193-194; writes *A Credit Union Primer* with Leonard G. Robinson, 193; and Myron T. Herrick, 194-195; background of, 214-215
Hammurabi's Code, 89
Harbison, L. C., 141-142, 153
Harper's Weekly, loan shark articles in, 63
Henderson, Byrd, 153
Henderson, Leon, 23, 87, 134, 150, 190, 197, 213-230; and Louis N. Robinson, 216-217; represents Sage Foundation on NRA Consumers' Advisory Board, 220; and career in government, 218-230; and campaign against salary-buyers, 232-241; and backing of labor leaders, 239; and Huey Long, 242-244; and F. D. Roosevelt, 247-248; and F. H. La Guardia, 248-251; and Regulation W, 263-265; advocates supervision of installment selling, 270
Henry VIII, 94-95, 297
Herrick, Myron T., 194-195
Hilborn, Walter S., 76, 122, 129, 133-134, 141-142, 145, 152, 167, 175, 245; and speech "The Philosophy of the Small Loan Law," 145-147
History of the Great American Fortunes (Myers), 26
Hodson, Col. Frank, 80, 140-144, 180-190
Household Finance Corporation, 108, 117, 152-153, 182-183, 189-190, 207, 210, 218, 254, 301, 311
Hubachek, F. B., 150, 233, 264
Hubachek, F. R., 139, 233
Hughes, Governor Charles Evans, 38, 118

Industrial Lenders' Technical Institute, 183
Installment selling, origins of, 204
Interest, history, of, 86-96; in early America, 97-105; Jeremy Bentham on, 101; Blackstone on, 101; Abraham Lincoln on, 103
Ittleson, Henry, 206

Jacoby, Neil H., 267
Jay, Pierre, 116, 192-193
Jefferson, Thomas, attitude towards credit, 98
Jerome, District Attorney, 77, 119, 130
Johnson, Arno H., 291, 294
Johnson, Lyndon B., 58, 152, 282, 288

Katona, George, 292-296, 314
Kennedy, John F., 59, 152, 282
Kennedy, Joseph P., 115, 181, 243
Keynes, J. M., 227, 256-262, 278
Kilgore, John, 238
King, Willford I., 253
Kuznets, Simon, 293

La Guardia, Fiorello H., 17, 248-252
Laidlaw v. Sage, 25-26
Landis, Kenesaw M., 144
Lee Higginson & Co., 190
Legal Aid Society, 119, 125, 134, 172, 177, 234, 299
Legal Reform Bureau, 174, 180, 185-186, 200
Legislation of lending, in New Jersey, 137, 252-254; in Ohio, 138; in Pennsylvania, 138-140; in Illinois, 143-145; in Missouri, 238-241; in Louisiana, 242-244; in Massachusetts, 157-179; in New York, 81, 120-123, 244-248; in District of Columbia, 178, 248-250, 300
Letters in Defense of Usury (Bentham), 101
Lincoln, Abraham, on interest rates, 103
Lindsay, Dr. Samuel McCune, 36, 81, 83
Loan sharks (see also Unregulated lending), articles in *Harper's Weekly* on, 63; and newspapermen, 64, 155, 167; clientele of, 68, 74; early reference to "shark," 105; and first lender to go to jail, 131; and prosecution of in Philadelphia and Atlanta, 130; and *Chicago Examiner* historic cartoon of, 144-145; and D. H. Tolman conviction, 131; and defense of, by Burr Blackburn, 152; named in *Financing the Consumer*, 236; estimate of volume of in 1930, 237; and Baumes Crime Commission in New York, 245-246

Mackey, Frank J., 108, 110, 139, 153, 182
Martin, William McC., Jr., 199
"Money Management" booklets of Household Finance Corporation, 183
Monti di pietà, established in Italy, 93
Monts de piété, established in France, 93-94, 113, 192
Morgan, J. P., 201
Morris, Arthur J. (see Morris Plan)
Morris Plan, 148, 172, 195, 246, 271-272; development of, 197-203; and conflict with Russell Sage Foundation, 148, 200, 272; sued by David Stein, 203; and development of credit life insurance, 305
Mosaic Code, 88-89, 90, 94
Muckrakers, 62-63, 69, 280
Mulholland, John, 109, 182
Murphy, Lawrence, 131

Nadler, Marcus, 266
Napier, Charles N., 239
National Bureau of Economic Research, 264, 266, 274
National City Bank of New York, 210, 246
National Conference of Charities and Correction, 29, 34, 44, 112, 118
National Conference of Commissioners on Uniform State Laws, 273
National Conference of Small Loan Supervisors, 255
National Consumer Finance Association, 141
National Federation of Remedial Loan Associations, 85, 112, 115-116, 136, 141, 163, 166, 174
Neuberger, Egon, 276
New York Globe, 121, 124
New York School of Philanthropy, 36, 41, 70
New York Times, The, 29, 42, 74, 132-133, 147, 195, 201, 259, 286
New York World, 108, 124, 128
Nugent, Rolf, 87, 109, 153, 197, 218, 252, 255, 263-264, 295, 300; writes *Consumer Credit and Economic Stability*, 263

Ottinger, Albert, 245-247

Pacific Finance Company, 310
Pawnbroking, in France (*monts de piété*), 93-94; in Italy (*monti di pietà*), 93; in England, 95, 114
Pei, Mario, 281
Persons, W. Frank, 31, 36, 70
Philanthropic loan agencies (see National Federation of Remedial Loan Associations), 84
Pope, Frank H., 167-176
Protestant ethic, and interest, 96; and consumer credit, 96, 285-286
Protestant Ethic and the Spirit of Capitalism, The (Weber), 96
Provident Loan Society, 29, 31, 70, 75, 112-114, 150, 192, 245

Raphael, Albert, 245-247
Regulation of the Small Loan Business (Robinson and Nugent), 87, 109, 153, 218
Regulation W, 263-268
Rendezvous with Destiny (Goldman), 53-54
Religion and the Rise of Capitalism (Tawney), 95
Robinson, Leonard G., 193-194
Robinson, Louis N., 87, 109, 153, 123; and Leon Henderson, 215-218
Roosevelt, Franklin D., and Glenn, 35, 247; and Henderson re N. Y. legislation, 247
Roosevelt, Theodore, and concept of regulation through strong supervision, 61, 158
Russell Sage Foundation, original directors of, 34; and first list of projects, 37-38; chartered by N. Y. State legislature, 38; and Forest Hill Gardens, 38-40; establishment of departments of, 41-42; and N. Y. School of Philanthropy, 69-70; and National Federation of Remedial Loan Associations, 85; and the Chattel Loan Society, 116; and credit unions, 125, 143, 147, 192; and salary-buyers, 232-236; and the Morris Plan, 148, 200; and survey of loan business, 217; and termination of Department of Remedial Loans, 255; and the uniform credit law project, 274

Sage, Margaret Olivia, 24, 28-40; as philanthropist, 28-30, 40; and W. F. Persons, 31, 70
Sage, Russell, 17-27, 69, 124, 126-127; and La Guardia, 17; and

Congressional career, 21-22; and Jay Gould, 23, 27, 124; and connection with railroad bribery, 23; sentenced as usurer, 24; and Laidlaw case, 25-26; in opinion of Gustavus Myers, 26
Salary buyers (see Salary lending), in the 1920's in New York, 245-248; and Sage Foundation campaign against, 232-236; and their specializing in railroad employees, 233, 245
Salary lending (see Salary buyers), nature of business, 75; prosecutions by District Attorney Jerome of, 77; compared with chattel lending, 85; advertising refused by newspapers, 124, 140; and opposition to Pennsylvania legislation, 140; proposed to be outlawed by National Federation of Remedial Loan Associations, 166; and inclusion of "purchase of wages" in Uniform Small Loan Law, 146, 233
Salary Loan Business in New York City, The (Wassam), 70
Sales finance business, 204-211; supervision advocated by Henderson and Nugent, 270; entry into loan business by, 208, 315-316
Savings and loan associations, 194, 251, 270, 316
Sears, Roebuck, 208, 286, 316
Shay, Robert F., 274
Small Loan Legislation (Gallert, Hilborn and May), 123
Smith, Adam, 101, 279
Smith, Reginald Heber, 172, 174-175, 177-178
Speyer, James, 113, 192-197
Spiegel, 311
Soviet Union, consumer credit in, 276
St. Bartholomew's Loan Association, 84
Statute of Anne, 97
Stavisky scandal, 94
Survey Research Center, 269, 292-296, 304
Symbols of Government, The (Arnold), 27

Ten Thousand Small Loans (Robinson and Stearns), 217
Tilden, Samuel J., 24, 29

Tolman, D. H., 76-77, 79, 109-110, 129, 130-133, 135, 144, 161, 171, 232
Toynbee, Arnold J., 284
Truman, Harry S., 265, 288
Truth-in-lending, 199, 270-274, 282, 295
Tucker, Frank, 36, 81, 112, 114
Tucker, Roy E., 182

Uniform Commercial Code, 273
Uniform consumer credit law, 273-275
Uniform Small Loan Law, original drafting of, 141-142; subsequent drafts of, 146, 254-255; and rate-making by commissions, 177; broadening of, 309
Unregulated lending (see Loan Sharks), early days of, 106-111; and number of firms estimated by Arthur Ham in 1911, 110; and volume in 1930 estimated by Henderson and Nugent, 237
Usurer's Grip, The, 125-127, 193
Usury, Russell Sage convicted of, 24; early references to, 88-89; and attitude of Medieval Church, 90-96; and Mosaic Code, 88-89, 90, 94; and Jews in relation to money lending, 94; and Jeremy Bentham, *Letters in Defense of Usury*, 101; and Massachusetts petition for repeal of usury act, 102; and Abraham Lincoln, speech on, 103; and *The Unjust Usurer*, 104; and *The Usurer's Grip*, 125-127; and the Morris Plan, 200; and "time-price differential" concept, 207

Van Kleeck, Mary, 42-43

"Wage-earner plan," 297-299
Ward, Barbara, 314
Wassam, Clarence W., writes *The Salary Loan Business in New York City*, 70-82; on D. H. Tolman, 76-77, 79; as an investigator, 81-82; dangerous activity, of, 252
Watts, Charles H., 141-142, 153, 182, Chapter 15, *fn.* 2
Weaver, L. F., 206
Wheeler v. Sage, 20
Whyte, William H., Jr., 286
Workingmen's Loan Association, 115, 117